3D TECHNOLOGY
IN FINE ART AND CRAFT

The possibilities for creation are endless with 3D printing, sculpting, scanning, and milling, and new opportunities are popping up faster than artists can keep up with them. *3D Technology in Fine Art and Craft* takes the mystery out of these exciting new processes by demonstrating how to navigate their digital components and showing their real world applications. Artists will learn to incorporate these new technologies into their studio work and see their creations come to life in a physical form never before possible. Featuring a primer on 3D basics for beginners, interviews, tutorials, and artwork from over 80 artists, intellectual property rights information, and a comprehensive companion website, this book is your field guide to exploring the exhilarating new world of 3D.

- Follow step-by-step photos and tutorials outlining the techniques, methodologies, and finished products of master artists who have employed 3D technology in new and inventive ways
- Learn how to enlarge, reduce, and repurpose existing artwork and create virtual pieces in physical forms through a variety of mediums
- Research your options with an accessible list of pros and cons of the various software, 3D printers, scanners, milling machines, and vendors that provide services in 3D technology
- Listen to podcasts with the artists and learn more tips and tricks through the book's website at www.digitalsculpting.net

Bridgette Mongeon is a master sculptor with over 20 years of experience in figurative sculpture. She writes and often lectures about the arts, technology and marketing in the arts and holds a Master of Fine Arts degree in combining 3D Technology and Fine Arts from Goddard College. She is a contributing author of *Digital Sculpting with Mudbox: Essential Tools and Techniques for Artists* and is the host of the *Art and Technology* podcasts.

Bound to Create

You are a creator.

Whatever your form of expression — photography, filmmaking, animation, games, audio, media communication, web design, or theatre — you simply want to create without limitation. Bound by nothing except your own creativity and determination.

Focal Press can help.

For over 75 years Focal has published books that support your creative goals. Our founder, Andor Kraszna-Krausz, established Focal in 1938 so you could have access to leading-edge expert knowledge, techniques, and tools that allow you to create without constraint. We strive to create exceptional, engaging, and practical content that helps you master your passion.

Focal Press and you.

Bound to create.

We'd love to hear how we've helped you create. Share your experience:
www.focalpress.com/boundtocreate

3D TECHNOLOGY IN FINE ART AND CRAFT

Exploring 3D Printing, Scanning, Sculpting, and Milling

Bridgette Mongeon

Focal Press
Taylor & Francis Group

NEW YORK AND LONDON

First published 2016
by Focal Press
70 Blanchard Road, Suite 402,
Burlington, MA 01803

and by Focal Press
2 Park Square, Milton Park,
Abingdon, Oxon OX14 4RN

Focal Press is an imprint of the Taylor & Francis Group,
an informa business

NOTICES
Knowledge and best practice in this field are
constantly changing. As new research and experience
broaden our understanding, changes in research
methods, professional practices, or medical treatment
may become necessary.

Practitioners and researchers must always rely on
their own experience and knowledge in evaluating
and using any information, methods, compounds,
or experiments described herein. In using such
information or methods they should be mindful of
their own safety and the safety of others, including
parties for whom they have a professional
responsibility.

Product or corporate names may be trademarks
or registered trademarks, and are used only for
identification and explanation without intent to
infringe.

Library of Congress Cataloging in Publication Data
Mongeon, Bridgette.
3D technology in fine art and craft : exploration of
3d printing, scanning, sculpting and milling / By
Bridgette Mongeon.
    pages cm
Includes index.
1. Three-dimensional printing. 2. Art—Technique.
I. Title. II. Title: Three-D technology in fine art and
craft.
   TS171.95.M66 2015
   621.9'88--dc23
   2014045695

ISBN: 9781138844339 (pbk)
ISBN: 9781315730455 (ebk)

Designed and typeset by Alex Lazarou

COVER IMAGE CREDITS
Front
(left) *Custos II* by Bruce Beasley
(top to bottom)
Victimless Leather by The Tissue Culture & Art
    (Oron Catts & Ionat Zurr)
Scanning of *David*
    by The Digital Michelangelo Project
Digital Model of Grambling University Tiger
    by Bridgette Mongeon

Back
(left to right)
Gold 2012 by Sophie Kahn
Akor Restaurant and Bar Walls by Matsys, 2013
Piranesi's Coffeepot created by Factum Arte

CONTENTS

FOREWORD

During 2009 I was contacted by Bridgette Mongeon with a request to include images of my digital sculptures in the gallery of her first book, *Digital Sculpting with Mudbox: Essential Tools and Techniques for Artists*. It was exceptionally compelling as a training manual for traditional figurative clay modeling as well as digital modeling with virtual clay.

The following year Bridgette invited me as a guest for one of the first podcast interviews that she has produced during the past several years. Her series of podcasts have proven to be a tremendous resource for anyone interested in researching digital sculpture as a significant contemporary aesthetic and emerging technological process for the production of sculptural forms with numerous choices of materials.

After recent review of early production drafts from her new book, *3D Technology in Fine Art and Craft: Exploring 3D Printing, Scanning, Sculpting, and Milling*, I am once again impressed that Bridgette successfully continues to advance research of digital sculpture with quality production, graphic layouts, comprehensive overviews of current technical processes, and extensive images of artworks by several renowned sculptors who have pioneered computer design and manufacture of 3D form.

I am particularly proud that she has included Autodesk sponsored "Digital Stone Exhibition" that toured China during 2008–2009 and the 2013–2014 Digital Stone Project Summer Workshops for Robotic Carving of Marble Sculpture at Tuscany.

This book also presents exquisite examples of digitally produced work from many other 3D design fields like the seminal "Out of Hand" Exhibition (2013–2014) at the Museum of Art & Design, New York City. Professionals in all 3D design fields will greatly benefit from this survey of CAD/CAM techniques. Likewise, this will be an invaluable textbook for academic programs that offer architecture, industrial design, furniture design, fashion, jewelry design, and especially sculpture.

Robert Michael Smith
Associate Professor, Fine Arts
New York Institute of Technology
October 20, 2014

PREFACE

I have been an artist ever since I could pick up a crayon and a traditional sculptor for more than 30 years. Working with 3D technology came through the influence of a friend, Mike de la Flor, and from my many trips to the SIGGRAPH (Special Interest Group on Graphics and Interactive Techniques) Conferences. I watched as the digital tools became more intuitive for a traditional artist, and in 2007 and 2008 I began using them in my own workflow; first for presentation purposes, and then, as the technology advanced, for creating my own work in a physical form.

I am known for my life-size bronzes and monumental sculpture as well as my portrait work. Digital technology expedites my process, gives me new tools and methods to explore, and in many ways saves me time and gives me many more hours to create.

A journey through the world of digital technology and marrying it to the traditional processes took a bit of boldness and self-esteem. The computer graphics world is primarily a male-populated area. I have joked that I have had to go through many tutorials of aliens, busty women, and monsters to get the training needed. At first, when I would approach the computer graphic artists and tell them that it was important for me to get the work out of the computer, they would ask, "Why do you want to do that?" They asked with a tone that made me think that my skin was turning a shade of pink polka dots. Creating work for animation, movies, and two-dimensional rendering, they just could not see why that would be necessary. As a traditional sculptor, the digital art is useless for me unless I can make it into a physical form. Eventually, the digital resources such as advances in 3D sculpting, 3D scanning, 3D printing, and CNC began to catch up with my needs. I continue, as many other artists do, to push the processes. As I embraced this new technology I noticed that many in the traditional art world looked on the idea of using digital tools in the traditional studio with a bit of hesitation. To my dismay, many turned away as they whispered the words "cheating" or "manufactured" and not "real art." I think it is important to bring these whispers of trepidation to light and create dialogues around them, and I have tried to do just that in Chapter 2: A World Turned Upside Down.

I'm not alone in having one foot in the digital sculpting world and another in the traditional sculpting world. There are many who have gone before me and have done the exact same thing. Through their efforts, exploration, communication, and sharing they have inspired me and many like me. There is no greater pleasure for me than to feature some of them and their work in this book. Talking with them on the online podcasts and hearing their journey through digital technology, a journey that in many cases began 20-plus years before my own, has deepened my respect and appreciation for each of them and their work. I recognize their creative process and what they have had to endure for the technology to get where it is, and for the general public, galleries, and museums to accept the work as legitimate fine art. I know that they paved the way for many artists that have come after. I feel honored to call them associates, and I hope I may also call them friends.

Incorporating the digital process into a traditional studio can be trying, but many artists have reported that it also can extend their careers. That is one of the motivations for me. Over the years, pushing hundreds of pounds of clay around had given me some pretty big Popeye forearms, and incredible hand muscles. After years of creative abuse, my passion also caused some internal injuries. Bruce Beasley, a pioneer using this technology, spoke of what he refers to as the "dancer's trap," but for sculptors. We have linked our creative expression, just as a dancer has, to our physical bodies. For many sculptors, over the years, our physical expression causes damage to our bodies, which can shorten our time to create. My body is my most important tool and, at the height of my career as a sculptor, injuries forced me to look at life without doing what I loved. "Allow me to hand you my business card," I would try to smile as I held the thin piece of paper between my index finger and thumb and grimaced at the immense pain. Incorporating 3D technology helped me to continue to create while doctors fixed my artistic body. I have found others on my journey that have had similar experiences. I'm careful about taking care of my most valuable tool—my body. I'm thankful for the digital tools, because with them—and some incredibly talented and devoted interns—I can continue to create work that will exist in the physical world, for many years to come.

This "sculptor's trap" also prompted me to go back to school and formulate what I believe was one of the first Master of Fine Arts degrees that combined traditional and digital art. Documenting my process for both my thesis and this book made me aware of things that one would not usually notice. The idea that while sculpting in the traditional studio, I would actually close my eyes to "feel" if I sculpted something correctly. Over the years, touch becomes as important to my process of sculpting as seeing. Alas, touch is lacking in a digital world.

Another aspect of working digitally that has vexed other artists as well is that, when an artist purchases a tool for traditional sculpting in the studio, it does not change. A caliper is the same today as it will be five years from now. This is not so with digital technology. The computers change and the software changes. There are advantages to these changes as the software and hardware designers push the limits and boundaries a bit more, allowing artists to do something else that, just a few months prior, they could not. This comes at a price; an artist incorporating these tools into their workflow is on a perpetual learning curve. Some of the learning, at times, can feel overwhelming.

I have often said, you don't know what you can do, until you know what you can do, and once you learn what you can do with this technology, the possibilities will blow your mind. For me, creating art is important, but sharing adventures and inspiring others are just as important. It is my hope that this book will inspire the reader and give them the courage and the tools to explore. Technology will change, and perhaps I'll be lucky enough to create an update of this book in a few years. The new book will feature the changes in the technology and may include artwork from those who used this book as their springboard, artists who were encouraged to explore and experiment.

My purpose for this book, the online podcasts, and the book's accompanying websites is to inspire and show the incredible possibilities. It is a one-stop guide for a traditional artist to begin in the digital world, or for digital artists to realize their artwork in a physical form. Have fun creating and be sure to drop me a line and let me know how this book has informed your own creative journey. I can't wait to see the art that you create.

Bridgette Mongeon

ACKNOWLEDGMENTS

This book is made possible with the help of numerous individuals. I first want to extend many thanks to my publisher Focal Press and my editor Haley Swan for believing in this book. Thank you for taking the steps to merge digital technology and fine art. I know this book was a bit beyond your usual scope of publications, but it is so very timely. Thank you for believing in it as much as my fellow artisans and I do.

> We are like dwarfs sitting on the shoulders of giants. We see more, and things that are more distant, than they did, not because our sight is superior or because we are taller than they, but because they raise us up, and by their great stature add to ours.
>
> *The Metalogicon*, John of Salisbury, 1159

There seems to be a need in us as humans to recognize the achievements of others. That is why we have banquets and develop awards. However, there is one group with no award and no recognition. As I think of this group, I feel compelled to give them that recognition. If I could have a banquet and invite all of them from around the world, I would. If I had a space where I could collect their work and show it to the world, I would. The only thing I have to recognize these people is a space in this book and the thankfulness of all of my muses. The individuals that I am speaking of are artists who have dedicated their life and passion to combining fine art and technology. These are the pioneers who have been working in 3D technology with their fine art for years. Many would ask, isn't this technology new? No, not really. These pioneers were doing it long before it was fashionable or fun. They have had the conversations and heard the dialogue about "am I cheating?" or "is it art?" along with other debates. They had discussed it long before this book came along, and they pushed for art shows and acceptance of the technology in the fine art world. They continue to push the boundaries of the technology, and they are open in sharing their work and their process. Unfortunately, I could not feature them all in this book, but there are many that I have featured. I am sad to say that some of them have passed on. To all of you I would like to say thank you.

Thank you to the many, many artists who shared their work, their thoughts, and their process and exploration in fine art technology. You have done so openly, both for the book and for the online podcasts. I look forward to continuing this conversation through the podcasts long after this book is in print.

This book would not be possible without my vendors who have put up with my many phone calls, and who have allowed me to hang out and watch, and ask numerous questions. They have been patient in helping me assimilate all of their processes over these many years so that I could help others to understand and explore. Thanks to Dan Gustafson at NextEngine digital scanning, Bob Wood at ExOne, everyone at Synappsys Digital Services, Vectric Aspire software, Agisoft, Mudbox, Autodesk, Pixologic, the folks at Carvewright and TXRX Hackerspace in Houston. I'd also like to thank all the incredible contributors from the 3D Printing LinkedIn Board.

A special thanks to Dave Morris for giving me the honor of being co-chair at 3DCAMP Houston. Being a co-chair gave me an opportunity to do what I love—encourage community, inspire, and educate. Thank you David, for being a beta reader on this book, your support means more to me than you will ever know.

Of course, I also need to give a shout-out of thanks to the other tech beta readers Dan Gustafson, Alan Ray, Brook Davis, and Johannes Huber. Thanks to Christina Sizemore of Diliberto Photo and Design for her work with the images in the book and support in exploring 3D possibilities. Sharing this with you made it all the more fun. Mike de la Flor I appreciate your companionship on the many trips to SIGGRAPH. These adventures allowed me to share, and gather resources, many of which are here in this book.

INTRODUCTION

You are about to enter a place where two totally different worlds meet. In *3D Technology in Fine Art and Craft: Exploring 3D Printing, Scanning, Sculpting, and Milling* the world of fine art and the world of 3D technology converge. Artists are creating some very interesting work using these processes, and have been doing so for many years. In some cases, the work that some artists create could never exist until recently, when these technologies matured and became available.

The possibilities are really hard to describe—you have to see them. And in this book, we do just that. Artists have shared their artwork, their software, their vendors, and even, in some cases, their tips. Artists are finding that these technologies can give them a new toolset. The technology also helps to expedite the creative process. This by-product of the technology leaves artists with more time to focus on creating.

Yes, it is true that you can take photographs of your favorite person with your phone and create a 3D image of them. Yes, it is true that you can "print" something in three dimensions, see it in a physical form, and do it in plastic, metal, ceramic, and even glass. Yes, people are printing biology with some of these machines. The technology that is in this book may seem like something from a sci-fi movie, but it is actually happening. It is not just available to engineers and scientists, but to everyone.

No, you do not have to invest your life savings in exploring some of the possibilities of using 3D technology. Some of the processes are even available for free. It has been the goal of this book to give the reader many options. Do you just want to dabble and get your feet wet without investing a tremendous amount of time and money? Then we give you those resources as well as the resources to dive in and create your own workspace using these tools and techniques.

Who Should Read the Book?

Traditional Fine Artists and Craftsmen

The author created this book for traditional artists and craftsmen interested in exploring digital technology in their work, but who may be unsure of how to go about doing it. They may not be aware of the processes or they may not know how to find the vendors. They may inquire, "What are the exact steps? How do I get from point A to point B, and what do I need to know to get started?" This book answers these questions.

Computer Graphic Artists
3D Technology in Fine Art and Craft: Exploring 3D Printing, Scanning, Sculpting, and Milling is also created for digital artists who may have the digital know-how, but are unsure of the possibilities or the processes of realizing their work in a physical form.

How Involved Are You?

There will be many different types of readers of this book. There will be those who are tinkerers and may want to create a piece of equipment from scratch, and on the other end of the spectrum there will be those who prefer to hand off their designs to a vendor or service bureau to help them with production. The author takes both of these readers into consideration as well as those wanting to know about an in-between solution—the possibility of using a makerspace to learn how to use the equipment without the investment of buying it or the headache of making a machine. Each section has taken these three types of readers in mind.

What Will You Learn?

This book's primary goal is to inspire and show possibilities. There are works of art from many artists, vendors and companies in this book, many of whom share their techniques and resources. Periodically you will find featured artists or organizations in highlighted sections of the chapters. Often those companies and individuals featured have also given an audio interview created into a podcast for your listening enjoyment. As you look through this book, you may find an artist who is creating and using a technique that you might like to try. *3D Technology in Fine Art and Craft* has removed some of the mystique from the art by sharing the processes.

How to Use This Book

There is a reason why the author has combined 3D printing, scanning, sculpting, and milling together in this book. Each of these is often used in the workflow or "pipeline" of a fine artist using the technology to create work into a physical form. They also inform each other. For example, learning about output devices like CNC machining or 3D printing will inform you as to the best ways to sculpt or to scan. If you are a traditional sculptor, then 3D scanning may be the way you would like to get your work into the computer. Once it is a digital model then the artist can send it for output created through a CNC machine or a 3D printer, but they will most likely have to do some preparation of the files using a 3D program.

Those new to 3D technology will want to start at the very beginning of the book, to get used to the terminology and ideas of 3D. Those already involved in 3D technology may want to skip the primer, and move right into the other chapters.

There are many types of 3D technology that artists use to make fine art, and many different final pieces of art that incorporate these technologies. These include two-dimensionally printed works, virtual art and others. The primary focus of the art featured in *3D Technology in Fine Art and Craft: Exploring 3D Printing, Scanning, Sculpting, and Milling* is artwork that is made into a physical form.

Using This Book in Education

Educators can use this book in both secondary and higher education. It is a primer for those wanting to use or explore these technologies. The vendors who provide this equipment have contributed their information in the hope of using this book to educate their potential clients. Educators can find resources for further exploration using this book, including study plans and outside resources in either the resource section of this book or on the book's accompanying website. It is easy to modify these principles for those working in primary education. See the book's accompanying website, www. digitalsculpting.net, for more details.

The Chapters

Chapter 1: Primer

If you have no idea what we mean by a polygon, or even how much memory is in your computer and why you might need to know this, then this is the place to begin. Everyone who works in 3D technology had to start somewhere. You want to be able to converse intelligently with the service bureaus, and if you can create a dialogue and understand the processes then you will soon be able to push past its limits as you create art.

Chapter 2: A World Turned Upside Down

For those working in the traditional field of art and entering a digital world, at first even navigation can be confusing. It is often hard to get your footing. This chapter is about more than working in digital space. It is about the merging of the two worlds. Using digital technology in the fine art world creates many more questions. Is it art? Am I cheating? What is the difference between manufacturing and fine art? How do galleries and museums react to 3D technology in fine art? Is it an accepted means of expression in the fine art world? These are all questions we try to answer in this chapter.

Chapter 3: 3D Scanning

There are many different types of scanners. What are the differences? With the flood of small studio scanners that are on the market now, how do you know what scanner you should purchase? What should you expect from a 3D scanning service bureau? For traditional artists, 3D scanning can offer a way to create traditionally and then bring your art into the computer without having to sculpt in the computer. There are also many applications for the use of 3D scanning such as art preservation, repurposing of art, and more.

Are there simple ways of scanning? How about scanning with my phone? What is photogrammetry and how is it used? These are all things that we explore in the 3D scanning chapter.

Chapter 4: 3D Modeling, Sculpting, and More

3D sculpting and 3D modeling in the computer offer a world of freedom and movement. One can quickly move around, zoom in, and create. There are no physical or material constraints. You have freedom to design without having to worry about the physicality or material properties. In this chapter, the readers learn about the software and tools. We also meet some incredible artists who have learned to make the technology work for them.

Chapter 5: CNC Milling, Routing, and More

CNC or computer numerically controlled machining is a digital process that has been around for a very long time. It is one way to get your work out of the computer and realize it in a physical form. The materials used with CNC are vast. We will visit the work of several artists and learn about their tools and processes. In this CNC chapter, we will also learn about CNC machining and where to find the resources to use it in your own workflow.

Chapter 6: 3D for Presentations and CNC Milling for Enlargements

Creating 3D presentations can assist an artist in securing commissions. In this chapter, artists share their process of creating 3D presentations.

Sculptors are finding that using the tools of scanning and CNC milling aids them in the recreation of life-size and monumental work. We will learn about these processes, as well as the tips and tricks of some of the artists using them.

Chapter 7: 3D Printing

Many think that they can 3D print at the push of a button. It is not that easy. There are many steps that an artist needs to take to get from a digital model to a 3D printed sculpture, and a variety of 3D printing processes and materials to choose from. In this chapter, we explore the many areas of 3D printing while learning how other artists are pushing the limits of the 3D printing process.

Chapter 8: The Foundry of the Future?

Artists use the lost wax method of bronze casting or investment casting, to create bronze artwork. It has changed very little over hundreds of years. This chapter follows that traditional process of creating bronze sculptures to see how digital technology is infiltrating each stage. These new processes and the technology may end up creating a foundry of the future.

Chapter 9: Copyrights, Ethics, Responsibilities, and 3D Technology

It is paramount for an artist to protect themselves and their work. It is also important to realize when you might be committing a crime with the use of these new tools. In this chapter, we look at copyright as it relates to 3D, along with the questions of ethics and responsibilities. What about those who are using these technologies to create Frankensteinian art by printing biology or those using 3D printing to create their own guns? This chapter poses difficult questions, such as, "Just because we can create using 3D technology, should we?"

Appendix

It is difficult to create using 3D technology without the resources to do so. This section, along with the book's website, lists many resources including software, vendors, and educational material available to the reader. Make this the last stop as you prepare your ideas and search for the tools to materialize your own creative designs using 3D technology.

For those desiring further education in these processes there is both formal and informal education available. STEAM is an educational initiative that focuses on incorporating science, technology, engineering, art, and math in education. This chapter looks at education and STEAM resources including formal education and colleges working with 3D technology in the arts. Don't forget makerspaces and hackerspaces. Learn what they are, where to find them and how they can help you to create your art.

Other Supporting Material

Where to Go From Here?

WEBSITE   It is impossible to put everything that one needs to understand all of these tools and processes in one book. We can't teach you everything you need to know about 3D printing, scanning, sculpting, and milling, but we can get you started and point the way. For further support, please visit the book's accompanying website at www.digitalsculpting.net. There you will find links to tutorials and videos that further define the topics. We have also included information from vendors and software companies. Looking at art and getting inspired is important. Visit the website and take the time to see what other artists are creating using both traditional and digital processes.

PODCASTS   The author has interviewed many of the artists and vendors in this book for the online *Art and Technology* podcast. You can find the links to the podcast at www.digitalsculpting.net or on iTunes. The author makes the links to these podcasts available for anyone to use on their website or in their online publications. Simply copy the link, place it on your website or blog, and the podcast opens up an additional browser and plays for your visitors. The podcasts are a personal touch; a way to get to know the author, artists, and vendors in a more intimate way: a fireside chat where art and technology meet. The author publishes regular *Art and Technology* podcasts. To stay up-to-date, subscribe to the podcasts in iTunes.

Contacting the Author

It is with great excitement that the author presents this book to the public. If you have comments on the work, or if you are an artist inspired by the work and tools presented, please feel free to contact the author through her personal website at www.creativesculpture.com. If you are a vendor offering some new processes or advancements in the technology or an artist that has created work using digital processes, Bridgette Mongeon would like to hear from you for inclusion in possible future editions of this book or for inclusion on the book's accompanying website.

Bridgette Mongeon is available for speaking engagements on a variety of topics.

Disclaimer

Working with tools and in a shop that explores new materials and processes can be fun, but an artist should be cautious at all times. Some materials can pose a health risk, and machinery can injure and kill. Please take all safety precautions when using materials. Artists enter these processes at their own risk.

Many featured artists recommend their tools and software. Including these resources in this book is not a personal endorsement by the author, unless otherwise stipulated in the book, or the book's accompanying website.

It is also recognized that the author and publisher are not lawyers and cannot be held liable for suggestions in this book. It is always recommended to artists to seek help from a competent attorney in legal matters, concerning copyrights and intellectual property rights.

Those using this book cannot hold the author, publisher, and all those associated with *3D Technology in Fine Art and Craft: Exploring 3D Printing, Scanning, Sculpting, and Milling* legally responsible for injuries or infringements caused by the use of this book or the associated technology.

DEDICATION

I would like to dedicate this book to those many pioneers who have gone before me and encouraged individuals to merge traditional and digital technologies to create incredible fine artwork.

I'd also like to dedicate this book to Mike de la Flor, who said, "Maybe you should look at digital sculpting."

To Debbie Lloyd who is one of my favorite art teachers. And to all of the art teachers who spend countless hours sharing their passion and being advocates for learners, especially those who break new ground with new tools and techniques.

CHAPTER ONE

PRIMER

———

"It is like a composer sitting down with notes and chords to get a feel for where the music is going."

Bruce Beasley discusses the freedom of creating fine art in a computer without any physical constraints

facing page
Custos II by Bruce Beasley.
Photograph: Lee Fatheree

When a traditional artist enters into the world of 3D technology and they begin to listen in on a dialogue between seasoned 3D technicians and/or computer graphics (CG) artists, the conversation might begin to sound more like the wah-wah-wah of Charlie Brown's teacher in the *Peanuts* cartoon. Those entering the world of technology and hearing such discussions can quickly become overwhelmed and feel that they need a translator or a crash course in computer graphics before they can continue. Relax and take a deep breath, this journey will be as painless as possible. We structured this book to give the reader inspiration in the world of 3D art and we break down the processes, steps, and technology. The resource section and the book's accompanying website hold even more information, including links to videos that will help to get you up to speed. Take your time. Use this section of the book to become familiar with 3D technology. Refer back to this section when necessary. Meanwhile, enjoy the artists featured throughout the book. They all share their process, tools, and vendors, which takes the guesswork out of your creative exploration. You might even try some of the free options for software and other tools to get your feet wet. Once you proceed past the unknown and familiarize yourself with the tools, along with dabbling a little in the processes, you will find a world full of possibilities.

There are certain terms that relate to 3D technology that will be helpful for you to know as you travel on your journey of incorporating 3D technology into your traditional art and craft processes. If you are already working in computer graphics, then this chapter will be very elementary, and you can probably think of a dozen or two more things to add to it. However, this chapter is a very basic primer to assist those who are working with a traditional artistic background. It is here to help you begin to understand this new virtual world. To those traditional artists, this chapter may seem daunting. Don't let it scare you away from the wonderful possibilities available to you. You don't have to know everything here to get started. This book and your vendors, the service bureaus, and support team can assist you in creating some marvelous projects while becoming more familiar with the technology. As the technology grows and becomes more accessible to the general consumer, the learning curve will decline. The technology will even become easier. Vendors are providing a great deal of assistance. With many vendors, their technical support team takes care of the back end of the business of incorporating the art and technology. The vendors realize the importance of educating the public in this new technology, and many take the time to do so. Also, as you will see in other chapters, new businesses are positioning themselves as middlemen between artist and vendor. They understand that not everyone thinks in the same way. Some artists may not want to immerse themselves into the technology; they just want the technology to work for them. They can visualize the final product but don't know how to get there, especially when they only have the experience to create in the traditional fine art sculpting world. Dependable individuals and companies that offer their service as a go-between for the artist and service bureaus, help to take the mystery and confusion out of the technology. However, if you plan on using the computer to create digitally, you will need to become more familiar with the digital world. You will also want to translate your ideas succinctly, and the most exciting part about this new technology, that you will see demonstrated over and over again in this book, is that if you know how it works, you can manipulate it, change it, and push it to do things that have never been done before. To do this, you will need to communicate in the language from this other world. This means learning the dialogue. Consider the digital processes as just another tool that you are trying to master. Now, let's familiarize ourselves with some things that at first may seem confusing, but eventually will become clearer on your own creative journey of using 3D technology.

Open Source

Open source is a concept for development of software, hardware, and other items. It is a great concept and for many it means "free" software. When the public considers software open source it means that not only is the software free, but the code that runs the software is also made available. By making both the code and the software free, the software or product will evolve and improve through shared development. People from all over the world will be contributing to improving the product.

A user of open source software may think that because there is not one owner, there is no support. However, open source often brings a strong community of followers. The followers have a commitment; they feel invested as if they own a part of the product. The community wants it to grow and get better, to be the best that it can be. Usually documentation, forums, videos, and other tools for users are readily available. For example, the software Blender became open source in 2002. Artists use Blender for modeling, animation, and movies. In this book, we will refer often to another open source software called MeshLab. MeshLab began as a course assignment at the University of Pisa in 2005. Artists may use MeshLab to change files from one extension to the other, or reduce the polygon count. Extensions, polygons… don't let these terms confuse you. These are covered further in this chapter.

You are probably getting excited thinking about the possibilities that are available to you, and that you can use these tools with no cost. Let's look at a few more things in the digital world first.

Open source has grown from just free software and hardware. Open source is now considered more of a movement in technology. For example, in 2007 Adrian Bowyer and a team at the University of Bath created the RepRap (short for Replicating Rapid Prototyper) as an open source 3D printer design. Many of the parts that are available for the RepRap are actually made by a RepRap 3D printer. In other words, it reproduces itself. The hope of those that created the first RepRap 3D printer is that it will develop and grow as others work with it and modify the design.

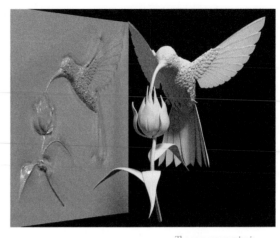

The user community is involved in the advances of open source software. For example, Vilem Novak developed a Blender CAM add-on that can export the code needed for CNC milling.

There are many quality open source products that this book will refer to and that we will list on the accompanying website. What that means to the artist or craftsperson who might like to use these tools is that there may be little or no cost involved with obtaining and using them. Those artists or craftspeople that think that there will be a large investment into using technology in conjunction with their traditional methods of creating can put their minds to rest. Yes, you may need a computer, but investment into expensive equipment and software may not be necessary, due to the increased participation in the open source movement.

Hacker

The word "hacker" has had negative connotations. We all dread hearing "someone hacked into your system." We picture dark basements with seedy characters trying to get into our checking accounts and draining our savings. We see hackers as the invisible Internet black-hat bandits versus the white-hat good guys.

But the word "hacker" has another meaning entirely. In another, more positive and adventurous, light the word "hacker" refers to a person who modifies software and hardware or other things to make them better. This "hacking" is at the root of how art and creativity help the technology evolve. The technology must change to suit the needs of the user. Creative people push the limits. In the case of art and technology, "hacking" is a term that can make things exciting. Hacking is solving problems creatively.

Jonathan Keep, *Iceberg*, www.keep-art.co.uk, self-build DIY delta ceramic 3D printer and *Iceberg*. Artist 3D-printed porcelain clay and glaze, 16 × 12 × 24 cm.

It is what this book is about. For example, Solheim Additive Manufacturing Laboratory in the Mechanical Engineering Department at the University of Washington has pushed the limits of their 3D printing machines. In Chapter 4 we will see how they are using ceramics, glass, and other materials in their 3D printers. They share their progress in "hacking" as they push their machines and the technology. They encourage others to share their development of open source technology through their blog and through collaboration with other universities and individuals.

The combination of open source, hacker, and sharing is a progressive and creative endeavor. Ceramic artists at Unfold featured in the 3D Printing chapter share their process of ceramic 3D printing openly online. Artist Jonathan Keep was able to create his own work environment and experiments using 3D printing of ceramics because of the willingness of others to share in the open source community. Keep now shares his exploration in 3D printing from his website. For links to these websites and information on how Keep or Unfold built their 3D ceramic printers, visit this book's accompanying website at www.digitalsculpting.net.

The educational initiative of STEAM featured in the appendix incorporates art with the former STEM educational initiative of science, technology, engineering, and math. In STEAM, the art element encourages us to be creative thinkers. Art helps us to look at things in a different light, to creatively hack our thinking.

Makerspaces, hackerspaces, or the maker communities are other revolutions that combine creative collaboration, hacking, and often open source software and hardware. Creative individuals combine their resources—including knowledge, art supplies, machines, and tools—and make them available, usually for a fee, similar to a club or creative co-op. The Appendix goes into more detail about makerspaces, hackerspaces, and the maker community.

Hacking and collaboration can have powerful results. Jordan Miller is a great example of those who wanted to think outside the box for creating bioprinting. Yes, with the advances of 3D technology they are 3D printing biology. It has developed into an entirely new form of medicine called regenerative medicine. Miller, a professor of bioengineering at Rice University, was trying to create something very delicate, a network of blood vessels. All regenerative organs, organs that they print using bioprinters, will need working blood vessels to be of use. Miller combined the hacker mentality and hacked an open source RepRap 3D printer with an extruder that can extrude fine sugar and gels that will make a vascular system. Discovering the strength in sharing of information, open source, and hacking, he has developed the Advanced Manufacturing Research Institute (AMRI) at Rice University, an entirely new program that combines scientists and the maker community. The results of this combination might just be lifesaving. Hacking and open source is an excellent concept, especially when, in the past, individuals, companies, and universities would like to patent, save, and distribute their knowledge for commercial gain.

3D printing has been around for several decades but commercial, closed-source companies didn't want us to modify their printers and wouldn't make the printer schematics available to us to modify on our own. So, I brought my scientific challenge to our local hackerspace Hive76, and we learned how to use the open-source RepRap printer and modify it to extrude molten sugar for our scientific experiments. Makers and Scientists are on a quest for knowledge, and through sharing and learning together we were able to push bioprinting to a whole new level.

Jordan Miller

ESTUDIOS DURERO
HELPS THE BLIND TO SEE

Sometimes hacking and collaboration come out of a creative necessity. That is the way it was for Estudios Durero in Spain. Sparked by the need of photographer Juan Torre, who was losing his eyesight, Estudios Durero created a new process for blind people to "see" photography through touch. The Didú technique gives textures and relief of up to six millimeters to flat images. Estudios Durero creates the image from a high-resolution photograph. Their trained technicians select the most suitable textures and volumes to guide the blind person's hands. They understand that small details may appear insignificant at first sight, but can be fundamental in understanding the composition or the theme developed in each image. They define the volumes and textures and print with special ink. Then they apply a chemical that gives volume to the initially flat elements. On these, they print the real image with the original colors, at a suitable size. The artwork takes on a three-dimensional quality in relief format so that the "viewers" can explore the textures and the volume of the reproductions by touch. Estudios Durero continues researching to develop and improve their technique, always with the same philosophy: "touching to see in a different way."

Photographer: Chema Madoz (top left + bottom); Clive Egginton (top right)
www.EstudiosDurero.com

How to Get Your Work into the Computer

If you want to use some of the technologies mentioned in this book such as 3D printing, CNC milling, laser cutting, and more, you will need to get your work into the computer. There are a few ways to do this. You can create artwork in the computer using a 3D sculpting or modeling program. You can find and use existing models and scans from the Internet—many of which are free—or you can use 3D scanning to scan existing work. Don't let the idea of 3D scanning frighten you. Now, you can even scan on your cell phone. You will find an introduction to each of these technologies within the chapters in this book.

A Workstation

If you are a traditional artist or craftsperson entering the digital field you may, at one point, ask the question, "What kind of computer do I need?" The answer to this will depend on what you want to do when you combine 3D technology and your fine art and craft. Do you want to sculpt in the computer, or do you plan on doing your work traditionally and then scanning it in? Are you going to buy your own scanner, or have a vendor do it for you? If you are planning on purchasing such things as scanners, 3D printers, CNC milling machines, and other external 3D products (peripherals) then you will need to think about these things in advance. If you plan on buying your own equipment you might work backwards. Research what requirements are necessary for each of these machines before upgrading or buying a computer.

There are many types of workstations. A workstation consists of a computer, monitor, keyboard, and other devices. This workstation features an iMac and a Intuos3 graphics tablet by Wacom. When you are working in a 3D program, a tablet is easier to use than a mouse, and a lot less expensive then a Cintiq.

It is interesting to note that as you make a transition into a digital world you may not need a new computer at all. How is that possible? Makerspaces and hackerspaces are popping up everywhere. You can even find makerspaces and 3D printers in libraries across the country. If you want to get your feet wet, but don't want to invest into a computer, try these spaces. Another option to purchasing or updating a computer to handle robust software is that many of the service bureaus offer programs online. For example, if you go to the Shapeways website (www.shapeways.com), you can create using a computer and their online software programs. There is a list of these in the Appendix of this book and on the book's accompanying website.

If you are using vendors to scan, prepare, and print your files, there may be a chance that you don't need any computer at all. The point is, don't let the thoughts of expensive equipment dissuade you from the adventure of using these technologies, but if you do decide to invest into these new and exciting tools, you may need to update your computer or invest into a new one. Maintaining digital tools is just as important as maintaining traditional tools. That means it will be necessary to update computers and software when needed. This should become a part of your studio budget.

If you already own a computer, it is important to know what your computer can do before giving it a program and a task. Otherwise, the entire process of sculpting, modeling, or posing in the computer will be very frustrating. There is nothing worse than getting so far on a project and feeling like you are beginning to get a grasp of the software only to have it freeze or crash. When you are comparing software or peripherals to the computer that you will need, or your own computer, there is a list of things you may want to consider.

Getting to Know Your Computer

OPERATING SYSTEM   The operating system is the communication hub of your computer. It manages memory, software, hardware, and everything that your computer will do. You will need to update your operating systems every few years. As new software becomes available, the software may require a newer operating system. Be sure you know what operating system you have or what operating system you will need for the software and the peripherals that you desire to work with. Not all software is cross-platform. Cross-platform software works on Mac, PC, and Linux. Some of the software for machining is not even available for the Macintosh operating system. If you are unsure of your present operating system on your computer, you can easily find this information. For a Mac simply click on the Apple icon in the left-hand corner, and then click on "About This Mac." A window will come up in the center of your screen with the version of the operating system. On a PC, right-click on "My Computer," and then click on "Properties" then review the information under "System."

PROCESSOR   The operating system communicates, and the processor or central processing unit (CPU) is the brain of the computer. There are many different kinds of processors. People refer to the processor speed of a computer in hertz (Hz), megahertz (MHz), or gigahertz (GHz). A hertz is a way we measure the frequency in the computer. One hertz is a cycle or refers to the instructions per second. A megahertz is one million hertz, a gigahertz is 1,000 MHz or one billion Hz. The higher the CPU's processing number, the faster the processor. When you are preparing to purchase

Many artists travel back and forth between the tactile traditional world and the digital world. Andrew Kudless, from Matsys Design, will sometimes experiment in the traditional and then try to replicate the effects digitally, or—as in the case of *P_Wall*—create a design in the traditional process but use a master pattern through a computer algorithm to work out the entire design. To learn more about Andrew Kudless and his process, listen to the *Art and Technology* podcasts and visit the videos at www.digitalsculpting.net. *P_Wall*, 2013, by Matsys, 2013, photo by Andrew Kudless.

peripherals or software, knowing your computer's processor or the required speed for the software or peripherals will be necessary.

32-BIT OR 64-BIT? There are two types of CPUs—32-bit and 64-bit. Around the mid-1990s, computer manufacturers introduced 64-bit computing to home computers, and it will eventually become the mainstay. Unfortunately, the transition is here and does cause a bit of confusion. "32-bit" and "64-bit" describe how the CPU handles information. If your computer is older, there is a good chance it is a 32-bit operating system. The difficulty is that some software and peripherals are 64-bit and will not run on 32-bit. However, some 32-bit software will run on 64.

Basically, a 64-bit computer can handle larger portions of information and will work faster. Understanding the architecture of your computer's processor, and the needs of the software and the peripherals, is something to consider. Whatever software you choose, be sure it matches the bit rate of your computer.

GRAPHICS CARD/VIDEO CARD   A graphics card is the graphic processing unit (GPU). It helps the processor to display images properly. Those individuals who play games on their computer may be familiar with a graphics card. If an animation or game is robust, it will require a good graphics card. Without a good graphics card, the computer tries to render the graphics, but there are interruptions; so the gamer may be right in the middle of shooting someone and the screen will look all fractured. For the most part, understanding a graphics card or changing your graphics card is not necessary. It comes into play more with those who play these video games or those who are creating video or animation. Changing or modifying your computer graphics card is not usually a concern for a fine artist or craftsman working in 3D on a computer. However, some 3D sculpting programs and peripherals do demand a specific graphics card, and you may find you need a graphics card for rendering your presentation, which we mention below. So, when comparing your computer and desired 3D sculpting program, be sure that you note the graphic card requirements or suggestions.

MEMORY   There are many traditional artists who may use a computer and never think about how their computer works. When they search the Internet, they simply turn on their computer and wait. Not until they want to use 3D sculpting programs or 3D modeling programs or add peripherals will they begin to think about memory.

Here are the basics of memory. RAM stands for random access memory. Programs will require a minimum amount of RAM so that they can run properly and with speed. The more RAM you have, the faster your computer will run. Your CPU or processor uses RAM while it is accessing everything to create on your computer.

You store your information on your hard disk drive (HDD). When you are writing a paper, using RAM, and the power goes off, if you have forgotten to save your file to the hard drive then you have lost your document. In the simplest terms, your processor is the worker. Your hard drive is where you store everything that you need to work, and your RAM is the place where you are working on things. When the work is complete, or when you shut down your system, everything goes back into the hard drive, unless, of course, your computer crashes and you lose everything from the RAM before saving it into your hard drive.

A computer can have multiple hard drives. There are external drives and internal drives. A boot drive is the hard drive where you store your operating system. Your computer starts up from this drive. There are some drives, such as solid state drives (SSDs), that can make your operating system and applications run faster. SSDs are more expensive, but worth the investment.

Increasing the memory of your computer is not that hard. RAM has gotten much less expensive over the past few years. You may not even know that you can add or change your RAM, and you can often do it yourself. Increasing the amount of RAM on your computer may increase the speed of your computer. If you are unsure how much RAM you have, or how much your computer can hold, you can check for yourself. Your computer has a series of slots inside of it. Depending on your computer, the slots or bays may be full, or some may even be empty. A user can add DIMM modules in the slots, or they can replace existing modules in their computer with modules that have more memory. When purchasing RAM, it is important to note that some computers require that you add the DIMMs in pairs. For example, if you want to add RAM you might purchase two 4 GB DIMMs and insert them in separate slots. Some retailers sell them this way. But you would not buy a 4 GB and an 8 GB DIMM. Again, check with your manufacturer or retailer for their suggestion, and always buy your hard drives and RAM from a reputable dealer. When it comes to purchasing hard drives or memory, this is not a place to try to find the "best deal."

There are many tutorials online for those who would like to add memory themselves, or you can take your computer to a service center to add memory. To find out how much memory your computer has and the capacity it can hold there is no need to unscrew it and look inside. Instead, follow these simple instructions or call the maker of your computer. If you are on a Mac go to "About This Mac" in your Apple menu and when the window comes up, click on "More Information." There are four tabs, "Overview," "Displays," "Storage," and "Memory." If you click on "Memory," it will tell you how many slots your computer has and how much you can install. If you are unsure, you can call your Apple dealer, or Other World Computing (www.macsales.com). They will help you to figure out how much memory your computer will hold and how many slots you have. To find how much memory your PC has or can hold is a little harder; it will depend on what version of Windows is on your computer. In Windows 8, right-click on the windows icon in the corner of your screen and then choose "System." In other versions of Windows, choose "My Computer," and then "Properties." If this is confusing, don't worry, just call the maker of your computer or a vendor that sells RAM and ask them to help you figure out these details. This book's accompanying website has a list of vendors. When considering adding software or peripherals, check out how much RAM or memory you need to run them. If your computer has sufficient memory, and you have checked the other suggestions such as the operating system, CPUs, graphics card, and the type of computer, then you are good to go.

TABLET Many artists working with 3D in the computer find it easier to use a pen and a drawing tablet instead of a mouse. For those sculpting or modeling, it may feel more intuitive than pushing a cursor around with a mouse. There are different types of tablets. Tablets have two parts: the pen or stylus and the flat tablet. Many of these tablets have pressure sensitivity, which may be more enjoyable for creating artwork. A Cintiq is a computer screen where you can draw directly on the screen. Just as with the tablet, you draw with a stylus pen.

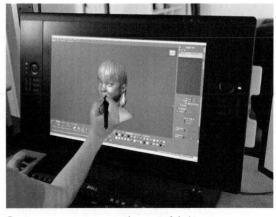

Creating art on a computer can make an artist feel a bit detached from their work. Incorporating a Cintiq in an artist's workstation, such as this Cintiq 24HD, feels more natural as the artist sketches and sculpts directly on the screen.

Software

A fine artist or crafts person has a variety of tools to choose from when entering the digital world. We have listed a few of them in the Appendix and on the website. Exploring the software applications listed in this book is a good place to start. However, it will be necessary to conduct your own investigation into your future software tools. It will, after all, be your time and your money that you will use to make these tools work for you. If a particular software program interests you, spend time researching the relationship between the software and the user community. Visit online communities of users of the programs. Register and ask questions or search their forums for the questions you may have. Check out the online videos to see how easy the program is to use, and to be sure that the software does what you need. A strong user community means that if you have problems with the software, you may be able to get help quickly. Sometimes you can join the user groups and either post your question or search the group for the answers. You will want to know: How often is the software updated? Do updates come free or do you have to pay for them? How steep will the learning curve be? If you are a student, you will want to research if a student version is available for a lower cost. If you find an artist who is doing something similar to what you would like to do, ask them about their software, hardware, etc. Some sculpting programs may be good for designing jewelry, but not as good for creating art that is CNC milled. We have asked all of the artists in this book to share the software that they use.

Many of the software companies offer free trials. Carve out a month of time to check out the free trial version before purchasing. If it is your first time using any program dealing with 3D art, you might also try open source software. This allows you to experiment and get your feet wet with no out-of-pocket expense. There is a list of software programs in the Appendix and on the book's accompanying website (www.digitalsculpting.net). Whatever programs interest you, often using the tool on a trial basis is the only way to know if the tool is right for you. A great example of that is the difference between what users say about ZBrush and Mudbox. ZBrush and Mudbox are the two top sculpting programs on the market. Many will say that the comparisons are hard to make. Each software program seems to work differently for them, even though they do very similar things. Sometimes, it may just be an interface, or the way the program looks that shows a user's preference. With these comparisons, ZBrush has many hidden drawers of tools, which can be overwhelming for some, yet others swear it is the best program. Others describe the simpler interface of Mudbox as less chaotic and more enjoyable. When it comes to the software choices, it may be a matter of your personal learning styles and individual preference, and these can only be experienced from taking the software on a trial run.

Although different 3D sculpting programs may do the same thing, their interfaces can vary. Often it is a matter of preference. Mathieu Gautier's sculpture *Dog* exhibits the Mudbox interface and Magdalena Dadela's *The Straw Hat* exhibits the ZBrush interface.

It is unfortunate that you will not be able to find just one software program that will fit all of your needs. It seems to be a recurring complaint with the many artists interviewed for this book. On average, the amount of programs each artist in this book uses to create their work and realize it in a physical form is approximately three to four. With certain programs, the artist may only use one or two things in a software program. A few years ago, the amount of programs an artist might need was more than three. Many artists have additional programs to make sure that their files are sufficient to be able to print on a 3D printer or be CNC machined. Today, the amount of programs needed to complete all of the tasks necessary to realize the work in a physical form is fewer than just a few years ago, because as software developers understand the needs of the users, they change and incorporate other tools into their programs. Each chapter in this book will introduce you to many different programs and you will begin to understand their use.

When comparing your needs as a traditional artist or craftsman entering the digital field it may not help to ask a computer graphic (CG) artist. Those individuals working in computer graphics for animation or gaming need a lot more out of their computers and software than someone who is simply working with a 3D sculpting program or bringing models into a computer. The workflow, "pipeline," or steps of those working in computer graphics to render images for a movie are different than the steps needed by an artist to create artwork using traditional and digital processes and to realize artwork in a physical form.

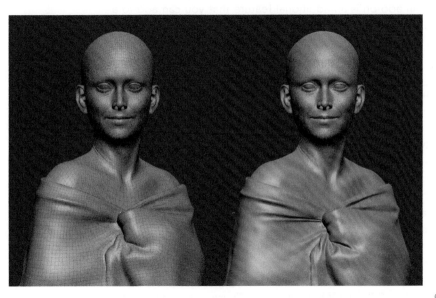

CG artists have a specific workflow to complete an image. Often this incorporates many different software programs. Dan Roarty sculpted the image *Freckles in a Blanket* for *3D Artist Magazine*. It was modeled in a software called Maya, textured in another software—Mudbox—and rendered in Vray. The hair was created with Shave and for the haircut and spec maps he used Knald. A link to the tutorial for this project is found on this book's accompanying website.

With that said, some 3D sculpting programs do have special requirements. Figuring the specification may feel overwhelming at first. When you are sorting out the question of what type of computer you need, you will be comparing. You will compare the needs of software such as 3D sculpting programs or your new and marvelous peripherals, such as 3D printers or CNC milling machines, to the computer required to run them.

Beta Test

Sometimes a software program will be a beta version. If software is considered a beta version then it is not officially released. Beta testing is when a software company or designers offer the software to certain end users who will try the software in real world settings to see if it functions as it is supposed to. Alpha testing is for those end users who have positioned themselves as experts. Become known for your work in a certain program and program developers will take note and make it worth your while to be a beta or alpha tester of their software.

Add-ons/Plug-ins/Extensions

"Add-on," "plug-in," and "extension" are terms that you will often see in association with a software program that you might choose. Although it may depend on the software program that you are using, these terms are very similar. An add-on is an additional feature that you can add to a software program. It is usually a script or coding created to add functions to the program that you are working with. Often a program can have many add-ons. These add-ons can do many different things, and these are usually free. For example, Blender has an add-on called "Add Mesh Walls." So, if an artist were creating a castle using the software program Blender, they might want to get this add-on to quickly be able to make the brick walls.

Many software programs—both the programs that you purchase and free programs—have add-ons or plug-ins. Developers create "extras" that they think complement a program. Users can usually self-install the add-ons simply by clicking on the add-on link. Other add-ons might require that the user install the add-on into a designated folder.

A software company may eventually merge the add-on or plug-in into the program. But add-ons can give great functionality to a software program and are worth checking out. A ZBrush plug-in called "3D Printer Exporter" was available with ZBrush 2009. This plug-in allowed a user to export their ZTool into STL or VRML file formats. These are the file formats that an artist will need for having a 3D model printed with a 3D printer. Another necessary plug-in with ZBrush is "Decimation Master." Sculptures created using a computer program can be very large, much too large to transport or often to use with a 3D printer or milling machine. "Decimation Master" preserves the detail, but lowers the polygon count, making the files much smaller. Unless the program offered these two plug-ins it would be necessary to move the project to another program to do these steps before the file can be output for printing and milling.

An extension is something that the software company may release that will add one or more things to the software that you already own. The maker of the software usually sends out a notice to those who own the program to let them know that the extension is available for download.

As you read this book, you will continually find that many artists have tweaked software to get it to do what they wanted it to do. If you are new to the world of technology, this may seem like an overwhelming endeavor. However, we have listed some information on learning code and creating with code that is quite simple. This new endeavor just might entice some readers to go a bit further with their creative involvement with their software.

Many applications have scripting environments and application program interfaces (API) embedded in them for developers to write custom plug-ins or add-ons themselves. And on top of that, many companies offer entire software development kits (SDK). These kits allow developers in the community (i.e. not employed by the company) to develop all kinds of plug-ins and extensions that access very low-level functionality in the application.

A creative person that is interested in getting more involved with their software would use an SDK to develop a plug-in or extension that has a deeper or lower level of functionality or integration into the core application. A scripting environment or API is a way for community developers to interact with the application at a higher level.

Many artists go back and forth between digital and traditional. You might not recognize how their work is done, and not know that new digital technology was a part of the creation process. *Dichotomy* by Gil Bruvel, 28 × 14 × 27 inches, stainless steel.

3D Sculpting vs 3D Modeling

Although the terms "3D sculpting" and "3D modeling" are often used interchangeably, they do refer to two different types of processes. A bit of history on 3D might help. It all began with a teapot. What does a teapot have to do with 3D sculpting or modeling? In 1975, a computer scientist named Martin Newell created one of the first graphic elements; a simple teapot using math and three-dimensional coordinates in the computer. The teapot was a great subject to represent graphically as it presented many design challenges. The teapot is now a sort of computer icon or inside pun in the computer world. *The Simpsons* features the Newell teapot and designers have slipped it in some of the first computer-generated films. 3D technology has come a long way since 1975. Software evolved; now creating a 3D model or design does not depend on an advanced degree in math and geometry. With 3D sculpting and 3D modeling the software automatically does all the mathematical equations to create your 3D object using the Cartesian system and the x, y, and z axes.

3D modeling was the precursor to 3D sculpting. The description of modeling versus sculpting is debatable. Also up for debate is which is more important to learn. Modeling works with the underlying structure. In modeling, the modeler creates with the polygons, faces, edges, and vertices. 3D sculpting is often described as a more organic process like traditional sculpting where one pulls and pushes on virtual clay. With 3D sculpting programs polygonal modeling and the geometry behind the art are not an issue; instead, the artist shapes the form that they desire.

Entering the process of creating digitally does not mean spending a great deal of money on software programs. As we have already pointed

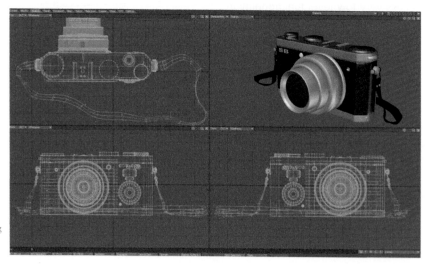

When creating with a modeling program like Lightwave 3D, the artist creates using the underlying geometry. *Camera* by 3D artist Marco Valenzuela.

out, there are many options that are free. Chapter 4 will feature more about the details of 3D sculpting and 3D modeling. Now, let's look at a quick and basic geometry lesson about 3D.

Looking at the Structure of 3D Technology

Entering the digital world is a different environment entirely. There are things that may take some time to get accustomed to. There is terminology that will at first be hard to understand but, as you work through the processes, it does become clearer. Once again, be responsible for your own education with your new tools. When a word or process comes up during your workflow, create an investigation and learn around that process or word. There are also links to several excellent online tutorials about 3D technology basics. You can find these on this book's accompanying website. One such resource is the Guerrilla CG Project, created by Andrew Silke. Both Vimeo and YouTube have these videos. It is difficult to comprehend some of the terms that pertain to 3D space on this 2D page. However, the Guerrilla CG Project tutorials on such things as "Subdivision Topology: Artifacts," "The Polygon," "Object," and "Multisided Polygon" describe these things in 3D on the screen. Accompany these videos with the tutorials in this book and you will have a much clearer understanding. To watch these videos, visit this book's accompanying website at www.digitalsculpting.net.

X, Y, and Z Axes
The term "3D" refers to three-dimensional objects using the Cartesian coordinate system, in the computer. The Cartesian coordinate system is a geometric system that works on three points or axes. Don't fret. Working in the computer is not going to require that you brush up on geometry or work with math. The process is much simpler. The geometry related to the Cartesian coordinate system is not something you will need to know in order to create in such programs as Sculptress, Mudbox, or ZBrush. You won't need to know it to pose a model using Poser or DAZ 3D, or to have something scanned or printed using 3D printing, but the understanding of these systems will be helpful.

When you create in the computer in sculpting or modeling software, the computer software calculates the coordinate system for you. Whether you are scanning an object or making one in a computer graphics modeling or sculpting program, what is happening behind the scene is code— numbers in Cartesian space.

RIGHT-HANDED RULE Hold up your right hand with the middle finger horizontal to the ground, the index finger pointing up, and your thumb pointing to you. In this configuration, the thumb is the y-axis, the pointer finger the z-axis and the horizontal middle finger the x-axis. The "origin" is at the center where the x, y, and z coordinates meet. Coordinates can be expressed in negative and positive numbers depending where they fall in comparison to the place of origin. These coordinates and right-handed rule apply in many cases; however, some applications will show their coordinates differently.

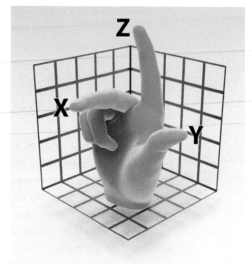

The right-handed rule.

As an artist gets deeper into the process of creating in 3D, the x, y, and z axes may become of interest. Knowing the Cartesian coordinates will also be helpful when you are sending your objects to the CNC milling machine or a 3D printing vendor. For example, CNC milling machines always mill on the z-axis. Even the description of a CNC milling machine uses the term "axis." There are three-axes, five-axes, even seven-axes milling machines. The number refers to the number of axes in which the machine works. Understanding how the 3D equipment will print or cut your object may help you to obtain a better final product. However, don't fret. When you begin using these processes, the computers, vendors and service bureaus often do all of the Cartesian calculations and thinking for you.

Now, let's take a look at some more terms that you will come across when hearing people talk about the topology of a 3D object.

Edges, Vertices, and Faces

An edge, in the underlining geometry found in 3D technology, is the line between two vertices. A vertex or vertices in 3D is a meeting of two or more straight lines in the corner. The faces in geometry are the flat surfaces between the edges and the vertices.

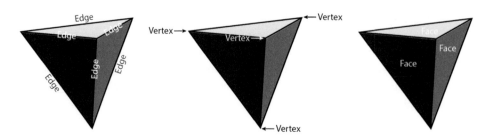

Polygons

The prefix "poly" means many. A polygon is a two-dimensional shape that consists of three or more vertices. The polygons that we use most often in 3D are those with three edges or triangles, or those with four edges known as quads. However, in 3D modeling and 3D sculpting it is best to use polygons with four vertices or quads.

The preferred polygon for 3D sculpting is quads.

Topology

When someone refers to the "topology" of a 3D object, they are talking about the geometry that makes up the surface. Good topology for sculpting in 3D has several characteristics.

1. The mesh consists of quads instead of triangles.
2. There is an even distribution of polygons.
3. The topology has edge loops.

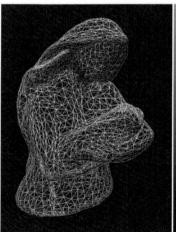
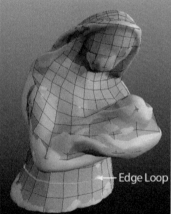
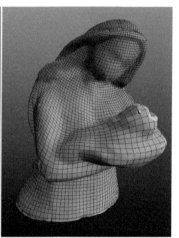

← Edge Loop

If you are sending your artwork to a company that creates 3D scans, and enlarges or reduces your 3D scan to send to a 3D printer or for CNC machining, you won't have to worry about the topology or the mesh, the service bureau may do that for you. But if you are creating work in the computer or modifying scanned work for 3D printing and CNC milling you will have to work a bit with the topology software programs to prepare your work. We will cover this in greater detail in Chapters 4 and 7.

- Tris or triangle—triangles are polygons with three vertices and three sides.

Retopology by Mike de la Flor using 3DCoat. When 3D scanning an object, the scanner creates a mesh made in points or triangles. If you want to sculpt on that 3D scanned object in the computer you will need to retopologize it and make it into a mesh with quads and good edge loops. Retopologizing in this manner will also prevent subsurface artifacts from appearing and annoying you when you sculpt. We will learn more about retopologizing and preparing files in Chapters 3, 4 and 7.

- Edge loop—an edge loop in the topology is a loop that goes around the object in one continuous flow and is not interrupted.
- Quads—are the preferred polygon for sculpting. Artists prefer them because they can easily divide. Sometimes, dividing a mesh may cause triangles to appear. These tris can cause bumps on the surface known as "artifacts." An artifact in 3D sculpture is like having a foreign object in your traditional clay. No amount of smoothing will get rid of it until you remove the artifact. If you continue to subdivide the mesh, it may only compound the problem.

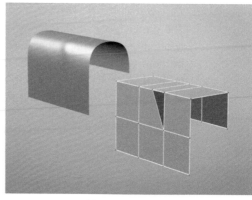

A bump or a smoothing artifact occurs when a three-sided face causes a bump in the mesh. For a clear and animated explanation of artifacts and topology, visit this book's accompanying website at www.digitalsculpting.net and watch the Guerrilla CG video prepared by Andrew Silke. This image was created for Guerrilla CG by Greg Petchkovski.

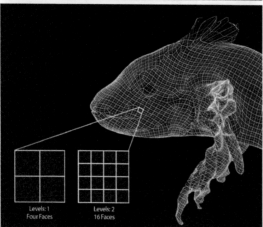

3D models built in the computer start with a mesh that has a low poly count and large quads. Subdividing means that the computer divides the faces on the object. When you divide the model, you get more polygons and, in turn, you will get more detail. The computer takes one quad on the model and divides it into four sections. In another subdivision, the computer takes that same surface and divides it again into 16 sections. The image becomes smoother with each subdivision. The higher the resolution in the models, the more faces it will have. High-resolution models also take up more memory in the computer. Once

(above left) With a polygon mesh, the mesh becomes smoother as you subdivide. 3D artist Marco Valenzuela.

(left) When sculpting in the computer, you can make a model smoother by adding more subdivision. A polygon mesh made up of quads is easily divided. Each subdivision is a division of four.

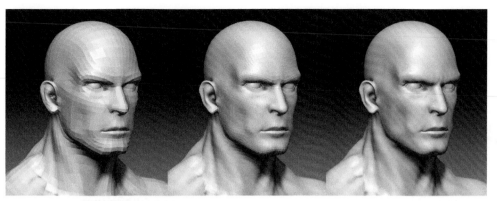

Artists who sculpt in 3D in the computer begin by roughing the sculpture in at a low resolution. As the artist needs more detail, they will subdivide the model. Subdividing allows them to sculpt more detail: more quads make for a smoother surface. Artwork by 3D artist Marco Valenzuela.

again, depending on the software, all of this geometry happens behind the scenes; you never have to worry about the math to create it. All the artist needs to know to subdivide the surface is how to press a button, how many times to subdivide, and the best time in the sculpting process to press that button.

Normals and Reversed Normals

You may hear the term "normals" or "reversed normals" when you are trying to get your model or sculpture out of the computer through 3D printing or CNC machining. Polygons are two-sided, and the "normal" is the face of the polygon that faces out. During the process of sculpting in the computer, the computer may reverse a face normal. Then the surface points to the inside on that polygon. Sometimes a 3D model might even be missing a face. These incidents are not something that you will necessarily see while sculpting or modeling, but the 3D printer and CNC machines will detect these. There are free software programs that will help you to locate and fix such things as reversed normals or missing faces. You may need to take your model into these free software programs when preparing files for 3D printing and CNC milling, or your vendor may do this for you. See Chapters 4 and 7 for more information.

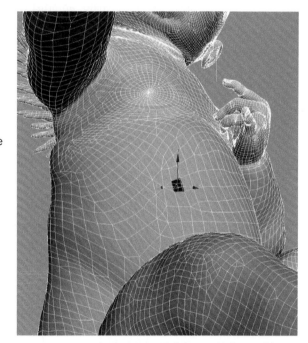

A polygon is two-sided; the normal is the part of the polygon that faces out. If there are reverse normals or missing faces in the model then a 3D printer cannot print and a CNC machine cannot mill. Reversed normals and missing faces are hard to see, but there are programs that help you fix your files for 3D printing and find the reversed normals and missing geometry.

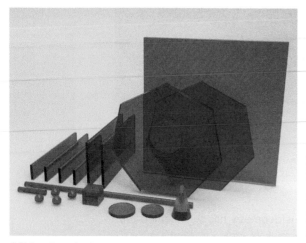

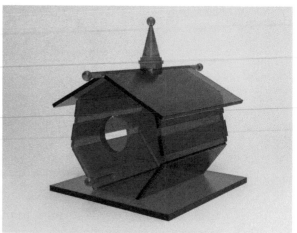

(left) An artist can break down most images into basic shapes. We call these basic shapes "primitives." Primitives are very helpful in creating a digital sculpture or model quickly.

(right) 3D artist Marco Valenzuela creates a birdhouse from simple primitives.

Primitives

Primitives are usually simple objects like cubes, cylinders, or spheres. Just like in sketching, an artist will use simple forms to block-in a drawing: a cylinder for the legs of a fat rabbit connected to an oval. Primitives come with the computer program. A 3D artist uses them to rough-in a model.

Decimation

We have seen how we start at a low polygon count or low resolution and then slowly build the polygons by subdivision to get more detail. However, when a 3D sculpture has a high poly count, an artist cannot send it to a 3D printer or CNC milling machine. The files may be too large. It is an art in itself to be able to determine how far you need to push the polygons and subdivisions to get what you need, without overloading the system. Remember that, as the technology is today, there is no output device able to create with the same detail with which the computer can create the model inside the computer. The detail of the output devices will change, as technology advances.

Each of your vendors will have a maximum size polygon count that they can handle and will let you know in advance. If your file is too large then you can reduce the poly count without affecting the overall look and detail of the art. Decimation is the process of reducing a poly count. Some 3D graphic programs have a decimation tool within them. There are also free tools like MeshLab, where you can bring your 3D file in and decimate it. We will look at decimation more in Chapter 4.

Rendering

We have already stated that it takes a lot of RAM to work on 3D models or scenes in the computer. The image that you see on the screen is often an approximation of what you are creating. To work on the image, as it would appear, would take too much time and slow down the computer. When an artist finalizes a figure, they may want to render it. An artist creating something in the computer to go to a CNC milling machine or 3D printer will not need to render. Rendering would be necessary if an artist were creating a presentation for a client to see what a sculpture or object may look like in its final physical form. The artist chooses materials and the lighting for the model. They can then render the scene and provide this render or photographic image for the client's approval. Rendering is one of those things that is affected by the graphics card. If rendering is something that you are considering in your regular workflow, then it will be important to pay attention to your computer's graphics card.

Mike de la Flor renders several views of a proposed panther for Prairie View A&M. Sculptor Bridgette Mongeon. See complete bronze on page 32.

Retopology

Retopologizing is the changing of the topology of a 3D sculpture or model. There are several instances where retopologizing becomes necessary. Imported models from other programs may have bad topology. A scanned model can come in with triangles or points. Pushing and pulling on the vertices while sculpting in the computer can change the underlying topology. There was a time, not long ago, when retopologizing seemed to be the holy grail of 3D sculpting, or at least the missing element. Computer graphic artists would describe the process of sculpting in the computer as organic, but if an artist destroys the sculpture's topology when they are moving the clay, it is hardly like traditional sculpting. In the past, an artist retopologized a sculpture by drawing each point, edge loops, and vertices all around the sculpture. Now, in some programs, an artist does it with a push of a button.

Navigation in 3D

Digital artists create 3D models and sculptures in a computer program. For an artist to create a digital model, it will be necessary to learn to move around or navigate in a 3D program. The terms found in these 3D programs are similar to terms used by cameramen. Each software program will have its process for the artist to navigate. It may be a keystroke accompanied by a mouse movement or a tool that the artist selects in the navigation screen. Another way to navigate is to use your tablet and the keys provided on your tablet. Your software and tablet tutorials will explain these types of navigation. Using a tablet or stylus pen to navigate is similar to using a right-click or left-click with the mouse. Some graphics tablets have programmable buttons on the side for easier navigation. This type of navigation offers a way to navigate without having to move your hand to the keyboard. Until an artist masters stylus pen clicks while working on a tablet in a computer 3D sculpting or 3D molding program, they will be moving the object around with their stylus hand, while they balance their other hand on the computer keyboard ready to push the memorized keys. As you develop a workflow and your workspace, you will find a navigation flow that fits your preferred sculpting software, your personal needs, and your working style.

Camera

Many 3D programs will have camera views and refer to these views such as "top view" and "side view" in the navigation window. When creating work in 3D, just as sculpting in a traditional studio, it is necessary to work on more than one view, moving back and forth. A sculptor in the traditional studio trains himself or herself to move back and forth between views of their physical model. They make changes to a portrait, checking it from the front, and then rotating the object to look at it from the side to see if these same changes look good from all views. Just as in the traditional studio, a digital artist can work on one area and then rotate the object in the computer. Some software programs will allow the user to alternate between views. With a couple of windows on the screen at the same time, the user may be able to look at both views simultaneously. So, while they are changing the nose while looking at the front of the face, the artist will see the same changes taking place to a profile image.

It is difficult, at first, to know where you are in the virtual space. It may look like you are clicking on the object from one view, but once you rotate the sculpture you may find that you are far away from the object. For someone just entering 3D sculpting or modeling and becoming used to the navigation, it can be a challenge at first. Terms to look out for include:

- Rotate—rotating simply means rotating around the object or turning the object. The object rotates on a predetermined pivot point. The user may change the pivot point. For example, instead of an object pivoting around its center, it may pivot around one edge.
- Zoom—as simple as rotating, zoom does just what it says it will do. Zoom makes the camera or the viewer zoom into a 3D model. You may even zoom so close that you end up inside the model.
- Pan—pan means to move the camera back and forth or up and down with your object staying in the same place.

Lighting

Lighting is important in any scene. It would make sense then that 3D sculpting or graphics programs offer the user different lighting. With 3D, the shape and form can change and pop out as the artist lights it. Sculptor Augusto Rodin would place a candle on the side of his work so that he could see the shadows. Placing lights around your digital scene will help to illuminate and shade the work while you are sculpting. Later, if an artist needs to render the scene for presentation they can arrange the lighting so that it highlights the art.

Mapping

UV Mapping

You will hear the terms "UV mapping" or "texture mapping" often in the 3D world. As mentioned before, CG artists or those working in the film industry, animation, etc., will use UV mapping much more than an artist who is sculpting in the computer and going to have their sculptures CNC machined or 3D printed. For the most part, an artist who is working with 3D scanning, 3D printing, milling, or even 3D sculpting to create their artwork into a physical form will not need to know about UV mapping. The exception to that is when you are working with photogrammetry or other scanning where you are collecting not only the geometry of the subject but also its color. We will also talk about UV mapping when you want to create a 3D print in full color—at the writing of this book, there are only a few ways to 3D print in full color.

Because there are few times when an artist will need UV mapping, we include it here. UV mapping is a type of texturing. Some may also refer to it as texture mapping. Let's try to simplify just what UV mapping is. Do you remember those globes that you might have had as a child or that were in school? You could run your hand over the mountains and feel their

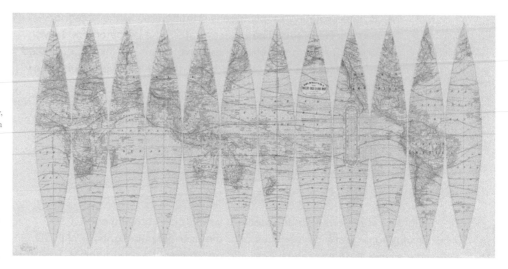

UV mapping or texture mapping is similar to unwrapping the color and texture from a globe. When you learn to work with UV maps you can unwrap the color and/or texture of your object that you sculpt in the computer, and bring it into a program such as Photoshop. There you can add more color or adjust the color, before bringing it back into a sculpting program. Then the artist applies the UV coordinates to the 3D geometry. That way, if you make changes to the 3D object, the changes will also apply to the UV map. Source: Geography and Map Division, Library of Congress.

texture. You could look at the blue and know where the lakes or oceans were. Hauling a globe around was not possible. The traveler needed a two-dimensional map. But how do you depict three-dimensional information in two-dimensional space? What if we sliced the globe apart? We know that the world is round, but to make a flat image of the world it might look like the image of the map above. It would become a two-dimensional representation, both in color and texture. What we did to this globe is similar to UV mapping in 3D. UV takes a three-dimensional object and creates maps that are in two dimensions. We learned about the x, y and z coordinates earlier. In UV these are also coordinates. Thinking of our world map again, consider the "V" coordinates the longitude or north and south or up and down and the "U" coordinates the latitude or east and west. When an artist puts the color and texture back on the object they align the UV coordinates with the x, y, and z coordinates.

Most of the 3D sculpting and modeling programs will create UV maps for you, should you need them, and you can then modify the UV map. Working with UV maps can be tedious when it comes to a complex shape. Keep watching the technology though; there is no doubt someone will eventually develop a better process for texturing and adding color. At that time, UV mapping may become obsolete.

Projection Mapping

Although projection mapping is not used anywhere in this book, you may come across the term as you are learning about 3D technology and beginning to socialize with those working in 3D. Projection mapping is another way of texturing an object. In projection mapping, the two-dimensional texture is projected on the image. This type of texturing will not apply to art that is coming out of the computer using 3D printing or CNC machining.

Projection mapping also has another meaning. 3D projection mapping is a form of audiovisual performance art that uses technology and specialized software to project images onto objects. This type of projection mapping is something to see. For example, in 2010 the Macula and Tomato Production used AV equipment and a computer to project images onto the old Prague clock in celebration of its 600th birthday. In 2013, Bot and Dolly took projection mapping and robotics and made them interact with an actor to create the work known as *Box*. For an interesting reflection of how technology and another form of art meet, check out the projection map videos on this book's accompanying website.

See, this primer in 3D wasn't that bad. But take a deep breath, we are about to get into the real creative process. There is quite a bit of information in this primer chapter. As we said, it is not necessary for you to understand everything in this chapter for you to proceed with incorporating 3D technology in your art or craft, and there is probably much more that we could put in this primer chapter to help you. This primer should help you. You may begin to see 3D a little clearer, and you now have a starting point from which to work. You will continue to add to your knowledge every time you incorporate a 3D process into your traditional workflow.

Perhaps you still feel a little apprehensive about using 3D in your studio or workshop. You are not alone. Before we look at some of the incredible art and processes created with 3D scanning, sculpting, and milling, let's take a moment to review the internal conversations that others who enter this 3D world have had. Let's also look at the dialogues that have been taking place between artists, collectors, and museums since the introduction of these processes. And finally, lets talk about the physiological challenges as well as the psychological and social aspects of marrying the digital world with the traditional world to create incredible art.

BRUCE BEASLEY

Bruce Beasley is one of the United States' most prominent sculptors. He is also a pioneer and has been working using 3D technology and fine art since 1987. The software company Autodesk created one of the first art shows incorporating 3D technology in 2008, featuring the work of several artists including Bruce Beasley.

Bruce describes sculpting in 3D as a process that enables him to make more subtle or complicated changes without material consideration. When he creates, he does not see the work in his head ahead of time. Instead, the tools give him a place for discovery.

Bruce Beasley and the assembly of *Arpeggio IV*, www.brucebeasley.com. Photograph by Lee Fatheree.

Bronze sculpture *Tenacity* by Bruce Beasley. Photograph by Lee Fatheree.

In the *Coriolis* series, Bruce creates fine art using Autodesk software Alias, 3ds Max, and Inventor. The pieces are then 3D printed. This 3D printed fine art takes 3D printing to an entirely new level.

Coriolis VII
by Bruce Beasley

BRIDGETTE MONGEON

Sculptor Bridgette Mongeon uses ZBrush and Mudbox to create digital designs, or sculpts them and has them 3D scanned. She enlarges the 3D designs and CNC mills in foam. After carving the foam and adding detail with a thin layer of clay, molds are made of the art and the sculpture enters the lost wax process of bronze casting.

Prairie View A&M Panther by Bridgette Mongeon. Photograph by Bill Petty.

Called to Pray by Bridgette Mongeon. Photograph by Christina Sizemore, Diliberto Photo and Design.

ANDREW KUDLESS
of MATSYS DESIGN

Andrew Kudless of Matsys Design moves back and forth between digital and traditional processes to create unique designs. For Kudless it is more than 3D, he also uses algorithms and physics when working on his art.

Kudless made *Chrysalis III* out of composite paper-backed wood veneers from Lenderink Technologies (www.lenderink.com). It contains cherry veneer (exterior) and poplar veneer (interior). To create each of these designs Kudless used the software program Rhino with Grasshopper, Kangaroo, Python, Lunchbox, and Rhinoscript.

Chrysalis III by Andrew Kudless, Matsys, 2011. Photograph by Andrew Kudless.

On the book's website at www.digitalsculpting.net you will find:

* Links to further descriptions on the process of creating the artwork featured in the galleries.
* Podcasts with the artists.
* Videos featuring the artists at work.

CHAPTER TWO

A WORLD TURNED UPSIDE DOWN

———

"It is an important token reminder for the younger generation and their tutors, that above and beyond the abundance of electronic marvels, the human vision and imagination remains the most important element, and that its nurture should not be replaced by excessive reliance on devices."

Erwin Hauer

facing page
Design 201 by Erwin Hauer.

Incorporating digital practices in a traditional studio is like entering a different world. It may, at first, feel like a world turned upside down. Imagine a dream place where you can float, where heavy is light, and light is heavy. Imagine a place where you can walk inside something solid or sit in a chair and instead of resting your head on a desk your head can penetrate the surface. Imagine an existence where you can create things that have never been possible, until this moment. A world limited only by your own imagination and creativity. For some, this is the place of virtual space. This new world gives the artist an opportunity to play, explore, and realize things they could never comprehend in any other way.

There are many possibilities in traveling to a virtual world and back to the physical world, and there are many possibilities in using the tools of each in the process of creating. There are some difficulties that a traditional artist or craftsperson may have to overcome. There are also some psychological and even social conversations that arise when an artist combines 3D technology with fine art and craft.

Incorporating 3D processes is like working in a different medium. There is a learning curve, and many adjustments for a traditional artist. A traditional artist and craftsperson may be able to bring their knowledge of form and use of traditional tools into the digital world, but there are still some challenges. When entering this world it is comforting to know you are not alone, and that others have gone through the same transitions and asked the same questions of themselves and the technology. Some of the topics in this chapter include internal dialogues that a traditional artist or craftsperson may have when entering the digital world and going through the learning processes or when straddling these two worlds of fine art and technology. There are also external dialogues that are continuing as the technology matures. Let's take a look at a few of the barriers, dialogues, and challenges.

Out of Sight, Out of Mind

Pressure of the deadline and/or inspiration propels some artistic endeavors. The artist is so driven; they will finish the artwork within a sitting or two. Yet, they may not complete other works in short durations and, instead, the creator works on them over long stretches of time. Inspiration strikes, but some pieces of art take a long time to complete. Each stage of the creative process ferments into the next, culminating in a finished piece of art. Some art may turn into masterpieces; others may be experiments. When you walk into a traditional sculpture studio, you will see surfaces lined with both old and new work. New commissions or inspirations of wet clay sit covered in plastic and may keep company with dried clay busts from previous commissions or inspirations and experiments of years gone by. All these works watch the progress of new creations brought to life with the artist's hands. A work in progress is not hidden away in a deep, recessed corner, forgotten. It sits awaiting attention. The physical existence of these unfinished works is a personal reminder of the inspiration that brings it to life. The dust accumulating on their surfaces is the solid physical reminder that prompts the artist back into activity. If pushed aside, the artwork pleads through its physicality, "Remember me? You loved me once. Finish me."

Traditional sculptor studios have physical reminders of work completed or work that is in need of completion. The studios have changed little over the years. *Elisabet Ney in ihrem Atelier*, Texas, 1875.

When turning to the digital process you store your work deep in a folder in the recessed corners of your computer's hard drive. There your inspiration waits, no longer visible. The artist must remember that the work is there and click on multiple folders to be reunited with their inspiration. The artist must remember the art, with no visual clues other than an unopened folder. Some artist may miss the visual reminders; they may even depend on those reminders to progress with their work and career. Working on a computer, an artist may feel they have nothing to call to them, unless they can remember what they have done and feel connected to the code within the computer. Traditional artists and craftsmen may find the transition to digital creations motivationally difficult. Artwork filed away is "out of sight and out of mind." There is a calmness in the visual clutter found in traditional processes that some may experience as lacking in the digital world. Perhaps a suggestion would be for someone to create a computer app that automatically flashes your work in progress across the screen. The stored art on your computer will come forward, giving you a visual reminder of a passion once expressed.

Loss of Data

Those individuals that create work in the computer or with a combination of traditional processes and computer-generated processes may feel very confident in saving their art. In fact, it is much easier to save a sculpture intended to be a 50-foot sculpture as a digital file, than it would be to store a 50-foot sculpture in real life. Even if an artist makes several backup files in the appropriate and recent file formats, there is no certainty that, over the years, the artist will ever be able to retrieve the work. In the 1970s and 1980s, individuals stored their work on a floppy disk first at 5¼ inches and then at 3½ inches. If an artist stored their work on those discs, is it still retrievable with computers that have a CD, DVD, USB flash, or USB pen drive? How will the future storage of data differ from how artists are storing their inspiration and life's work today? Besides the storing of the data, there is also the problem of being able to open that data. If you are trying to save your data, can we be certain that there will be a program on your studio computer that can open the data five or ten years from now?

Space and Size

When sculpting digitally, the traditional artist enters a world in which the art defies natural law. When an artist first starts working in the computer's virtual space they will ask him or herself, "Where am I within this space?" They become the camera view to their sculpture. That is their physical connection. A traditional artist entering the digital world learns to navigate, not by walking, but by mouse movements combined with keystrokes. It will take time, and at first they will feel like they are stumbling around the virtual space, but they will eventually enjoy the ease of moving around a digital sculpture.

It's All About the Detail, or Not...

When working on a miniature sculpture, the traditional artist searches for a more powerful magnifier. They search for smaller tools—a dental tool or the fine tip of a pin—as they delicately caress and finesse the clay into a tiny replication of their creative thought. In the digital environment, the size is hard to determine. Is the sculpture big or is it small? In the computer, size is often a hidden or unused concept; not until it comes out of the computer is it given an actual size. Size and detail can become a stumbling block for beginners. They need to know how much detail they should carve digitally. When an artist tries to get the artwork out of the computer, can the vendor reproduce the detail the artist is laboring over? How much detail should they put into the sculpture? A famous quote is: "Art is never finished, only abandoned." The traditional artist may work for many hours on a sculpture and know intuitively when it is time to abandon the art. They know the level of detail they are obtaining for their medium. For example, the detail put in a clay sculpture that an artist will cast as a bronze is different from the detail put in a clay sculpture that the artist will cast in concrete. The artist understands the limits of the medium and how far they can push those limits. They can see what their eye can see because they are seeing the artwork in the size in which they intend the viewer to experience it. In the real world, it is easier to determine when the artwork is complete. However, a digital artist, with their capability of zooming in, may not know the threshold of detail necessary when exporting the artwork out of the computer for digital reproduction in such things as 3D printing or CNC milling. Also, in many cases, the present technology for output cannot give the detail in the size and material that the artist desires. As an artist becomes experienced with the process of output, they will know when they reach that threshold. Otherwise adding additional detail to a virtual model is a waste of time.

Artistic Vertigo: Connection or Flying?

For the traditional sculptor now in the digital world, the art of panning, zooming, and digitally revolving around a sculpture may bring on a type of artistic vertigo. They may also feel a disassociation from the art. If you don't know the physical size of the art, how can you possibly relate to it? A traditional sculptor has time to sit with a sculpture as it fills the space and breathes within the area where the artist is creating. By walking away and approaching the art from another direction, the artist may sense the changes that need to take place. They come back to the clay and move an arm here, push this piece there, and step back once again. At first, the relationship of size and space to a traditional artist working digitally may feel a bit confusing and unrewarding. Yet, for some artists, such as Bruce Beasley, who work their designs as they create them and whose physical work is large and heavy, working in a digital environment can feel very liberating. You might even describe it as similar to the ethereal feeling of flying. They don't have to physically move around large heavy sheets of metal, weld, and then dismantle them if they change their mind. They can simply create in the computer, moving shapes until they feel the cohesion of design.

The Smell of Creativity

Artists' and craftsmen's studios have a smell to them. There is no mistaking the smell of a woodworker's studio or an oil painter's studio. Even the art can have a smell; some of these smells may be particular to each artist. For example, the painter Robert Genn of the wonderful artist blog *Painter's Keys* writes about the smell of his oil painting:

> Odour might just be the unsung silver hammer of art. Who can resist the magnificent waft of a new oil painting? (Acrylics and watercolours are at a disadvantage here.) Back in my oil days, there were folks who came into my studio and actually paused to savor the Rembrandtian atmosphere. Were those flexing nostrils, I wondered, part of my sales team?
>
> *Painter's Keys*, "The Smell of Art"
> (http://clicks.robertgenn.com/smell-of-art.php)

It is difficult to say what effect the smells of a traditional studio have on an artist's creativity. It may be as simple as walking into the same room to create and the smells trigger neurons in the brain. Creativity bursts forth because of those neural connections and that entices the creative muse. Perhaps those sculptors transitioning from traditional to digital should bring some wood shavings or an open box of clay into the computer room when they create. If your creative workflow combines both traditional and digital then you always have the comfort of returning to the traditional studio to create and sniff.

Touch

Artists and craftsmen work with their hands. The sense of touch involves many different things; temperature, pressure, vibration, and even the tension of your skin. The artist's touch lights up when in the process of creating. Traditional artists working in a digital world may find the lack of tactile stimulation of the digital process a hindrance. A seasoned traditional sculptor of clay knows the results of the placements of their finger on a sculpture or the fattiness of their thumb depressed to make a crevice. These appendages are their most vital tools. They are extensions of their creativity. Exploring and sculpting by touch, with your eyes closed, is not unheard of for a traditional sculptor. They have trained their sense of touch and comprehension of form to such a level that things "feel" right.

Natural elements also contribute to tactile sensation in the process of creating; for example, sculpting in traditional water-based clay, an artist

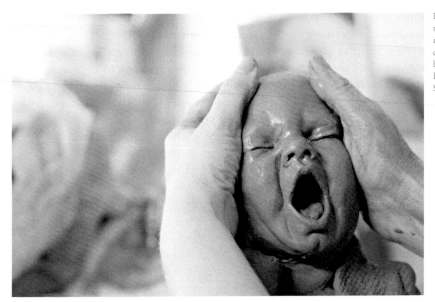

learns the stages of the clay and what they can accomplish in the sculpting process when the clay is soft as compared to when it dries and is "leather hard." The digital processes remove the tactile sensations of sculpting. Artists can feel some experience of tactile sensation through some software combined with specific hardware. Hardware such as a graphics tablet is the first exploration of most artists working in a digital environment. There are many makers of tablets; Wacom is a very dependable graphics tablet with a variety of options from which to choose. A graphics tablet may be a bit difficult to get used to at first. Tablets are input devices that work with a digital pen, which the artist moves, or strokes on the tablet. Using a tablet and pen is more natural than trying to draw with a mouse. At first, artists may find that stroking on a tablet and watching what happens on the screen is not pleasurable. This "disconnect" does subside after repeated use. There are other options; Wacom makes a Cintiq that allows you to draw directly on the screen, the screen is the tablet. A workstation that uses a Cintiq can be a great asset to those artists who have a difficulty of "sculpting" and looking at the screen, while working, creating movement on a tablet. The artist can configure the Cintiq or the tablet. When configured, the effects of the pressure sensitivity of the pen combined with the software can be quite a productive and enjoyable experience. However, this pressure sensitivity might not apply to all software programs.

Haptic devices are another type of navigation device used in the computer world. Haptic devices work on vibration or force to offer a tactile sensation to the user. Manufacturers of haptic devices intend for them to give a more realistic feel of touch. Although the technology is advancing with haptic devices, they are far from real touch. Using digital technology may be more about training yourself to create in a different way with less sensory input. Traditional artists retraining to use haptic devices could be compared to a surgeon originally trained to open up the body and look inside to do his or her work, and then transitioning to performing "minimally invasive surgery" by looking at the camera while manipulating tools placed through small incisions. For an artist to use these devices in the digital world, it will be important to be less dependent on the touch that they are used to while working within the creative process.

For some artists, nothing gives the needed tactile stimulation and involvement with the materials as much as the traditional processes do. In the case of incorporating digital tools in the traditional studio, this lack of tactile stimulation is simply a deal-breaker. They cannot get past the lack of touch, but for every negative there are positive things about using digital technology. If you feel like you may be one person that feels they cannot get past that lack of touch, hang in there. Maybe some of the positive parts of using digital technology will outweigh your intense need for the tactile sensation you crave. Let's take a look at a few of those.

Navigation and Traditional Acrobatic Sculpting

There are advantages to the virtual space. For example, when sculpting the underside of something in a traditional studio, the artist becomes an acrobat or muscle man. Flipping a traditional sculpture may not be possible. Instead, flipping the artist is necessary as they contort their bodies to sculpt hard-to-reach areas. In contrast, with digital sculpting, an artist can hide parts to get to other parts more easily. Hiding parts digitally is like cutting away in the traditional sculpture process. If the traditional artist can't reach the folds tucked in the crevice of the arm, the sculptor cuts the arm away, fixes the folds and then attaches the arm again. However, the artist will also have to repair the damage of the clay caused by cutting the arm away. In the case of a digital model, the sculpture is never harmed. The artist selects the piece with the cursor and temporarily hides it from view. A traditional artist will soon find that this maneuverability in a digital world is an absolute pleasure.

In a traditional sculpture studio, an artist revolves around the subject. They walk away to view the entire sculpture and come back to the sculpture again to make changes and work on details. In the computer, navigating a sculpture is no longer done in the traditional way. In the digital environment, an artist can enlarge the sculpture to create the smallest detail. They can zoom out to see how the sculpture will look from across the room, across a field, or even flying above the art. Computer navigation offers advantages over traditional space, because physical space in a traditional studio often has limitations. When working on a monumental sculpture in a traditional studio, it is sometimes impossible to back away far enough to be able to view the entire sculpture. It is hard to imagine what it will look like from the observer's viewpoint, or how it will look mounted onto a large pedestal. Navigation in the digital studio helps the artist to see all of these things. However, time and time again artists report that they truly don't "see" the sculpture until they are experiencing it with their own eyes in a physical form.

The Benefits

One only needs to view the incredible possibilities and art in this book to see the benefits of incorporating digital and traditional processes. Digital processes have an "Undo" button so you can undo things that you do not want without damaging the work. You can also make modifications to the work and bring back the original file to compare. Symmetry opens up a world of possibilities and saves time. It is possible to sculpt, not only on two sides of an object at the same time, but in some programs an artist can use three, six, or even 12 brush strokes in perfect symmetry at the same time. There are times when even a seasoned sculptor will create a sculpture and wish they could enlarge or reduce it. Digital processes allow an artist to enlarge and reduce. Many other processes such as copy and paste, mirror, even deforming or reducing parts of a sculpture are all possible and very easy with the digital process of creating. The weightlessness of the material and creative possibilities of not having gravity offer a new way of creating. Many of these advantages of sculpting and creating may just outweigh the artist's need for touch.

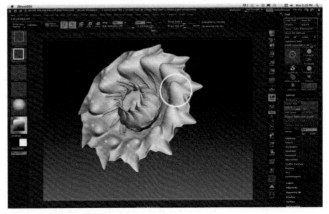

When working in the computer an artist can sculpt in symmetry using multiple points.

Is it Art?

Art should, in any case, transcend the medium.
Technique always has been and probably always will be confused with art.

Digital sculptor, Keith Brown

(Christiane Paul, *Fluid Borders: The Aesthetic
Evolution of Digital Sculpture*)

The artwork created by artists using 3D technology is intriguing and in some cases the artwork is outright stunning, but many have asked, "is this art?" Of course, the question is subjective and depends on the viewer. Is a woodworker any less of an artist than a glassblower? Is an artist specializing in miniatures less of an artist than one working on a monumental bronze? Does the art created with the 3D tools somehow have less value because of the process? Digital tools are just another medium, another tool. The art should rise above the medium in which the artist creates.

The conversation of "is it art?" is not a new conversation. Every time tools change, the conversation repeats. In 1848 a French writer, Alphonse de Lamartine, wrote about the new invention called photography:

> It is because of the servility of photography that I am fundamentally contemptuous of this chance invention which will never be an art but which plagiarises nature by means of optics. Is the reflection of a glass on paper art? No, it is a sunbeam caught in the instant by a manoeuvre. But where is the choice? In the crystal, perhaps. But, one thing is for sure, it is not in Man. The photographer will never replace the painter, one is a man, the other a machine. Let us compare them no longer.
>
> *Cours familiar de littérature: Entretiens sur Leopold Robert*, 1858

Yet over the years, individuals, collectors, and galleries have accepted and celebrated photography as a creative form of expression and viable art form. In 1910, the Albright Knox Art Gallery in Buffalo, New York, was one of the first museums to bring photography into a fine art collection, although it still took some time for many to accept photography as an art. The tools of photography began to change in 1975 with the introduction of the first digital camera. Soon using a camera and shooting with film and processing the work in the dark room became nearly extinct as the digital process began replacing the film process of photography by mid-2000. Some photographers believed that it wasn't truly art without the film part of photography.

When you involve a machine in the process of creating the work, does it depreciate the value of the work? "The value of 3D art" is a conversation many people continue to have. When a sculptor creates a limited-edition bronze figurine with the traditional process of the lost wax method, as

(top) In the Remington sculpture comparisons, each of the images are the same sculpture; they are, however, different numbers in the edition. The nuances of the process of the lost wax method of bronze casting assure us that no two are exactly alike. Frederic Remington, *The Broncho Buster*, 1895, bronze. Cast by Henry-Bonnard Bronze Company, ca. 1895–1898. Amon Carter Museum of American Art, Fort Worth, Texas, 1961.

(middle) Frederic Remington, *The Broncho Buster*, 1905–1909, bronze. Cast by Roman Bronze Works, ca. 1910–1914. Amon Carter Museum of American Art, Fort Worth, Texas, 1961.

(bottom) Frederic Remington, *The Broncho Buster*, 1895, bronze. Cast ca. 1920–1952. Amon Carter Museum of American Art, Fort Worth, Texas, 1961.

shown in Chapter 8, each copy in the edition will not be exact. There will be nuances created through the process. The artist and the foundry labor over each wax, trying to make them look alike. (The artist requires one wax for each number in the edition.) When looking at a series of Remington bronzes, it is fascinating to see how each bronze, with so many little pieces and details such as guns, rope, etc., changes over the life of the edition. In some cases, the differences are so vast it does not even appear to be the same edition. When comparing 3D printing, and the traditional lost wax method of bronze casting, John Frembling, archivist and reference service manager of the Amon Carter Museum, says that he feels the digital process "takes the artist's process and diminishes it into another industrial application."

When using 3D printing or CNC milling, without any additional handwork, all of the sculptures, whether there are three or 30, will all be exactly alike. The untrained eye might not be able to see the difference between 3D digital print in bronze and sculpture that the artist has cast in the lost wax method of bronze casting. What if an artist who has sold work to galleries, museums, and patrons only as fine art bronze now creates their work as a 3D printed in bronze? Would it still be as collectible? It is interesting to note that there are many artists who embrace the technology in their workflow, and sell their artwork as fine artwork. The museums, galleries, and patrons collect the work and the artists simply do not publish how they create the art. The collectors never know.

Is there a way that artists can insert differentiations within each exact 3D print so that they do not appear

manufactured or will collectors and others begin to accept 3D printed artwork as fine art? How do we, as artists and creators, push the limits, explore, and create incredible art that encourages others to think differently about what is art? There are some artists who are using 3D printing and CNC milling as just a portion of their process. They then enhance the artwork by hand after they incorporate the technology. Some materials such as 3D printing in clay or wood may warrant this type of post-processing. In the future, it will be interesting to see how artists work with post-processing to make the artwork created in 3D more "one of a kind."

Up until the point of creating digitally, collectors, galleries, and art curators knew all of the processes of creating art. They were familiar with the materials that the artists used. Curators understand the value of a good bronze sculpture. With digital technology, whether it is 3D printed, CNC milled, or even two-dimensional work created with software and printed on canvas, it will take education and eventual acceptance by curators, critics, and collectors for "value" to be placed on the work. Some museums are already beginning to recognize the work and the value of the medium. The Museum of Modern Art and Design featured the work of 3D artists in their 2014 show "Out of Hand." In 2008, MoMa's exhibit "Design and the Elastic Mind" featured a variety of work using 3D technology.

> The most interesting and most important technological innovation in the field of design and the field of manufacturing is 3D printing.
> Paola Antonelli, curator, Museum of Modern Art (MoMa),
> MOMAMultimedia, Design and the Elastic Mind Video, 3-D Sketching

If you look at the history and work of just about any artist featured in this book, you will find a great deal of them collected and represented by museums around the world. Is the artwork that an artist creates digitally now accepted as fine art of value? The pioneers that we mention and showcase throughout this book have successfully combined fine art and 3D technology and have contributed greatly to the changes and acceptance that we are now seeing with collectors and museums. They have worked diligently as they pushed the technology and labored over their own works. They educated while converting others to explore the possibilities and helped others to comprehend the value of the art. Software companies such as Autodesk also contribute to the acceptance and marriage of 3D technology and fine art when they invest time and money into such explorations as the "Digital Stone" exhibition. Great progress continues as many not only give value, but also celebrate these works as an art form.

"DIGITAL STONE" EXHIBITION

Autodesk, the maker of professional 3D software, has continued to lead the way in the diversity of software for professionals. They also encourage consumer and amateur 3D exploration with their free apps such as their 123D suite. In 2008, Autodesk reached over another chasm to embrace and encourage the merger of digital technology and fine art by creating the "Digital Stone" exhibition. They invited four artists—Bruce Beasley, Jon Isherwood, Robert Michael Smith, and Kenneth Snelson—to create digital designs in virtual space. Autodesk then helped the artists realize the works in the real world by creating 3D prints. Finally, the series was then enlarged and reproduced by Dingli Stone Carving Company in Fujian Province. Dingli Stone Carving used traditional methods of the art of stone carving to reproduce the fine artwork created through digital processes. Samples of these designs are shown on the right. To see the entire collection, visit this book's accompanying website.

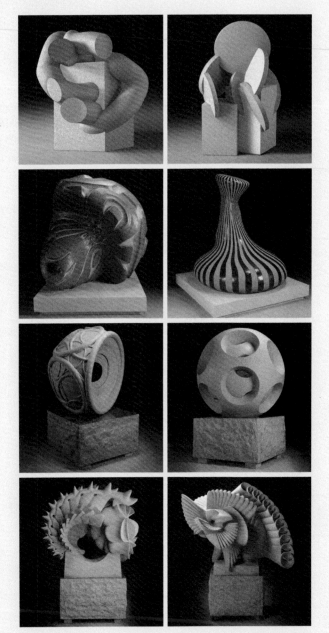

OLD PROCESSES AND NEW TECHNOLOGY

On display at the 2008 SIGGRAPH (Special Interest Group on Graphics and Interactive Techniques) convention was the work of traditional sculptor Erwin Hauer. Beginning in 1950, Hauer created works of modernism. Each modular sculpture of looping and repeating shapes changes as the viewer interacts with the piece, light bouncing off form, shadows moving and blending, creating an entirely different piece of artwork from every angle. Many of the original screens have disappeared or are in disrepair, and the laborious task of making molds and casting these screens had not taken place in nearly 40 years. In 2003, computer technologist Enrique Rosado began working with Hauer creating digital files of Hauer's original work. Using the

Boston Museum of Fine Arts, *Design 201* by Erwin Hauer. This panel is based on the original 1954 design. The screens are produced by Enrique Rosado- Erwin Hauer Studios using CNC milling, 2010. Architects Foster & Partners.

new technology of digital files and computer numerically controlled (CNC) milling machines, the team is working to recreate the works of this master. The journey of translating the designs into a new technology was not easy for Rosado. He found what others have found; often you must push the technology to do what you need it to do, and then wait until it can catch up and become affordable. In the wonderful magazine article "Sculpting Infinity" (Metropolimag.com, October 2006) it states, "These subtleties of balance and proportion were difficult to translate into the software. 'The computer wants to do what it wants to do,' Rosado says. 'And if you're fastidious, you have to beat it into submission.'"

Design 306, 2004. CNC milled Indiana Limestone panels. At CENTRIA Installation, 2007. Architect Philip Koether.

Never-ending Learning Curve

In the traditional artist's studio, once you learn to use calipers and sculpting tools they never change; not so with digital tools. Software companies and computer manufacturers are always searching for "better" ways to do things. These changes have advantages for the consumer, but they come at a price. Once an artist incorporates digital technology in their process, there is a constant learning curve. The digital tools, unlike the traditional studio tools, are always changing. This means that the artist has to continue to learn, and this can be a maddening process.

Am I Cheating?

There are several ways of creating traditional, figurative, life-size sculpture. Some artists create an armature and then sculpt the details, clothes, and accessories. Others create a "body" armature and clothe them in real clothes, stiffening the clothes with wax, and then make a mold of the entire piece for bronze casting. Many sculptors would look down their noses at an artist who clothes their figures like dolls. "It is cheating and not real art," they would exclaim. Some sculptors even use mannequins, dress them, cast them in bronze and call it a fine art bronze. Are all of these processes fine art?

Is using the digital technology cheating? Perhaps the term "cheating" is just as subjective as the idea of "is it art?" If an artist finds a digital model of a young girl, manipulates it in the computer, and then has it 3D printed, is it their artwork? Are they cheating or just streamlining the process?

Is the cheating determined by how much or how little the artist does? One of the tools that we discuss in this book is the scanning of a small maquette so that the artist can enlarge it, mill it in foam, and cover it in clay. These processes are discussed throughout the book; see Chapters 3, 5, and 6. Some sculptors that are unable to accept the new tools would feel that this process is cheating, and prefer the old time-consuming process of pointing up.

Ownership and Digital Art

The traditional process of moving around a sculpture, adding and removing clay is a kinesthetic, tactile dance and an integral part of the creative process. Some artists fear the new technology will divorce the artist from that process, no longer allowing a transfer of soul to the subject, a relationship each artist feels as they enliven the clay with emotion through the dance.

As with any tool, 3D technology takes time to be able to master. It also takes time for it to become an extension of the artist's creative process. An artist can learn to use the tools and processes to make the artwork their own and take ownership of the art even if the learning process may, at first, make them feel disconnected from the art. The internal dialogue a traditional artist has when entering the digital field, along with navigating their way through the combination of both traditional and digital, can make them, at times, feel like their world has turned upside down. The conversations on cheating, ownership, and value will continue to take place. Visit this book's accompanying website to contribute to these dialogues.

There are so many possibilities when it comes to the incorporation of digital and traditional processes. The art that is being created is incredible and the possibilities that are open to the reader are endless. Let's see what others are doing, and how 3D technology is influencing their process and work.

> Our fine arts were developed, their types and uses were established, in times very different from the present, by men whose power of action upon things was insignificant in comparison with ours. But the amazing growth of our techniques, the adaptability and precision they have attained, the ideas and habits they are creating, make it a certainty that profound changes are impending in the ancient craft of the Beautiful. In all the arts, there is a physical component, which can no longer be considered or treated as it used to be, which cannot remain unaffected by our modern knowledge and power. For the last twenty years, neither matter nor space nor time has been what it was from time immemorial. We must expect great innovations to transform the entire technique of the arts, thereby affecting artistic invention itself and perhaps even bringing about an amazing change in our very notion of art.
>
> Paul Valéry, "Pièces sur L'Art," 1931, *Le Conquete de l'ubiquite*
> (from Walter Benjamin, *The Work of Art in*
> *the Age of Mechanical Reproduction*)

KEITH BROWN

Keith Brown is a pioneer in the industry. He began using computing technology to create sculpture in the early 1980s. Keith uses 3DS Max and prints his work on a Stratasys FDM Fortus 360mc and a Matrix300 A4 3D paper printer by Mcor in Manchester Institute for Research and Innovation in Art & Design (MIRIAD), where he is a professor.

Sweep
by Keith Brown.

MARY VISSER

Another pioneer of 3D technology and fine art is Mary Visser. Mary has been working with computers to create her art since 1985. The software that Mary uses now is Materialise Magics 18 for file repair and preparation for printing. She creates using different software and finds that each does a different job than the other. She uses Carrara Studio Pro, Cheeta3D, SketchUp, and 3DS Max, but she is always looking for a different Boolean function. (A Boolean is when you combine two objects, either subtracting one from the other or adding it to the other. You always need clean geometry under the art to be able to realize it in a physical form. See the 3D sculpting chapter for more about Boolean functions.)

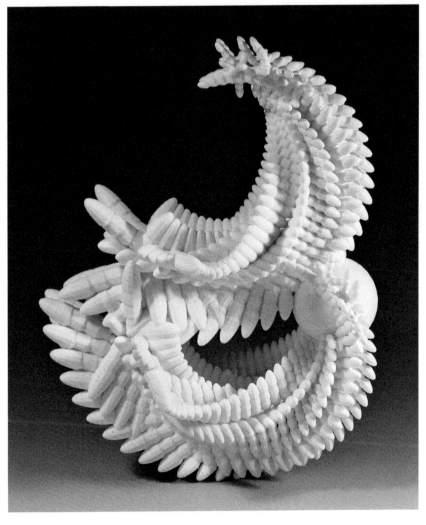

Reflections by Mary Hale Visser. Process: 3D printed SLS, printed at University of Texas, 16 × 12.5 × 6 inches.

MARY NEUBAUER

Mary Neubauer often uses data as art. As she describes it:

"My recent sculptures, prints, and public artworks use information
obtained through digital and numerical processes to create visual
imagery. Illuminated photograms, laser-scanned images, animations,
and rapid prototypes are combined with more traditional casting
and replication techniques in artworks that address the natural
world as well as the metropolitan environments in which many
of us now live. I am interested in contemporary science and its
data-gathering methods. My artworks take a new and highly visual
look at constantly streaming information about our surroundings.
I believe that scientific, numerical, and technical data may be
interpreted in a visually compelling manner, and that these new
visualizations can aid in a deeper understanding of the world,
including its long-term geophysical transformations as well as its
daily cycles and rhythms of growth and change."

Desert Rain by Mary Neubauer,
bronze, 15 × 20 × 20 inches.
Photograph by Jacob Sterenberg,
the Bollinger Atelier.

NATHALIE MIEBACH

Creating data as art is a fascinating exploration, but it is not new to 3D technology. Though Nathalie Miebach may not be using 3D digital processes, she demonstrates how visually stimulating the capturing and weaving of data can be. There are other artists featured in this book and on the book's accompanying website who also bring data and code into a physical existence using 3D technology.

Antarctic Explorer—Darkness to Lightness by Nathalie Miebach. Reed, wood, plastic, data, 4.5 × 3 × 2 feet, 2007. A portable data device for the Antarctic explorer, this piece explores the transition from complete darkness in June to 24-hour sunlight in October. Data translated include weather patterns, temperature variations, barometric pressure, wind data, azimuth of the sun, sunrise in relation to cardinal directions, tides, moon phases, moonrise, and sunrise. Using a base of 24 hours, every weave represents one hour.

On the book's website at www.digitalsculpting.net you will find:

* Links to further descriptions on the process of creating the artwork featured in the galleries.
* Podcasts with the artists.
* Videos featuring the artists at work.

CHAPTER THREE

3D SCANNING

———

"I work with all of this imagery not because I want to be morbid, but because I am interested in exploring the ways that technology can fail to capture life, and what the poetics of that failure might look like. We live in a world where we are so bombarded with claims for all seeing, all-powerful, imaging technologies. It is my belief that as artists destabilizing those, through poetics, might actually prove to be the strongest weapon that we have."

Sophie Kahn, from the Digital Scanning Leaders in Software and Art Conference, Guggenheim Museum, New York

facing page
Triple Portrait of E by Sophie Kahn.
3D print from 3D laser scan. Life-size, 2013.

Creating artwork in the computer is one way to obtain a 3D model. An alternative way of bringing a 3D model into the computer is through digital scanning. Digital scanning is the process of taking an existing physical object and creating a digital representation of it as a 3D model using data that the scanner collects.

3D scanning was created for industry but, as with other forms of 3D technology, others have adopted the technology and use it in many different disciplines. It was not long ago that 3D scanners were hard to come by, and it was cost-prohibiting for a small studio to purchase a 3D scanner. Today, high-quality digital scanners are more affordable. Another option to making an investment into a digital scanner is a scanning service bureau. One day, scanning an object may be as easy as taking it to your local office supply store, but even if you don't have a scanning service bureau near you, with some preparation you can send small maquettes or sculptures to a scanning bureau for detailed scanning. For those interested in creating a basic 3D model from a real object, you can find the novelty of 3D technology right in your phone. Phone scanners do not provide the fine detail of the high-end scanners, but they may be sufficient for getting a base model. It is also worth noting that the technology is advancing at an enormous pace. Even as the author writes this book there is cutting-edge technology being beta-tested. Now, let's look at 3D scanning in more detail.

The Digital Michelangelo project (http://graphics.stanford.edu/projects/mich/) is just one of many different ways the technology of 3D scanning and fine art are coming together. Documentation, preservation, and creating art combine perfectly with the technology of 3D scanning.

Scanners

There are multiple ways of making a 3D model using scanning processes. There are two types of scanners—contact and noncontact digital scanners. The difference between the two is that the contact scanners are scanners that collect information through physical touch of the object. A 3D probe touches many points. The scanner uses collected points to digitize the object and translate it into a 3D model. Engineering, machining, and manufacturing may use probe scanners. A scanning facility may use a probe scanner on geometric shapes, but they do not recommend contact scanners for organic shapes. Just as with other scanners, contact scanners come in a variety of styles and prices.

Noncontact scanners are the preferred type of scanner for scanning art, and they come in two types—active and passive. In very simplified terms, active noncontact scanners use structured light or lasers that pass over an object. The scanner measures the time that it takes for the light or laser to bounce or reflect off the object and come back to the scanner. It collects this data as points to make a 3D shape of the scanned surface.

Another form of noncontact scanning that we will review in this chapter is photogrammetry. Photogrammetry is considered passive noncontact because a light source does not actively probe the surface. Rather the shape is generated using algorithms that combine multiple 2D images to interpret a 3D shape. You might think of photogrammetry as a combination of photography and geometry. The artist takes many overlapping photographs of the image, and a software program splices these images together to create a 3D model.

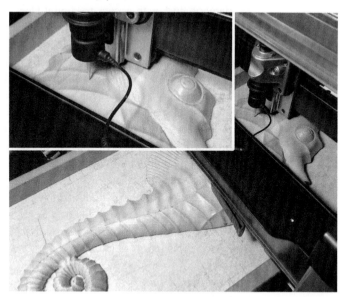

As we walk through the many examples and tutorials of scanning in this chapter, you will begin to become more familiar with the scanning process and perhaps see the many options and ways that you can use 3D scanning as you incorporate it into your art or craft.

The CarveWright CNC System (www.carvewright.com) has a scanning probe that attaches to their 3D CNC milling machine. This addition offers the home user an opportunity to scan and create.

Saving Cultural Heritage

Tsunamis, earthquakes, floods, wars, and hatred can have detrimental effects on art, artifacts, architecture, and culture. When these treasures are gone, they are gone forever. Preservation of art, history, and culture is important for many different individuals and organizations working with 3D laser scanning using noncontact scanners. For example, the Smithsonian is beginning to scan their collection. They provide the 3D models online and believe that offering their collection in this format makes it more accessible. Students anywhere can see it. Touching an artifact with our hands causes deterioration and damage, but in the computer individuals can rotate and examine the 3D collection without ever causing any

Smithsonian X3D (http://3d.si.edu) offers online visitors a chance to explore the collection of the Smithsonian in a digital world. The Smithsonian makes Amelia Earhart's suit and Lincoln's life mask, as well as many other historical artifacts, available online. Educational material for teachers is also available. To find out how to download digital models for printing or educational resources, visit this book's accompanying website at www.digitalsculpting.net.

damage and, with access to digital files, anyone who has a 3D printer can print the models. The Smithsonian provides educational resources so that students can learn from the data, and they hope that students will even join the Smithsonian in investigation and exploration, making discoveries. Being able to interact with the art or artifacts digitally gives us a connection to our history. Many believe that having access to other people's culture and being able to interact with it digitally from anywhere in the world gives us a greater understanding of who we are as mankind. The history, the art, and the cultural artifacts are a part of our "cultural DNA."

Humankind takes for granted that these wonders of architecture, art, and cultural significance will always be available. The sad truth is that they will not. Such things as time, environmental factors, and vandalism can destroy these objects, and we will lose them forever. This loss is painfully apparent in the following sections.

Buddhas of Bamiyan

In 2001, the Taliban declared a spiritual war against idolatry and dynamited the Buddhas of Bamiyan. The two Buddhas standing at 55 meters (180.446 feet) and 38 meters (124.672 feet) were colossal, ancient, carved sandstone figurines that were a fine example of Gandhara art, and estimated to be more than 1,500 years old. The Taliban declared the Buddhas to be idols

In March of 2001, the Taliban dynamited the Buddhas of Bamiyan, estimated to be more than 1,500 years old.

and destroyed them. In one act, they destroyed ancient monuments that have stood for thousands of years.

Saving Mes Aynak

In 2007, there was another threat to the heritage of this region. This time it was not incited by warfare, but by economic gain. The Afghanistan government awarded a contract to the China Metallurgical Group Corporation. Mes Aynak, "Little Source of Copper" outside of the desert of Kabul, is not so little—reports state that it is one of the largest untapped resources for copper with an estimate of value of more than $100 billion. Archeologists consider it a treasure. Thousands of years ago, the site was the home of a Buddhist monastery and archeologists believe it was also a hub of commercial interaction. Archeologists are working to uncover the site's treasures, despite death threats from those wishing to halt their efforts. They labor on through unbearable heat, all the time watched by armed guards. They work to document and save this cultural treasure of Afghanistan's history. However, after much excavation they have discovered that they will only get to approximately 10 percent of the excavation before the China Metallurgical Group will destroy the site in search of copper. They are certain that they would find more treasures deeper if they had time to excavate. Also, many of the artifacts are either too fragile or too big to move and will, like the Buddhas of Bamiyan, meet their demise.

> I feel like a mother whose child is going to die. We work so hard uncovering the artifacts and protecting them, they have become like children to me. Seeing the artifacts getting destroyed would be like a mother watching her child dying in front of her.
>
> Abdul Qadeer Temore, lead Afghan archeologist, from Brent E. Huffman's documentary *A Chinese Threat to Afghan Buddhas*

Archeologists estimated the excavation project would take ten years minimum, and more likely 25–30 years. However, the Chinese mining company scheduled the destruction of the site to create their open pit style of mining to begin in three years. Political unrest in Afghanistan caused a delay in the project. Desperation motivates those whose interest it is to preserve the site. Instead of just saving artifacts, teams are pulling together to try to quickly document this lush cultural heritage before the Chinese mining company destroys it. It is possible to use 3D scanning to preserve what archeologists cannot move.

The same alloy that drew the monks to this site two thousand years ago, and caused them to make such incredible art, is what threatens the continued existence of that same art. Some artifacts are too fragile to move. Archeologists believe they have not scratched the surface of the treasures of Mes Aynak, but we may never know. Brent E. Huffman, from the documentary *Saving Mes Aynak*, www.savingmesaynak.com.

CyArk

In 2003, spurred by the destruction of Bamiyan Buddhas, individuals with a love of cultural heritage created CyArk. CyArk is a not-for-profit organization that specializes in using cutting-edge technology to preserve the world's heritage sites digitally. Their mission is to use emerging technologies such as 3D laser scanning to create a free, 3D, online archive of cultural heritage sites from around the globe before they are lost to natural disasters, destroyed by human aggression, or ravaged by the passage of time. In 2013, they launched the CyArk 500 Challenge, an unprecedented initiative to digitally preserve 500 heritage sites from around the world in five years.

For example, the Black Hills of South Dakota is the backdrop for Mount Rushmore. Sculptor Gutzon Borglum directed the carving of the 18 meter (60 foot) high heads from 1927 to 1941. CyArk scanned Mount Rushmore in 2010. The data collected on Mount Rushmore took CyArk two and a half weeks. It consists of more than 200 georeferenced laser scans along with traditional photography.

CyArk offers many different resources for educators interested in culture, art, and the technology of 3D scanning. CyArk's initiative does not stop at documentation. Educators are using the 3D data captured of heritage sites to create interactive curricula for many different age levels. CyArk offers these free on their website at www.cyark.org.

CyArk's mission has already been invaluable. In 2009, CyArk went to Kampala, Uganda, to scan the tombs of Buganda kings at Kasubi, a UNESCO World Heritage Site. The tombs are considered one of the most religious and spiritual locations within the Buganda culture. From 1884 to 1969 four *kabakas* (kings) of Buganda were interred in this structure.

In 2009, a partner of CyArk traveled to the tombs at Kasubi and conducted 3D laser scanning of the entire UNESCO site. A year after CyArk completed the onsite preservation and processing of the 3D data, fire consumed a portion of this grass-thatched cultural heritage. There are plans to rebuild the tombs using the 3D data stored securely in CyArk's archive, which contains measurements of the site down to millimeters of accuracy.

Your Own Scanning

There is much more that individuals can use 3D scanning for besides capturing culture. Artists are using 3D scanning in a variety of ways. They use it to create art, to enlarge or reduce designs, to repurpose artwork, and in the preservation of design; they are even using it as part of their legacy and inheritance that they leave to their children. Perhaps further exploration of 3D scanning will spark creative inspiration and collaborations in the readers of this chapter.

Service Bureau

Creating a good detailed 3D scan requires a good scanner and considerable time. If an artist is not yet ready to invest into a scanner, a 3D scan created through a service bureau that offers high-powered processes is an option. Sending the work to a 3D scanning service bureau relieves the artist from having to have the tools or technology and the patience that it takes to get a good 3D scan. The scanning service bureau will look at several factors when they estimate the cost for scanning. The amount of time that it takes to scan, the size of the object they are scanning, and the color or texture of the objects are all considerations. Some objects, such as those that have a shiny or see-through surface, do not scan well. The scanning service bureau may be able to dust the surface of the object with powder to kick back the shine. When using a service bureau for a 3D scan, schedule a consultation session. Also remember, if an artist is scanning art that they already installed, there may be travel charges incurred from a scanning service bureau.

Using a service bureau is convenient. Farming out the 3D scanning and leaving scanning to the experts frees up creative time for the artists. For a list of 3D scanning companies and those that sell scanners check the resource chapter or the book's accompanying website (www.digitalsculpting.net). Many scanning companies work in industry rather than art, but it is worth getting to know your local scanning company, if you have one.

When using a professional scanning company, often their scanners provide huge amounts of data. A scan that comes from a consumer scanner that you purchase for the art studio and the scan that comes from a professional high-end scanning service may be different. When working with a scanning service bureau requesting a high-resolution scan may be more data than the artist needs. As always, it is important to develop a working relationship and clear communication with your service bureau to obtain the best results.

Fine artists that are enlarging artwork through 3D processes such as those featured in Chapter 6, will first need to scan a small sculpted maquette. The artist, with the help of vendors, will later translate these maquettes into a sculpture that is different in size from the original. The artists can create monumental works using 3D scanning combined with other resources in this book, such as CNC milling. If a sculptor creates a maquette in soft clay or water-based clay, it cannot be shipped to a scanning company without causing damage to the original. The alternative to scanning the fragile original at a service bureau is for the artist to make a mold of the original art and then cast a wax or plaster to send to the scanning company. Digital scanning is rarely

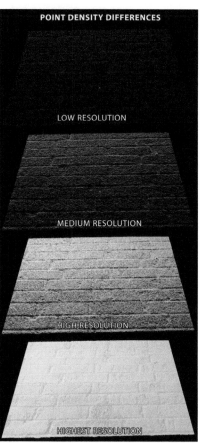

POINT DENSITY DIFFERENCES

LOW RESOLUTION

MEDIUM RESOLUTION

HIGH RESOLUTION

HIGHEST RESOLUTION

When using a professional scanning company it may not be necessary to request the highest resolution scan. Doug Smith from Smart Geometrics uses a Leica C10 scanner. He reports that 95 percent of the projects created through Smart Geometrics for industrial applications only require medium resolution.

done with just one scan. Instead, the scanning service bureau creates many scans from all directions. Once the service bureau scans all the pieces of the sculpture, they align the scans and splice them together in the scanning program or additional software.

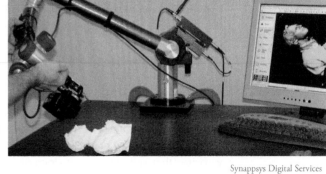

Synappsys Digital Services scans Harry Weber's artwork using a Model Maker laser line scanner mounted on a Faro Gold Arm to create a digital file for CNC milling.

Having a cast model that the service bureau can cut apart before they scan is helpful. For example, it may be necessary to separate an entire arm that rests close to the body. This process will help the scanning service bureau to obtain an appropriate scan that will also include all the undercuts. Without these sculptural divisions, the laser or light beam must squeeze into these areas and, if the scanner cannot read the area, it will appear as a hole in the scan.

It is interesting to note that by the very nature of making a mold of the original art to send to the scanning company, it is now a generation away from the original. Each generation may mean loss of detail. Therefore, having a good studio scanner is another option.

The process of scanning using your own studio 3D scanner has its advantages. A digital scan of a small maquette of a full figure that measures 12–14 inches tall may cost between $500 and $1,000 to scan at a service bureau. Unless you have a service bureau around the corner, it means you may have to ship something to the scanning company to scan and, as we said, you may also need to make a mold.

As is the case with most of the 3D technology in this book, 3D scanning is slowly making its way into homes and studios. Also, as 3D printing becomes more commonplace, so is 3D scanning. Unfortunately, desktop 3D scanners are flooding the market, which may lead to confusion among the consumers. A high-end professional scanner

For the best scan from a service bureau, send artwork that they can divide into pieces. *The Pledge* by Harry Weber.

can cost hundreds of thousands of dollars and home/studio scanners range from a few hundred dollars to several thousand dollars. When looking at noncontact scanners on a general consumer budget, those scanners with the best advertising budget are not necessarily the best choice for the home studio. If you are in the market for a scanner, then you will certainly be asking the question, "how do I choose a 3D scanner?"

Your Own Studio 3D Scanner

Gathering information to compare 3D scanners is extremely confusing. Spatial resolution, field of view, scan volume, dimensional accuracy, scan speeds, and scan volume are some of the terms that you will find on websites that sell scanners. It does make a consumer's head spin. Let's break this down a bit differently. When researching the purchase of a home/studio 3D scanner it is important to look at a few things not mentioned in the specs of the many 3D scanning websites. The criteria we suggest to review are quality, flexibility, and ease of use.

Quality—or Quality of a Scan

When researching scanners, it is intuitive for a buyer to look for a number, such as the resolution. The buyer uses these resolution numbers, as advertised on one scanner ad, to compare to the resolution numbers advertised on another scanner. When the buyer gathers and compares numbers, they may feel they have done their homework and have purchased a quality product with the "highest resolution." The term "scanner resolution" can be misleading. As mentioned before, some scanners are better with close-up scans, and others are better at long range or distant scans. When referring to home scanners, "long range" in this instance is not referencing Mount Rushmore. The "long range distance" referred to with home scanners is the difference between a small 3-inch figurine and a person in the room. The sales material for home scanners may provide a number for "resolution"; however, it is difficult to know how this number applies to each distance.

It is better to look at other parameters in addition to the resolution. The most important parameter to look at is the quality of the scan. It is difficult for the average consumer to scan the same item with a few different scanners. A picture is worth a thousand words. We have included some comparison scans from readily available desktop processes of 3D scanning.

Flexibility and Ease of Use

Don't let advertisers persuade you by "click of a button" scanning. "Click of a button" is not what we are referring to when we say "ease of use." As you will see in the scanning tutorial of the concrete children in this chapter, scanning with your own home scanner is a process. The artist does not

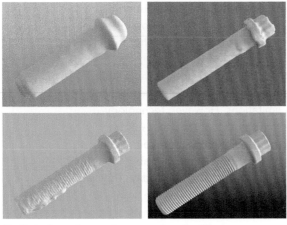

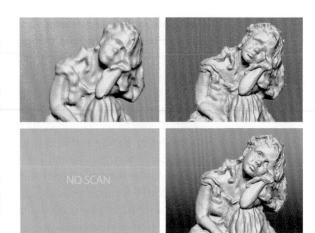

NO SCAN

NextEngine Scanner has created some tests of scanning different objects with four different scanners. The orange is the Sense Scanner, priced at $399. The red is MakerBot, priced at $799. The green is the free app 123D Catch from Autodesk, and the blue is the scan with the NextEngine Scanner $2,995.

Sculptor Bridgette Mongeon conducted her own research with three scans of a broken sculpture for repurposing. The orange is the Sense Scanner, the red is the MakerBot, and the blue is NextEngine. There was no scan created with 123D app. The artist could not use the 123D app on her personal work because, according to the terms of service on the Autodesk site, if she creates a model using 123D Catch and uploads it to their server, she may be giving up her rights to her creation.

create a good scan by just a push of a button. In fact, scanners that claim to have an automatic process can have a detrimental effect on the scan. How much control an artist has and how flexible the scanning system is during scanning, as well as in the post-processing of the scan, can play a large part in the quality of the scan. Therefore, when picking a scanner, it is good to look at the software behind the scanner. How easy is the software to use? Do the process and the software allow for some flexibility and interaction by the user? Also, be aware of the limitations of the scanner's scanning size. Artists create in many different sizes. Don't let your choice of scanners limit your creativity. It will take time to compare scanners, but be sure to choose a scanner that will encourage your inspiration, not frustrate you.

Scanning Considerations

When scanning either through a service bureau or in your studio with your own desktop scanner, there are some things to consider.

Quality and Use

Quality is the sum of the errors that are possible and the resolution, also referred to as "accuracy and resolution." As stated before, the artist's intent for the scan may determine what amount of detail they will need. If they are going to retopologize a rough maquette and then bring it into a sculpting program for further refinement, they will not need a high-resolution scan. However, if they are trying to obtain as much detail as possible for restoration or documentation of art, then they may need a higher resolution scan.

It is important to note that what limits an artist, at the time of this writing, is the resolution of the output devices, as well as the size of today's output devices. A 3D printer has size limitations. However, technology is changing rapidly and who is to say that the technology that will be available in two, five, or ten years will not be able to output your art in different mediums and sizes? In the future, your heirs may be able to reproduce your work in ways you would not even dream of today. They will be able to do so because they documented and preserved the scans of your inspiration and creations.

Management of the Data

As we stated, the 3D scanner measures many points on an item. The larger the item, and the higher the resolution of the scan, the more data the scanner will capture. If you plan on working on this data in your computer, then you need to understand whether or not your computer can handle this data. That is why Chapter 1 stated that familiarizing yourself with what you want to have your peripherals do for you and even perceiving what you may need them to do in the future will be important to understand when you are purchasing your computer, software, and peripherals. You may start out scanning small objects, but later find that you need to scan life-size pieces. The processing of scan data takes a good deal of computer power. Plan ahead. It is also necessary to know how far you need to go with a digital scan to get the optimal resolution necessary without bogging down your system.

Size and Material

The size of the object does not matter. Depending on your scanning company, they can scan a jet or a piece of jewelry. Remember dark, shiny, or transparent objects are difficult to scan. Knowing your final output of the project when scanning will help you decide which scanner or scanning service will fit your needs.

Color

Most scans provide a colorless digital model. If you need to preserve the color with the geometry in your scan, this is another element to consider. If you have a service bureau scanning your work and you desire color, ask them if this is a possibility. If capturing color is something that is important to you in your home/studio 3D scans, consider purchasing a scanner that also scans for color.

File Formats

Scanners can produce files in many different formats. Again, knowing what you are going to do with your scan will help. If you need color in your scan for 3D printing in color and a 3D scanner captured the color with the object, you will want to have the appropriate file format for this (see Chapter 7). Do you need to do additional work with the files? Are you going to want to change or manipulate the design in a sculpting program? If so, then you may want to use polygonal models. Do you need to obtain measurements from the data? If so, then you will want the raw point cloud data to bring into an appropriate CAD (computer-aided design) program. If you are unsure what file format you need, just ask your service bureau what they recommend.

Changing a File Format

Even if you do not have the file format you need for the next step in the process, you can always change the format of the file using several free software programs. MeshLab and MeshMixer are two such programs.

Photogrammetry/Stereophotogrammetry

Another way of creating a 3D model is a process known as photogrammetry. Photogrammetry is a combination of photography and geometry. The artist takes multiple photographs of an object all around the subject and common points are referenced in the computer. Photogrammetry can be done as aerial shots for larger scans or at close range. The advantages of photogrammetry are that it is accessible. If you have a camera and the software, you can use photogrammetry to obtain a 3D model. Of course, the better the camera, the better the detail in the model.

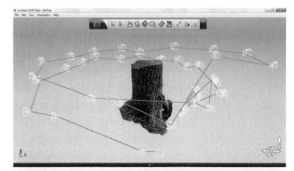

Several websites offer free photogrammetry software. 123D Catch is a well-known free and easy photogrammetry software. Here it is used to scan a tree, which is brought into ZBrush and hollowed out. *Tree* by Bridgette Mongeon and Katherine Dewey. Photograph by Christina Sizemore.

Free Photogrammetry Software

There are several free photogrammetry software sites on the Internet. One of the leading software companies providing 3D software internationally is Autodesk. They have a suite of tools that they offering for free and one called 123D Catch works with photogrammetry. For example, with 123D Catch you simply take many incremental, overlapping photographs 360 degrees around the model with your phone and the 123D Catch application. When you are done simply upload the files to Autodesk's 123D Catch and wait for it to process. Autodesk even has a web application where you can clean up your scan. The plus side of 123D Catch is its simplicity. You really need little training to make 3D models with your phone. The downfall of 123D Catch is that you can only load a small amount of images using your account.

Free online photogrammetry websites may have their limitations. They do not compare to high-end scanner files. Also, check to see what type of file the "free" sites will let you export. If you can only create the file but can't export that file then it is useless. Also, the free version of 123D Catch cannot be used for commercial purposes.

But there are even more things to be aware of when using online services providing photogrammetry processing. Some photogrammetry sites require that you upload your image to their server to process your 3D model. It is easy to be persuaded to use such accessible tools, especially if they are free, but be sure to read the fine print in the box of "terms of service," which most people skip over, and some sites make it impossible to understand and follow all of the links. In many cases, the "ownership" of your scans is in question. That means the scans you are processing on their server, once they are uploaded, you may have just given away. The software company may now own them. It appears that offering the free service may be a way to gain the rights to many 3D models. According to the "terms of service" they might just be able to do what they want with your images. That means that if you scan your own artwork or ideas with these tools and upload them, you just might be giving them away. Or if scan your child, their image may, one day, be available to anyone.

An alternative to a free photogrammetry site is to purchase photogrammetry software. Photogrammetry for the studio is not just for art studios with big budgets. There is reasonably priced photogrammetry software that allows you to create 3D models with textures from photographs. Agisoft is such software. This software works on your own computer. The standard edition costs $179 and a professional version costs $3,499 (www.agisoft.ru). Because you are processing your images on your own computer, there is no concern about you uploading and processing elsewhere or the possibility of you losing or "sharing" the rights to your files or accidentally transferring your copyrights. Agisoft runs cross-platform.

You will have to take note of the limitations of your personal computer. When using Agisoft the processing of splicing of the photographs will be done in the computer instead of, as 123D Catch does, in the cloud. The more photographs you have, the larger the memory needed and the more time that it will require to process. Of course, these types of software programs are memory hogs. Agisoft will require a computer with a great deal of RAM. The Agisoft website suggests up to 32 GB of RAM for basic configurations.

Type of Camera

A consumer digital camera is suitable for most photogrammetry. Of course, you can hardly expect a good scan if you have poor pictures. The higher the resolution of the image that you are shooting, the better the scan. At least a 5-mega-pixel camera is suggested.

Taking Photographs

When taking photographs for photogrammetry it is important to get the correct images for your needs. When shooting an area, stay perpendicular to the surface. In the case of shooting a sculpture or a person, it is important to take photographs at an equal distance around the subject, including the top. Each photograph should overlap the previous photograph by 25–30 percent. Taking photographs for photogrammetry is not like taking personal photographs. When you are taking a picture, the camera focuses on the center or the focal point. For example, if you take a picture of a face, the subject's ears and shoulders will be not be as sharp as the face. Therefore, overlapping images give the software sharp detail and shared reference points.

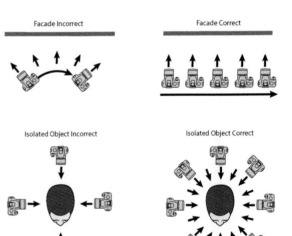

When taking photographs for photogrammetry it is important to get the correct images. For a façade, it is necessary to photograph the façade with a minimum of 1/3 overlap of photographs. Each photograph must be taken parallel to the surface. To take photographs of a single object, move around the object shooting photographs at the same distance.

There are more details on shooting photogrammetry on this book's accompanying website.

SERVICE BUREAUS
FOR PHOTOGRAMMETRY

A service bureau such as Captured Dimensions is an alternative to doing your own photogrammetry (www.captureddimensions.com). Captured Dimensions uses 80 DSLR cameras that shoot simultaneously. Once the 3D photo sitting is complete and an image is chosen, Captured Dimensions cleans up the files and the color using ZBrush, Mudbox, and Photoshop. Photogrammetry with Captured Dimensions can provide much finer detailed models than we are showing here. There are many uses for fine artists using 3D models created with photogrammetry. Many are mentioned in this chapter.

The final output of our sitting is a miniature 3D print. A full color 3D mini selfie is a novelty, but it will be interesting to see how artists creatively incorporate photogrammetry into their fine art. Using a service bureau that offers photogrammetry has an advantage as it can capture data even with movement, something that most scanners cannot. Movement is not a problem because the camera is shooting all sides at the same time. The disadvantage to this type of service bureau is that they are not mobile.

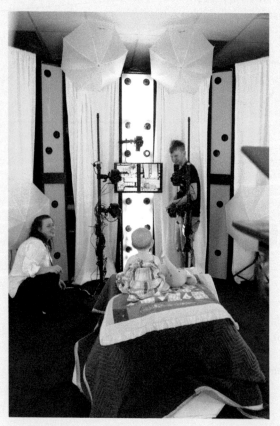

Photogrammetry captured with this type of system offers many advantages. 80 DSLR cameras take pictures simultaneously. Because photographs are taken from all sides at the click of a camera shutter, there is no worry about movement. It makes capturing a 3D model of such things as gesture, activities, and even pets or a crawling baby, quite easy.

Captured Dimensions uses Agisoft software incorporated with their own scripting to splice all of the images together (www.agisoft.ru). The software shows all of the many camera angles. After splicing the shots together, Captured Dimensions cleans up the scans using other 3D sculpting programs such as Mudbox and ZBrush.

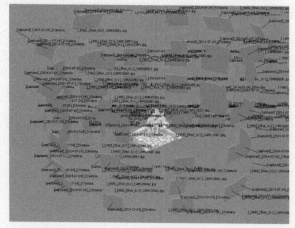

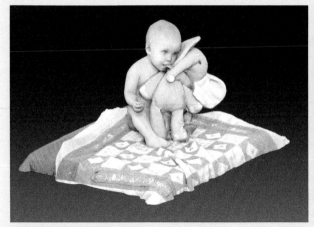

The process can capture color and great detail. As with most 3D scanning and modeling, the amount of detail depends on the needs of the client for the final output. Captured Dimensions will create this model as a 3D print with color and does not require that much detail in the model. The color on the 3D print helps to fool the eye into assuming there is a lot of detail; however, before the scene is printed in 3D the experienced 3D modelers will clean up the file.

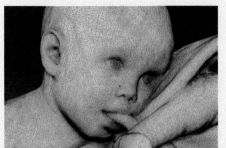

The mesh is created using triangles or points. The detailed point cloud is very dense.

The final output for this process is a small 3D model printed with a 3D Systems printer in a gypsum powder with a CMYK colored binder (glue) injected.

Enlarging and Reducing—History of Art Enlargements and Reductions in Fine Art

Over the years, sculptors and craftsman have been enlarging and reducing work in a variety of ways. Traditionally, the artist first creates a smaller version of a large or monumental sculpture. With this small maquette, the artist can focus on the composition, movement, and proportions of a sculpture. It is much easier to modify a small maquette than it is to adjust a large or monumental piece.

Enlargement and reduction both in 2D and 3D has always been about measuring points and copying, enlarging, or reducing the distance and spaces. Artists and engravers use a pantograph invented in the early seventeenth century to enlarge or copy writing or two-dimensional art. A 3D pantograph similar to the seventeenth-century pantograph is one of the tools used by sculptors before creating 3D scanning and enlargements in foam. The 3D pantograph's predecessor, the 3D pointing up machine, was like the 3D pantograph. The pointing up system assists the artists in measuring each point on one three-dimensional model to a point on the armature of an enlarged or reduced sculpture. Linked mechanical arms in pointing up recreate motion from one end to the other. The motions, depending on the size and creation of the pantograph or pointing up machine, can give the appropriate points to enlarge or reduce a sculpture. In recreating a monumental sculpture, the studio apprentice holds one point to a designated part on the original maquette. The artist then recreates the thickness and recreates the design at the other end. This traditional process of enlarging or reducing is painstakingly slow and takes many man-hours.

There are other ways to enlarge and reduce. You can use calipers. Regular calipers can capture a measurement of point-to-point distance. The artist then holds the calipers to a ruler and notes the measurements. They calculate the enlargement and translate the new measurement to the larger sculpture. An artist's proportion wheel can also help artists with proportions

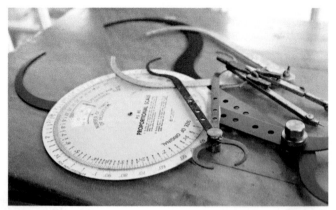

Other tools used for enlarging are calipers and reduction wheels.

when measuring points from one sculpture to another. Measuring this way is a time-consuming process.

Enlargement calipers have a designated ratio. The artists must measure a point with the smaller end of the calipers on the small sculpture and translate the distance that the calipers open up on the fixed larger end.

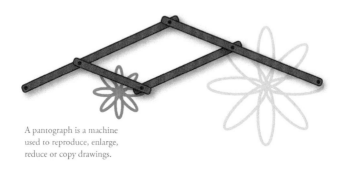

A pantograph is a machine used to reproduce, enlarge, reduce or copy drawings.

Michael Keropian Sculpture Studio uses a 3D pantograph to enlarge and reduce sculpture. Sculptor Berthold Nebel patented the original design of this particular manual machine on May 28, 1929. The sculpture shown is a reduction "in progress" of a sculpture created by sculptor Chester Beach called *Riders of the Elements*.

Photosculpture

Artists have been trying to capture the physical form of a person and translate it to appropriate dimensions in art for as long as they have been creating. One creative process found in 1864 has some very strong similarities to many of the chapters in this book—François Willème's photosculpture and mechanical sculpture.

In a traditional sculptor's studio, a portrait artist will move around their subject slowly, copying what is before the eye. The negative space or the space around the subject is as important as the nose or mouth. When trying to obtain the mass and contours of a sculpture, the artist finds these shapes by examining the space around the object. They look at the edges of their model and copy that to the clay. They move sequentially around the model while moving their sculpture in the same position and same angle. In other words, it is as if the artist is paying attention to all of the silhouettes of the figure and putting them all together. The silhouette from all sides will make

Twenty-four strategically placed cameras are hidden behind the walls of François Willème's photosculpture studio. Courtesy of George Eastman House, International Museum of Photography and Film.

up the figure. That is what transpired with François Willème, who applied for patents in 1860 and 1861 for his processes of photosculpture and mechanical sculpture.

The processes that Willème employed resembled photogrammetry, and one can even see similarities of 3D printing and CNC milling. There were several steps in the process of photosculpture. The first is to obtain the 3D model through photography.

Within Willème's specially designed circular studio, the subject stood or sat on a circular pedestal. The pedestal contained reference numbers and segmented lines that resemble 24 slices of a pie. Behind each wall, Willème hid cameras—24 of them. Within moments, Willème could create photographic reference material from every angle of the subject in a pose. This type of visual information is necessary and would be a luxury to even a sculptor working in today's world. And remember, prior to photosculpture, for dignitaries to have their image forever captured in sculpture they would have to sit for hours. They might also have to subject themselves to the

The subject sits or stands beneath a plumb bob on a platform divided up into the same number of sections as the cameras in the room. Admiral Garragut seated on a dais, posing for a photosculpture, Huston & Kurtz, ca. 1862. Courtesy of George Eastman House, International Museum of Photography and Film.

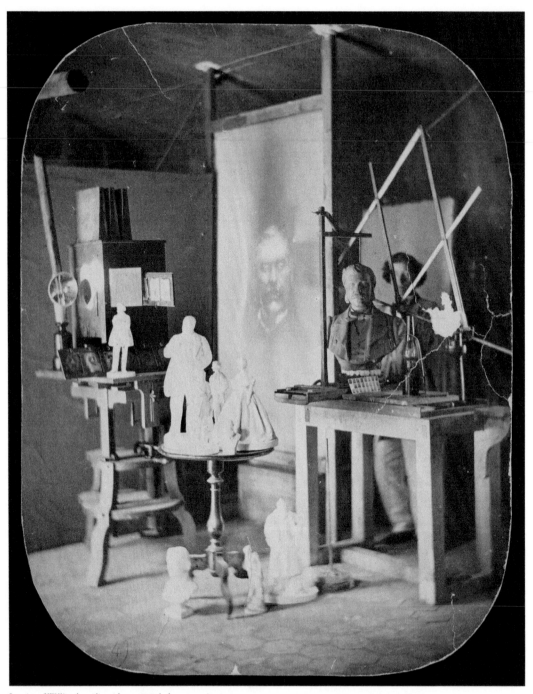

Interior of Willème's studio with pantograph, lantern projector, and example of photosculpture including a photosculpture of Willème himself, ca. 1865. Courtesy of George Eastman House, International Museum of Photography and Film.

process of having their face covered in plaster as artists often created a life mask to use as reference. For his elite clientele, Willème's photo sculpture promised accuracy and ease.

But this was only a part of the process. From here, Willème transferred the photographs to clay. Willème projected each lanternslide onto a large screen. Not far away from the screen, he placed a slab of clay on a round pedestal. The pedestal contained the same pie numbering system as in the photo gallery. The translucent quality of the screen allowed the craftsmen to stand behind the screen and copy the image with a pantograph from the screen to the clay.

Willème also had another process of recreating the form. In mechanical sculpture, Willème photographed the subject, but this time in up to 50 positions. Willème sliced the images and put them together to make a sculpture in the round. Although Willème made a positive, it appears by his patent information that he was trying to obtain the negative so that he could use the negative as a mold for reproductions.

Unfinished photosculpture: portrait head of a woman. François Willème, France, ca. 1865, oak maquette compiled of profiles. Courtesy of George Eastman House, International Museum of Photography and Film.

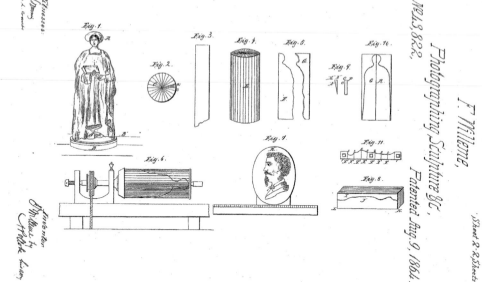

This Photosculpture patent dated August 9, 1864 depicts Willème's attempt to create mechanical sculpture.

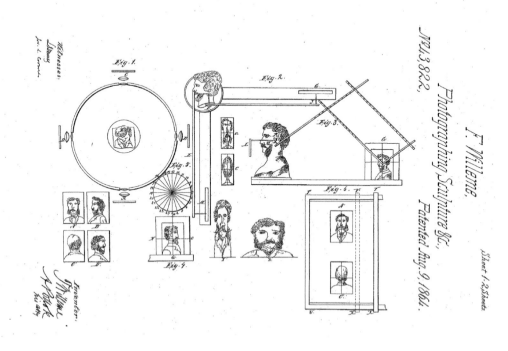

Photosculpture patent August 9, 1864.

In 2012, Ian Dawson, Louisa Minkin, and the undergraduate students from the Winchester School of Art, University of Southampton, recreated François Willème's photosculpture studio and the mechanical sculpture process. They built a round sculpture photography studio with 24 cameras. The students project the images on a translucent screen, and the artist transfers the dimensions of the subject to the clay using a pantograph. To read more about their results and to listen to a podcast about the process, visit this book's accompanying website.

PRESERVING ART—
THE DIGITAL MICHELANGELO PROJECT

In 1997–1999, students and staff of Stanford University and the University of Washington began a project that brought them to Italy to create 3D scans of the works of Michelangelo. Marc Levoy, professor of computer science at Stanford, and his team wanted to be able to work so closely with the works of Michelangelo while combining 3D technology that they would capture chisel marks smaller than a millimeter. The technology of laser scanners has been around since the 1960s but back then the technology was not as readily available. As we learned, a 3D scan is not made with one scan. There are multiple scans that require a great deal of post-processing. The scanning process creates large files that taxed the memories of computers of that time. The Digital Michelangelo project team was one of the first groups that felt it important to document art and culture. They wanted to preserve the cultural heritage in 3D.

With a variety of scanners made for this project, they made scans of many of Michelangelo's works. The sculpture of David has a very large dataset with two million polygons and 7,000-color images. The Michelangelo project has made its datasets available to "established scholars, for non-commercial use only."

It is the goal of the Digital Michelangelo project to capture all of the sculpting nuances with 3D scans, even fine chisel marks (http://graphics.stanford.edu/projects/mich).

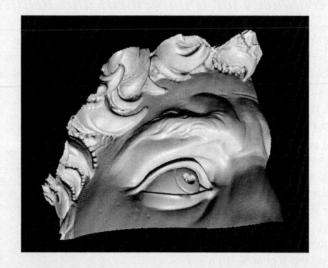

At 23-feet, no one gets to see close-up detail of the work of this master. The photographs and scans show drill holes under the hairline (http://graphics.stanford.edu/projects/mich).

3D Technology for Enlargement and Reduction

Now, thanks to 3D scanning, fine artists who are entering a digital world, who do not want to design in a computer program, can create a sculpture in traditional clay, another medium, or a mix of media. They can then have their work 3D scanned. Once scanned, the artist can add more details to the art in a computer-sculpting program. Or, the artist, in just a few keystrokes, can send the file to a vendor and have it enlarged and/or milled in foam, stone, or wood. Transporting the art is easy. The artist transports the work digitally. An artist in Texas can easily send the digital file to a stone-sculpting facility in Tuscany. The artist can also use these same digital files to create 3D prints in a variety of materials from the many vendors that we talk about in Chapter 7. To learn more about CNC milling of enlargements refer to Chapter 6: 3D for Presentations and CNC Milling for Enlargements.

Artists' work can fall into disrepair, but 3D technology offers the opportunity to repair and repurpose artwork. *Beach Girl* by Bridgette Mongeon.

You don't have to be a Michelangelo to think about preserving artwork. Over time, the artist's work can fall into disrepair or even deteriorate. 3D scanning of the art revives the inspiration. An artist can repair the artwork in the computer and 3D print or CNC mill it in another medium. Another option for artists and 3D scanning is repurposing of their art. An artist can take a life-size figurine created for one purpose, scan it and then recreate the art at a different size and medium.

Art that might be more transportable interested Jan Kirsh. She also desired to enlarge her artwork and create it in another medium such as stone. She had her red pepper sculpture scanned and modeled by Direct Dimensions. ExOne then repurposed her pepper artwork by creating it in metal as a small version.

Chile Pepper 2 by Jan Kirsh, 20 × 36 × 15 inches, cast resin with automotive paint, sealed with clear coat. Bronze and stainless steel with silver-tone finish, 1.75 × 3 × 1 inches.

She states, "I'm trying to have fun with my work and trying to take it to different levels. It means continuous exploration with a constant learning curve" (www.dirdim.com, www.exone.com).

Tutorial—Scanning for the Repurposing of Art

Sculptor Bridgette Mongeon creates digital files of old concrete sculptures of children and broken art. This gives the artist an opportunity to rework the art digitally and repurpose the figures.

Every sculptor knows that you must create art with the end product in mind. If you are creating artwork in clay, you cannot have a heavy figure balancing on a tiny ankle. The limitations of the medium of production and the modification of designs will become even more apparent in Chapter 7: 3D Printing. Whether creating art traditionally to be cast in bronze or digitally for 3D printing in ceramic, it is important to create and design the art with the final output in mind. The nuances of a piece of artwork created for a mold for concrete casting is different from the artwork created for 3D printing. With a sculpture created with the intent of concrete casting, the artist fills in undercuts, creating a design with more of a solid mass. However, as we will see in Chapter 7, 3D printers make art layer upon layer, and deep recesses are not a problem. With the use of scanning, the artist can scan the figure, then bring it into a sculpting program such as ZBrush or Mudbox, rework the designs, and repurpose the concrete children or broken art in other mediums with the final digital medium in mind.

Preparing the Art

There is no need to prepare the white surface. White surfaces will scan well, although shiny or transparent surfaces might need a coat of powder. The artist adds colored dots to the sculpture to help with registration. She places the art on a turntable for easier rotation and secures the scanner safely to a tripod.

System Requirements

As stated in Chapter 1: Primer, when it comes to having the right computer system, often it is best to work backwards. Find the peripherals such as a scanner or the software that you would like to use and then work backwards to find the type of computer that you will need. Will the computer handle the data coming from the 3D scanner? Users can find the system requirements on the peripheral or software websites. Presently, the minimum system requirements for using the NextEngine scanner on

Windows XP/Vista/7 are 2 GHz CPU, 3 GB RAM, and a 256 MB graphics card. The scanner connects to the computer through a USB port. Support from NextEngine lists the minimum requirement, but a quick phone call reveals that the computer may require more RAM to accommodate larger data rich scans created when scanning life-size concrete children. As stated in Chapter 1, sometimes you will need to modify or even purchase a new computer workstation to accommodate your intent. Because this is a larger sculpture, the scanner will collect more data, which means it will require more memory in the computer than if you were only scanning a smaller sculpture.

Scanner Setup

The NextEngine scan setup window has many options. The artist chooses the "Single" position. This means that instead of an object rotating on the turntable the scanner will create individual scans. In the "Points/In.2," the slider is set to the "High" range of SD. The higher HD settings would give more detail, but this is a case where that much data is not necessary. A single test scan shows that the middle-range SD, set at the high end, is sufficient. The "Target" is the material. This material is a bright white plaster sculpture and so the artist applies the "light" setting. We can already see that working with this scanner is giving us one of our criteria in searching for a scanner. We have "Flexible" options when scanning.

Range

The NextEngine scanner makes it easy to remember the positioning of the art. In the "Extended Mode," the scan's best image is at a range of 17 inches. The sculpture and scanner are then placed to accommodate the 17 inches.

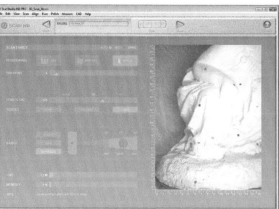

It takes many scans to move around the sculpture with a 25–30 percent overlap of each scan. The final count of scans to scan the entire figure using the NextEngine scanner and individual area scans is 22. It takes approximately two to five minutes to scan and align each section, depending on the experience of the user. Scanning is a fine art. It is important to get the overlap of each scan needed in the preferred range. Making excessive scan to align does not always mean a better digital file.

A scanner that offers flexibility may not be automatic. The options that the scanner offers can lead to a better scan. The artist scans the little boy at a range of 17 inches from the lens of the scanner. It will take quite a few sections to scan and align the entire large sculpture.

The Process

The steps in the scanning process are: scan, align, trim, fuse. The viewing window allows the artist to clearly see what data is missing or needed. The artist rotates the art and creates individual scans. Each scan may have excess data in the image, and this is easily deleted using the software's "trim" function. Registration dots on the scanned sculpture help the artist to visually align the multiple scanned images in the computer software program. These different images are then fused together using the software. There may be recessed areas in the art where the scanner cannot gather information. These hidden areas will create holes in the scan. If any holes remain, the program can fill these holes with the "fill" command.

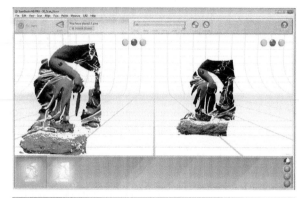

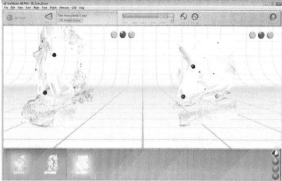

Output

The NextEngine scanner comes with operating software called ScanStudio that provides output of the following Mesh file formats: STL, PLY XYZ, VRML, OBJ, and JPG texture files. See Chapter 7: 3D Printing for further discussion on file formats. Other file formats are available for this scanner; for example, file formats for CAD programs are available with the NextEngine software upgrades. It is important to know the file output format available from either your scanner or your service bureau. To finalize the details within a sculpting program, the artist uses this digital model created by the scanner. It is important to be able to import the file into the sculpting program. Once the artist refines the 3D model he or she can send it to a 3D printer to print the art in other media and sizes. See Chapter 4 for information on sculpting or refining a file in a sculpting program, as well as preparing the file for printing.

The NextEngine scanner can scan color, which makes it easier to see registration dots on the sculpture. The artist matches up the dots on the scanned art with three dots in the software, placed preferably in a triangular position. The computer then aligns and fuses each of the scans. If any holes remain after all of the scans are complete, the scanner can fill the holes.

This tutorial of scanning concrete children has helped us to understand the process of scanning using a studio digital scanner that provides a quality scan, with ease of use and flexibility. Now let's take a look at some other types of scanning and the way that artists are using this 3D process to create incredible pieces of art.

OBJECT
BREAST CANCER

Leonor Caraballo is an artist who was diagnosed with breast cancer. As a visual person, she wanted to see her tumor, to give it shape, to know what it was instead of it being this unseen monster. In collaboration with her husband, Abou Farman, they took her MRIs and created a digital model that they then turned into a 3D print. The artist changes the cancerous mass into a bronze jewel. When viewing the tumor at an art show, breast surgeon Alexander Swistel told the artists, "These tumors are saying something." Through the art, another collaboration takes place. Because of this artwork, Swistel and Dr. Michele Drotman have decided to look at the volume of cancer and see if it can change the way doctors treat breast cancer.

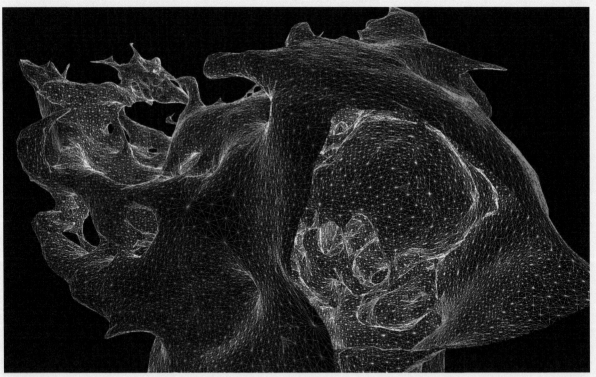

Object Breast Cancer
by Caraballo-Farman.

Object Breast Cancer
by Caraballo-Farman.

Other Types of Scanning and Capturing Data

Artists are taking more than 3D scans using scanners and photogrammetry to create art. They are also using such things as medical scan and motion capture. You don't have to have sophisticated equipment and medical software to work with your own medical scans. InVesalius is free software that can create 3D images from 2D medical files like CT or MRI scans (http://svn.softwarepublico.gov.br/trac/invesalius).

Motion Capture

The military, game developers, and those who work with robotics, medical applications, and film have all used motion capture. In film, motion capture or "match moving" on a computer records the movements of the figure, brings that information into a computer as data, and transfers that information to a character in animation. Motion capture does not copy the physical characteristics of an individual, but only their movement or actions.

There is similar technology used in the Xbox Kinect game console or the Nintendo Wii that copies the motion, movement, and gestures of the person and passes those movements on to the characters on the screen for use in a game or Wii sports activity. Hackers are already using the Kinect to create a room scanning system. It won't be long before we see artists begin to hack the Wii or Kinect to create their own motion art. On this book's accompanying website, there are links to hacker sites that show how to use your Kinect as a room scanner.

An artist who is taking motion capture and movement as data and translating that into art is Raphael Perret. Perret captures data not by scanning but by probes that he places on the body. This motion capture is then transferred into the computer and later printed out as a physical object.

Using 3D data capture with archeology, art, and cultural digital preservation of sites that are subject to deterioration through the elements is a way to preserve earth's cultural heritage. Using digital files in education to explore without damaging the artifacts and art has great potential, not only in education, but also in encouraging awareness and acceptance of other cultures.

The capturing of data, whether through scanning, photogrammetry, 2D data made into 3D files, or motion capture, opens up a world of possibilities for artists. It helps the blind to see and, who knows, as in the case of Leonor Caraballo and her breast tumor, the exploration and art might just spark a thought process that could have greater potential for mankind. 3D data for enlargement, reduction, repurposing, and documenting for a legacy for loved ones extends the artist's toolset and creative life journey. Whatever you see, you can now capture, change, and modify easily in a digital world. Put these tools in the hands of creative minds, and it is amazing what will come forth.

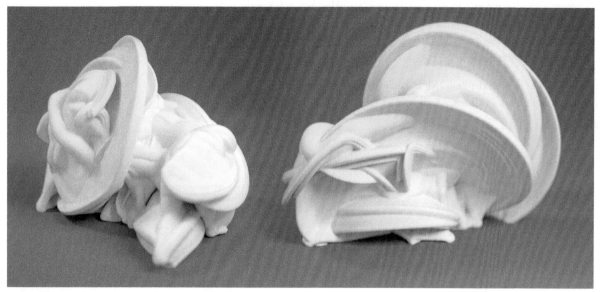

Motion Capture *Milton #10.2.1* by Raphael Perret. Rendering by Vladimir Jankijevic.

KEVIN BOX *and* ROBERT J. LANG

Kevin Box collaborates with origami artist Robert J. Lang to create monumental origami sculptures in metal.

There are several ways that Kevin Box and Robert J. Lang continue to push the boundaries of the process, art, and technology. Box and Lang incorporated 3D technology with laser scanning of a paper/wax original art titled *White Bison*. Thai Metal Crafters Co., in Thailand, enlarged and CNC milled the work in foam (www.tmcbronze.com). The artists finish the foam with clay and wax to restore edges and "wrinkles" before it travels through the traditional lost wax method of bronze casting. This process is similar to the process detailed by Bridgette Mongeon's tiger sculpture featured in Chapters 6 and 7.

Box continues to push the limits while exploring technology and his personal inspiration. In Chapter 8, we will see how Synappsys Digital Services uses Box's work to create yet another advancement in digital technology.

White Bison, bronze by Kevin Box and Robert J. Lang.

Origami Bison by Kevin Box
and Robert J. Lang.

Origami Bison, folded paper by
Kevin Box and Robert J. Lang.

3D SCANNING

BARRY X. BALL

Barry X. Ball is another pioneer who has incorporated 3D technology and fine art since 1997. Ball 3D scanned his own head with a Cyberware scanner at Cyber F/X in Burbank, California, then he had the head CNC milled in foam. He refined the foam heads and used them as models to create works like *Flayed Herm* found on his website (www.barryxball.com).

Ball created the artwork *Envy* from a scan of *La Invidia*, the work of sculptor Giusto le Court (1627–1679). Although these are scans of other artists' works, Barry and his team try to bring the work past what the original artist has done, past the compromises that the original artist made at the time of the commissions. In an interview for the recent Museum of Art and Design exhibition Out of Hand, Ball states:

> "I think I make a distinction in my work, between copies and what I do. I'm definitely not copying or re-presenting historical works. I'm using… historical artists' end point as my starting point. Trying to analyze what my historical fore bearers where trying to do, and attempting, in my way, to do it better."

Envy/Purity by Barry X. Ball. Pakistani onyx/Mexican onyx, 2008–2012. Private collection, New York.

Ball created the artwork *Purity* from a scan of the sculpture *La Purità* by Antonio Corradini (1668–1752). These two images quickly display Ball's influence on the work by the materials he has chosen.

Ball works with a variety of software including ZBrush and Rhino 3D. For scanners he prefers the Breuckmann white-light scanner and vendors that he has used are Unocad (European scanner, www.unocad.it/cms), Direct Dimensions (US scanner, www.dirdim.com), Fine Line Prototyping (www.finelineprototyping.com), Materialise (www.materialise.com), and Repliform (www.repliforminc.com).

Purity by Barry X. Ball. Belgian black marble. 2008-2010. Private collection, Paris.

ROBERT LAZZARINI

Robert Lazzarini creates art of distortion that invites a type of artistic vertigo in the viewer. These sculptures look like two-dimensional objects that a photographer might skew in Photoshop. They are instead, three-dimensional works of art. The art compels the viewer to walk around it. The viewer hopes to rectify the visual distortion as one would walk around a *tromp l'oeil* painting trying to find the artist's intended perspective. However, with the viewing of Lazzarini's work, rectifying the 3D image in your mind is impossible, no matter how many times you walk around it. They are spatial paradoxes.

Pay Phone, 2000, by Robert Lazzarini.

Lazzarini's process, although unique to each object, combines digital design, industrial processes, and hand-finishing. One of the aspects of his work is that there is no material translation. In other words, the sculpture that he creates is made from the same material as the object it is based upon. His series *Skulls* are cast bone.

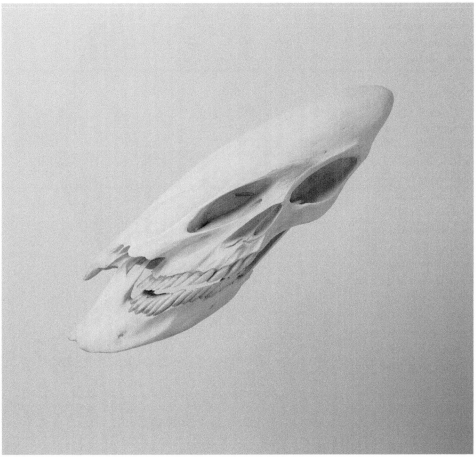

Skull, 2000, by Robert Lazzarini.

SOPHIE KAHN

Sophie Kahn comes from a background of capturing the stillness of life in photographic images two-dimensionally. What she now embraces while working with 3D technology is the movement of stillness. Kahn has incorporated 3D scanning in her workflow since 2010, combining the technology with bronze casting and other mediums. When using a 3D scanner, it is difficult to capture the human form. As we have seen, 3D scanning takes a bit of time and patience. When creating a 3D scan of a person, distortions of the image happen through subtle movement of the subject. What some might consider the limitations of the 3D scanner when trying to capture figures, Kahn sees as a creative part of the medium. The movement of the body makes what a scanning technician would refer to as noise or "motion blur." Noise is something a scanning company would try to avoid, or cut out of the project. However, Kahn embraces it. Kahn incorporates the noise from that movement in her work and creates new art that looks fractured, old, and broken, more like an artifact that an archeologist would find on a dig.

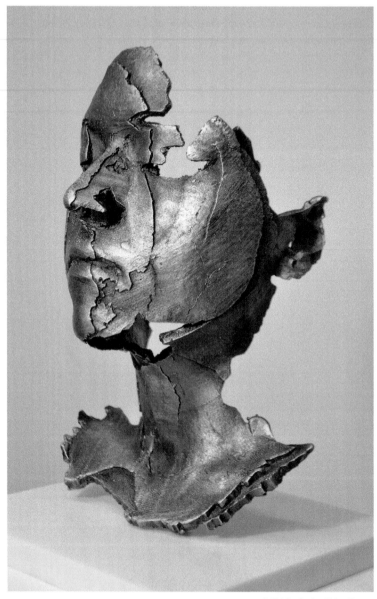

L:Gold by Sophie Kahn. Bronze (cast from 3D print), 2012.

She describes seeing a 3D scan of herself without color or movement, looking like a death mask—eerie and haunting. The technology of the 3D scanner strips the life away from the body, which intrigues Kahn. Using this new medium was a continuation of her exploration and questions about the human body, time, memory, loss, and history. She is also interested in how the advance of technology, the use of social media, becomes a way for us to "continue living" or entomb ourselves.

In a lecture at the leaders in Software and Art conference at the Guggenheim Museum in New York 2012, she states.

> "I work with all of this imagery not because I want to be morbid, but because I am interested in exploring the ways that technology can fail to capture life, and what the poetics of that failure might look like. We live in a world where we are so bombarded with claims for all seeing, all-powerful, imaging technologies. It is my belief that as artists destabilizing those, through poetics, might actually prove to be the strongest weapon that we have."

On the book's website at www.digitalsculpting.net you will find:

* Links to further descriptions on the process of creating the artwork featured in the galleries.
* Podcasts with the artists.
* Videos featuring the artists at work.

Période de délire, K, by Sophie Kahn. 3D print from 3D laser scan, aluminum base, 2014, 12 × 11 × 8 inches (without base).

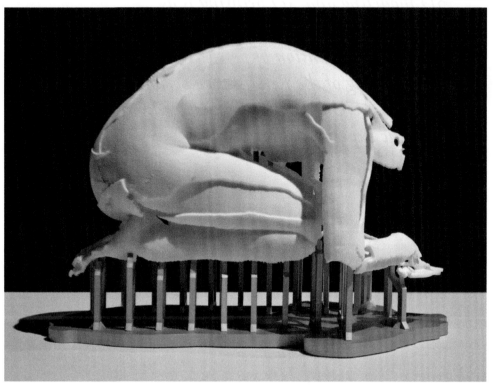

CHAPTER FOUR

3D MODELING, SCULPTING, AND MORE

———

"3D modeling and 3D printing is as much of a revolution as a creative tool for artists as the invention of perspective at the beginning of the Renaissance period in Italy. It has changed forever the paradigm of artistic expression."

Gil Bruvel

facing page
Check Mate by Gil Bruvel, 37.5 × 37.5 × 3¼ inches.
Mixed media: stainless steel and bronze, wood and resin.

Many artists who use digital techniques such as CNC milling, 3D printing, and digital scanning may never need to use digital sculpting, modeling programs, or 3D models. They will simply create their work in a traditional manner, then they will have it 3D scanned. The digital file may be required for enlargement or repurposing of the art. The artist can choose between the subtractive process of CNC milling and the additive process of 3D printing to create the artwork into a physical form. For others, sculpting in the computer may be the beginning of their creative process. They will create their designs in the computer without ever physically touching the design. Other artists may work with nothing but code to create their art. Some artists use a mixture of all of these processes. They may become adept at both traditional and digital and tweak code to get their final results. Or artists may use the digital part of their toolset as the steps before production where they can tweak the designs a bit further to obtain their desired results. They may experiment with something in the real world and then translate it to the digital world or vice versa. The combinations and possibilities are endless.

As you will see in Chapters 5, 7, and 8, some of the ways that are available to create artwork in physical form using 3D technology have limitations. Some of the processes of output are expensive, although they are changing and quickly becoming more affordable. The limitations and considerations for artists who want to realize their work in physical form revolve around what this book refers to as "the big three." This criterion consists of; the cost, build envelope or size, and the detail available in the desired material. The growing technology of 3D offers much, but as we will see, the costs of creating digitally can sometimes be more expensive than creating the art in a traditional process. By "build envelope," we are referring to the maximum size in which the artist wishes their object created. The final decisive factor is the quality of detail that may or may not be available for the desired material. The big three criteria are changing.

Jewelry by Lisa Krikawa, Krikawa Jewelry and Design.

We will also see that what material you want to create your artwork in may help to determine the type of software that you purchase. For example, Krikawa Jewelry—featured in Chapter

7 and interviewed in the *Art and Technology* podcasts—need to have precise measurements in their designs. They work with the CAD software Rhinoceros.

Many artists find that as the materials, processes, and tools of technology become more readily available, they may float back and forth between digital and traditional until they achieve the end results they are looking for. It is the author's hope that this book will prompt creative people to explore the processes and their limitations. Fine artists are using software and hardware intended for use in other industries such as animation, film, industry, architecture, and engineering. They combine that with a spirit of exploration and they achieve an original result that no one has seen before.

You may be starting out with incorporating 3D technology in your traditional workflow, or are entertaining the idea of making this technology a part of your creative process. If this is the case, then deciding on what programs to work in can feel overwhelming. Unfortunately, using 3D tools takes a bit of commitment. It is not like buying a pad of watercolor paper and watercolors and sitting down to work. It will take some dedicated time to learn these new tools of the trade. How do you know which tool is the right one for you and your process? Throughout this book, artists share their software preferences. This may help in making a decision on software. Cost of software may be an important determining factor. One must also weigh in other determining factors mentioned in Chapter 1, such as your computer, operating system, video card, memory, etc.

This chapter is by no means designated as a "how to" guide to sculpting or modeling in 3D. There is a generous amount of free information on the Internet for just about any program that you would like to learn. If a certain 3D sculpting, modeling, or design program interests you, begin learning by watching online tutorials. Links are available on this book's accompanying website. The videos will help you to see the interface of the program as well as its usability. Many of the software programs also have user forums. If a program catches your attention, join the user forum. Lurk and listen in on the conversations of the users. Searching out your questions in the forum search engines will go a long way to getting answers. If you have a project in mind, post that idea and ask the users for help in directing you. Do note that many of these individuals will be using the program with their agenda in mind. Your agenda will be different; you are using the program for fine art, not for animation, movies, or renders. Finally, you can't determine if the program is right for you until you try it out. Many programs are available on a free 30-day trial. Carve some time out and play.

There are many different types of programs, as you will see by the work in this book and the artists that are using the different software programs. Some do a specific thing, such as digital sculpting that feels like pushing around clay. Other software programs do more than just sculpting or modeling. The software's toolset may also include items you will never use, for example, animation. Some programs are free, others cost thousands of dollars. The Appendix has a list of the programs that many of the featured artists in this book are using to create their work.

Don't let the lack of a computer and software keep you from investigating. Try your hand at some free online resources for creating; there are many sites that offer you the ability to play with design in a variety of ways. Some websites also link many of these free software programs to an online service bureau so that you can then realize your artwork in a physical form. Perhaps you would like to learn how to create your art using code; this information is also available. A list of these resources is in the Appendix.

Digital Compared to Traditional

The author compiled this book in the hope of introducing individuals to new processes. In light of that, there will be readers who are considering adopting digital sculpting/modeling into their workflow. Let's compare and contrast digital sculpting/modeling to traditional.

Additive and Subtractive

Within traditional sculpture, there are two categories of sculpting—additive and subtractive. In additive sculpting, the sculptor will add material, building up layers to bring to life the object that they are seeking. For example, facial features are often created using different sculptural masses consisting of muscles and fat.

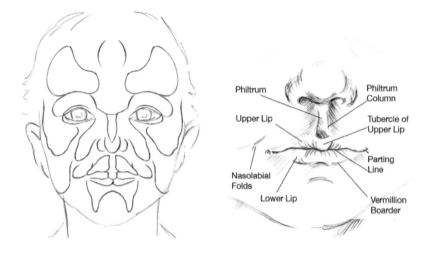

Sculptural masses make up the intricate details of facial features. From *Digital Sculpting with Mudbox: Essential Tools and Techniques for Artists*, Mike de la Flor and Bridgette Mongeon.

Philtrum

Philtrum Column

Upper Lip

Tubercle of Upper Lip

Nasolabial Folds

Parting Line

Lower Lip

Vermillion Boarder

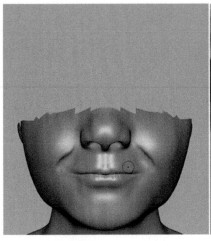
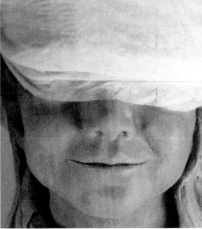

The sculptor may still carve away at areas or subtract clay from the mass that they begin with, but on the whole, it is a malleable process that starts with the addition of a material. Works such as Bruce Beasley's, featured in Chapter 1, could also be considered additive. The metals may not be malleable, but Bruce adds one piece to the next to form a specific shape.

In contrast, artwork created with a subtractive process is the removal of material. A stone-carver takes away material. He or she reveals the shape beneath, as does a woodcarver. The subtractive process of sculpting is far less forgiving as the wrong move or the wrong amount of pressure can be disastrous. There is also the unknown behavior of the material. Hit a knot in wood or the grain in stone and the creative subtractive process of sculpting can be temperamental and require a real master to achieve it.

Most of the artwork created using the digital sculpting tools is more closely associated with the additive process of sculpting. It does not mean that a digital sculptor could not use the subtractive process; it is just not a primary process of sculpting.

Arpeggio by Bruce Beasley. Photograph by Lee Fatheree.

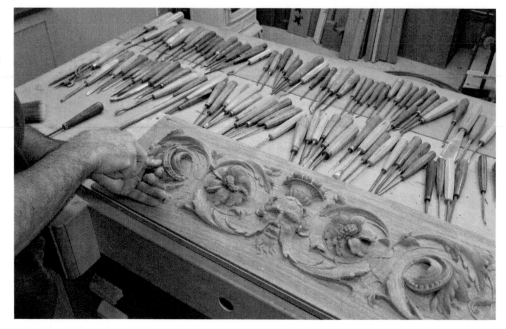

Master carver Patrick Burke uses the subtractive process for hand carving wood. Work in progress—over-door panel embellishment done in the Renaissance style, European walnut.

Although they may not use the subtractive process of sculpting within the digital world of sculpting, subtraction of material in production certainly plays a part in many of the final designs, as we will see in Chapter 5. In fact, incorporating digital processes with traditional processes can relieve the artist of the difficulties of using temperamental material. Barry X. Ball states that he believes CNC milling allows him to use stone with natural artifacts that would not easily carve with traditional methods.

The Traditional/Digital Studio

A sculpture is not created as a painter creates a painting. A painter stands in one position and the subject is in one position. The stance allows the painter to create a two-dimensional image, as it would appear flat; the color, shading, and contrast in the paint fool the eye to create a three-dimensional quality. Sculpture is by its very nature three-dimensional. A sculptor is much more physically active with the creative process. A sculptor who works in clay on such things as portraits or figures is working in three dimensions. In this traditional sculpting studio, an artist works on a rotating sculpture stand. Movement is a dance that happens between the artist, the clay, and the subject. The artist takes measurements and orbits around the stationary model, carving, adding, and moving clay as they also rotate their clay figure. The artist performs all of this dance and rotation many times as they interpret the model before them and translate that interpretation to the clay.

Digital sculptors do the same movement, but they do it in the computer. The digital sculptor can rotate an object, move in close to an object, or see what their sculpture will look like from 20 feet overhead. The artists might not get the same amount of exercise as they do in a traditional studio, but all of the navigation is possible.

Of course, a clay-sculpting studio is only one type of sculpting studio. There are metal sculptors who take large heavy pieces of equipment, hoist them on cranes and weld them together. Stone sculptors chip away at large slabs of stone in their studios. The variety of sculptors and studio space is as vast as the variety of media. There is a variety of media in which a sculptor can work, each medium and material depicting their process. Whether following an additive or a subtractive process of sculpting, each artist will look at their work from all sides, checking composition, light, and how the sculpture may interact with its surroundings.

Besides moving around the subject and back to the clay, the artist may need measurements. *B.B. King* by Bridgette Mongeon.

The very nature of the digital studio may at first feel contrary to the traditional process. The digital process tethers an artist to the computer, and they can't easily move around the model. (A digital sculpting class with a live model, one in which the tables and artists could rotate around the live model, would be a class to experience.) In the computer, the dance of the rotation of the sculpture is still done; however, the artist does it within the confines of the navigation on a computer screen.

Comparisons

There are many comparisons between the tools of digital and traditional processes of sculpting. There are strengths and weakness of both. Let's look at some tools and processes.

The tools of both traditional and digital sculpting are similar. As the technology advances, it moves more towards the traditional feel of sculpting—although nothing can replace the touch and smell of a traditional studio. Still, programs like Mudbox, ZBrush, Sculptris, and 3D-Coat have that organic feel of sculpting.

The traditional sculpting is tactile and physical. Sculptor Michelle O'Michael works in her metal shop creating *Blue Moons.*

The downfall of the digital software is that it changes. Software companies revise them often. Many of these revisions give the user more usability and features, but with each step there is a new learning curve. Many software programs offer more tools than one would ever use in a single sitting; there are tools to mimic each traditional tool.

Digital tools often feel like traditional sculpting tools.

Tools in Mudbox and ZBrush are similar to the tools in a traditional sculptor's studio.

Gravity Works

Traditional artists understand that the final material affects the design. For example, the way you create a design to be cast in bronze as compared to how you would create a design that is in terra-cotta clay is different. Unlike a virtual world where there are no real world limitations and gravity does not exist, it does exist in the real world. In the real world, the artist could not create a sculpture in a material that would not support the real-world limitations. For example, a sculpture of a child balancing on one foot, with thin ankles supporting the weight, may be possible, but not advisable. If the sculpture could make it through the sculpting and firing process it would always be a very fragile object where one bump would break and ruin the integrity of the sculpture. Breakage may not happen in another material. An artist can make that same sculpture in bronze (although, most foundries will suggest three points of contact in a bronze sculpture unless the artist engineers a substructure within the piece to accommodate the possibilities of balance and breakage). Foundries realize the demands that the real world can put on design. The traditional artist is familiar with gravity, if for no other reason than having a sculpture or armature collapse in the process of creating.

Real World

We have already spoken about some real-world concerns. In traditional clay sculpture, you will create an armature for your work. The armature is what will hold up the artwork, and they come in all shapes and sizes. It might be lightweight aluminum wire used inside a small figure, plumbing pipe, or welded rebar. It might also be CNC milled foam, as we will see in Chapter 5. Whether it is a portrait bust or a monumental sculpture, the armature is pivotal in the creative process. If the armature is not sufficient then the laws of physics will take place while the artist is sculpting. Adding a mass of clay to one area without support can bring on disasters. The clay may slide off of the sculpture; it may break at the weakest point. When it does, it takes everything else along with it, or it could just cause the entire internal structure to collapse, taking weeks or months of work with it.

In contrast, a virtual object has no physical bounds like gravity or the weight of the clay. An artist can add, subtract, and create parts hanging off other parts. In the computer, the artist can create objects in midair such as a splash coming off of a dog's wagging tail. However, to bring these virtual designs into the real world, one has to consider constraints such as gravity. Artists then have to find or invent a 3D process that is available to make their art a physical object.

Experimentation

In a traditional sculpture studio with a traditional sculpture, if the design is small enough and has an internal moveable armature, a sculptor can move appendages around to obtain just the right pose. However, the sculpture may suffer some damage, and an artist can only reposition a small figure easily. A larger figure with rebar as an internal armature will take muscle, a sledgehammer, and some power tools to move and bend. Needless to say, changes cause much more damage.

With digital processes, whether you are

- posing a figure, using models from DAZ and Poser for design possibilities for a life-size or monumental sculpture;
- manipulating primitives intended for large sheets of metal created in the software program Blender;
- sculpting organic shapes in such programs as ZBrush or Mudbox for 3D printing or CNC milling...

an artist can easily experiment. They can even save versions and compare.

(left) Working out designs in 3D sculpting, modeling, or posing software is helpful. Bridgette Mongeon art directs Mike de la Flor as they work out a running pose using Poser's run program and DAZ models for a sculpture titled *Lucas* by Bridgette Mongeon.

(right) *Lucas* by Bridgette Mongeon.

Symmetry

We mentioned symmetry in Chapter 2. Many programs allow you to sculpt using symmetry. This means if you are sculpting a face, you can sculpt both sides at the same time. Because faces are never completely symmetrical, the artist simply turns off the symmetry feature and manipulates the digital clay to give the specific non-symmetrical characteristics of their model. But sculpting on two sides at the same time is not all some programs can do. They can sculpt radial symmetry or they can sculpt in symmetry on different axes as shown in Chapter 1.

Mirror Objects

In traditional sculpture, if you create an eyeball on one side you must then spend the same amount of time sculpting the same thing on the other side. When you are working digitally, you can mirror objects.

Erase Mistakes and Undo

Wouldn't it be great if we had an "undo" button in traditional sculpture studio? If you happen to be carving in stone and accidentally lopped off a specific body part, you could press "undo." "Undo" in digital sculpture is a part of the process. If an artist needs to change a sculpture in the traditional studio, they scrape the clay off and start again, sometimes destroying the underlying work that they don't want to change. In a sculpting program, you can simply "undo" and go back in history until you reach a place where you want to start again.

Extension of a Career—Physical

Traditional processes of sculpting are very physical. For an artist creating a monumental piece of sculpture, they are climbing up and down scaffolding and ladders, they are crouching to reach difficult areas, and often acting more like an acrobat in Cirque du Soleil than a sculptor. Their job consists of hoisting tools, materials, and armatures, and always working with their hands. Injuries and hazards of a traditional sculptor's studio can be many, including: pulmonary problems from breathing in dust, burns from chemicals, eye injuries, muscle strains, and—because they work with their hands in repetitive motions—hand injuries.

A traditional sculptor's
workflow is very physical.

Artists that work with large sheets of metal and welding will find that putting together and changing the design in the computer is much easier than welding hundreds of pounds of metal. They may also find comfort in that they can fit everything together prior to fabrication instead of grinding it off later because the design doesn't quite fit, or does not look the way the artist intended as it is further reviewed from all sides.

Digital processes assist the artist in extending or even saving a career, depending on their physical capabilities. It is much easier to sit at a computer in front of a graphics tablet and push around a stylus pen than hauling material.

Just Like Real World Sculpting?

Whether the digital process is just like real-world sculpting or not is debatable. Software companies promote it as such, and digital sculpting has come a long way over the years. For example, let's take a look at the metamorphosis of one program, ZBrush, and its commitment to be like "real sculpting." ZBrush was released in 2007 and available for Mac in 2009. When ZBrush first came out, the process of creating your sculpture came from creating ZSpheres. ZBrush intended the creation of ZSpheres to give the artist a clean base mesh for their model. By moving ZSphere tubes, the artist created simple or complex armatures and base meshes of their design. With a few clicks, the ZSphere sculpture turns into a polygonal model for sculpting.

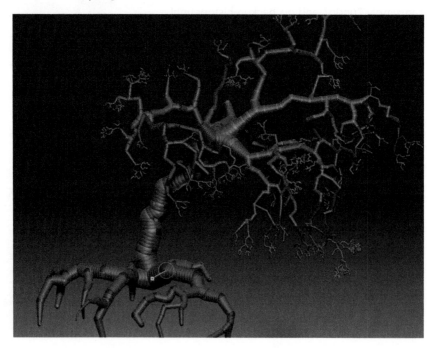

Sculpting with ZBrush ZSpheres.

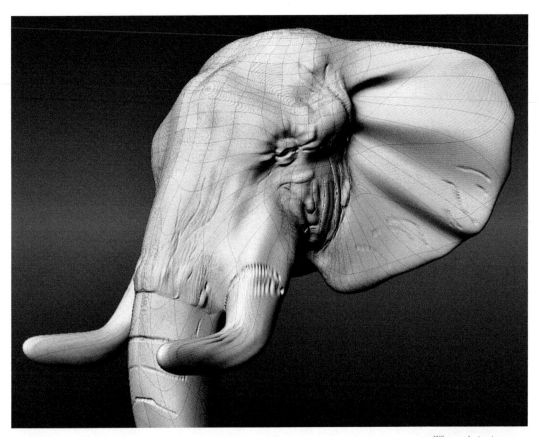

When sculpting in a digital sculpting program, pulling on the clay would destroy the underlying topology. This makes it impossible to sculpt. For traditional artists learning to sculpt using digital tools, the process can be frustrating.

The difficulty with the process of sculpting in ZBrush was also the case in Mudbox. Once the artist created the polygonal model, if they pushed and pulled on the clay, as one would in the traditional processes of sculpting, it destroyed the underlying topology. With a distorted geometry, the user could no longer sculpt smoothly without having to stop and fix the topology. The artist would have to recreate or retopologize the underlying mesh to be able to continue to sculpt.

Of course, it was possible to take the sculpture out of a sculpting program and bring it into a retopologizing program like 3DCoat, but this made the process less organic and fluid.

ZBrush's next transition was from spheres to a process called ZSketching in version 3.5R3 2009/2010. Remember how we said that there were continuous improvements and learning curves? ZBrush's improvements are a great example. With ZSketching one still had to use a ZSphere skeleton, but an artist could flesh out the sculpture using the ZSketch tools. ZSketch was more intuitive for the traditional artist. It was more like rolling out tubes of clay and adding them to their form as sections of mass.

ZBrush ZSketch of a fish, a sculpting skin, and a render.

ZBrush introduced Dynamesh in 4R2, which was a huge leap. The process of using Dynamesh finally became more like sculpting with a ball of clay in the traditional studio. Pushing and pulling and adding to the clay may still distort the underlying topology; however, the artist drags on the screen with Dynamesh turned on and the program will remove the artifacts and give additional geometry where needed. There is no interfering in the sculpting process. It is continuous. Dynamesh is different than ZRemesher, another tool in ZBrush that allows the artist to recreate the underlying topology with controlled polygon groups, directions, and even edge loops.

The digital sculpting programs are becoming increasingly more powerful and more intuitive. The technical aspect of creating in 3D is more fluid and more in tune with traditional sculpture. Do remember that each revision of a software program has a new learning curve. It is not like working in the traditional studio. Clay and calipers do not change.

Control

Though there are many things that you can do with digital technology, when an artist is working in the computer they don't have full control. They have to wait on a computer to process the art.

No Touch

We have already discussed the importance of touch in previous chapters. Some artists feel that haptic devices help them feel more connected to their work. Other artists find that the lack of touch in the digital process is one of the hardest things to overcome.

Heather Gorham works on *Flowering Lamb of Odd* using touch haptics and Geomagic Freeform.

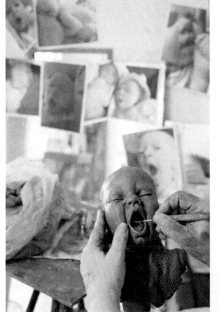

Yawn by Bridgette Mongeon. Photograph by Christina Sizemore.

Losing Your Work

Never in the entire time of the history of traditional sculpture has anyone claimed that, in the middle of the project, their work disappeared. Alas, with all of the things that we have discussed about digital sculpture, such a loss is a possibility. So are corrupt files. The remedy is to save your work and save your work often. You might also periodically save in different formats.

Visibility

In a digital sculpting program you can hide certain areas to reach and sculpt other areas. So, if you were sculpting the inside of the mouth you could hide portions of the lips.

Finding Software for Those Special Problems

As an artist creates using digital and traditional means, they will gather the best tools for each part of the job. With each project or design, new obstacles or challenges may arise. As they begin to incorporate digital tools in the process, they will start with one program. However, when the present software reaches the design limitation and does not have the capabilities the artist needs, they will seek out other programs that will fill in the gap. This scenario is a constant with all of the artists interviewed for this book and the artists interviewed for the *Art and Technology* podcasts.

One such incident for sculptor Bridgette Mongeon was incorporation of text in a digital model intended for reproduction in the real world. Mongeon found this challenge of creating and incorporating three-dimensional text in such art as medallions and memorials a challenge. Visit this book's accompanying website to follow the tutorial on how Mongeon experimented with traditional and digital processes of creating text in sculpture. She found Vectric Aspire, software designed for CNC (computer numerically controlled) machining, to assist her with her projects. She documents the process of creating text for a Bible in her sculpture *Called to Pray*.

When sculptor Bridgette Mongeon runs across a problem or a challenge in the sculpting process, she considers both traditional and digital processes that she may use in solving the problem. When sculpting *Called to Pray* and other pieces of art such as medallions and memorials, the incorporation of three-dimensional text for art is often a challenge. Visit www.digitalsculpting.net for the tutorial "Creating 3D Text For Sculptures."

There are many different ways to obtain a 3D model. We have looked at scanning artwork that artists have sculpted using traditional processes and even manipulating scans within the computer to repurpose artwork. There are also numerous free programs for artists to try. These programs help the traditional artists get their feet wet in a virtual world of creating before investing into expensive hardware and software. There are also programs for artists to learn and design with code. Check the Appendix and this book's accompanying website for software suggestions.

As you experiment, you will most likely find that you will need a variety of digital tools to get to the results you desire. If the program you chose is not giving you exactly what you need, don't despair. There may be a plug-in or additional programs that will help you fill the gap in your artistic process. Sometimes the needs of the artist will push the manufacturers of the software to change the software and provide the artist with their "wish list." Just look at how ZBrush morphed into a program that is more like traditional sculpting.

Whatever ways you decide to put creative inspiration into a digital form, you will eventually want to get it out of the computer and share it with others. In the following chapters, we will explore the many possibilities and resources of making your 3D artwork that is in the computer into a physical form. Combine these resources of creating and realizing artwork with the resources listed in the Appendix, and the tutorials and other information on the book's accompanying website. You will be well on your way to creating incredible artwork combining traditional and digital processes.

DAVID C. MORRIS

A pioneer of incorporating 3D technology into fine art, David C. Morris writes his own code to create his incredible art.

Columbia River Crystal by David C. Morris. Welded bronze, 12 foot. Built at Milgo-Bufkin, Brooklyn, 1997.

Matador's Cape by David C Morris. Cast bronze, 6 foot. Cast at Polich-Tallix, Rock Creek, New York, 2010.

3D MODELING, SCULPTING, AND MORE

KEVIN MACK

Kevin Mack creates his works of art using custom tools developed in Houdini for constrained random implicit surfaces, procedurally derived structures, and articulated turbulent noise advection. Shapeways is the vendor who created these works.

Standing Mind Over Matter by Kevin Mack, 14 × 19 × 7 inches. Selective laser sintered nylon print.

JOEL MONGEON

Joel works in ZBrush and Modo with a bit of Photoshop for
final compositing.

The Gallery by Joel
Mongeon.

GIL BRUVEL

Check Mate by Gil Bruvel,
37½ × 37½ × 3¼ inches,
mixed media: stainless
steel and bronze, wood,
and resin

Rain by Gil Bruvel.
20 × 17 × 14 inches,
stainless steel.

On the book's website at
www.digitalsculpting.net
you will find:

* Links to further
  descriptions on the
  process of creating the
  artwork featured in the
  galleries.
* Podcasts with the
  artists.
* Videos featuring the
  artists at work.

CHAPTER FIVE

CNC MILLING, ROUTING, AND MORE

———

"Opening the door of CNC machining an artist finds a world of possibilities."

Bridgette Mongeon

facing page

Vine Door by G. Watson Design. Traditional millwork produced in knotty alder. A door that leads to a wine cellar was enhanced by the incorporation of climbing grape vines.

Computer numerically controlled (CNC) milling and routing is a subtractive process that takes away material from stock to create a part. A CNC machine is similar to a router carving the edge of wood or a drill cutting a hole in a piece of plywood. In CNC milling and routing machining, the bit rotates as it moves across the object. The machine makes multiple passes over an item to remove the necessary material. This method of working can produce very detailed parts.

There are many different types of CNC milling and routing machines. Technically, there are both CNC routers and CNC milling machines, and they are different. Generally, routers cut soft material such as foam or wood and mills cut harder material such as steel. Both routers and millers basically do the same thing, but they also may have a different internal structure. Although woodworkers and machinists might differentiate between routing and milling, the term "CNC milling" seems to be the term referring to both routing and milling and the term that is most used in the arts. In this book, we therefore use the term "CNC milling."

There is a variety of materials that one can mill with CNC machines. The type of machine often depicts the type of material that a machine can cut. There are many options for artists who want to be creative with CNC. There are service bureaus that mill or an artist can own a low-cost CNC, or they can even make their own CNC machine. Another option for exploring CNC is to join a maker community.

CNC does not just relate to carving. There are several tools in the shop that are computer numerically controlled such as lathes that cut wood or metal while they spin, plasma cutters that use a torch to cut metal, and water jet cutters that use water and an abrasive substance to cut multiple materials. In this chapter we will look at CNC as it refers to the subtractive process of technology. We will explore some of the machines, materials, and processes of using CNC, while visiting the inspiration and incredible creations made with the combinations of 3D sculpting, scanning, and CNC technology. This topic is robust and diversified.

To help the reader with all of the topics such as software, service bureaus, hardware, materials, and expanded as well as additional tutorials you can use the Appendix or visit the book's accompanying website. As with all technology, it changes and new things become available daily. We will try to update the website with these new possibilities (www. digitalsculpting.net).

CNC Milling and Routing

When considering using CNC milling in fine art and craft, there are several choices for artists and craftsmen. It will depend on the level of interest and tinkering that each prefers. Do you want to own your machine? Do you prefer to share a machine or use a service bureau? Exploring these options can help you define your working process.

Service Bureaus

The easiest way to explore the processes of using CNC without a huge investment in equipment and time is by using a CNC service bureau. CNC service bureaus often specialize in the materials that they machine. For example, some CNC service bureaus cut only in foam, others specialize in wood, and still others carve only in stone. Of course, using a service bureau means that they are a professional service. They have experience in the process, and an artist can usually expect quality results.

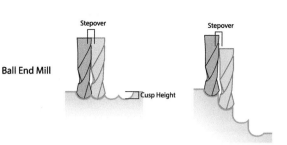

When an artist chooses this path of exploration of CNC milling, they need only to supply the file to the service bureau. They won't need to think about coding, toolpaths, or how to service the machine. However, communicating with the service bureau and becoming familiar with the process can assist in getting the results that an artist expects. Spend time in this chapter to become familiar with the terms, processes, and materials used in CNC milling. Understanding the process will help the artist communicate succinctly to their CNC vendor.

The downside to using a service bureau is that they may be expensive. The adage of "time is money" applies here. The more time the service bureau spends on your file—whether in fixing the files, milling and routing and post-processing, sourcing materials, creating toolpaths, machine runtime, or the part cleanup—the more it will cost you. The material you choose may also affect the time spent on the machine and, of course, the cost; however, service bureaus usually buy in quantity and can often get a better price on materials than an individual.

The CNC tool cuts a path. The G-code will determine the "stepover" or how far over the tool will move to carve the next path. The distance of the stepover, the tool size and the shape of the tool, as well as the material, will determine the cusp height and how much scalloping there will be. The stepover is usually set to 25–50 percent of the tool's diameter. The smaller the stepover, the smoother the surface will be when milling. A smaller stepover also means more time on the machine, and more machine time equals more cost.

Most CNC milling, no matter the material, requires some secondary post-processing or handwork after the machine completes the carving. An artist can reduce the cost of using a service bureau by understanding and being willing to do some handwork. Some service bureaus offer to do the handwork, but remember their time is your money.

Typically, a CNC machinist will start out with large bits that subtract large portions of the material. In general the larger the bits, the faster the machine can go. If the artist desires more detail in the milling project then the service bureau will use a smaller bit. As the bit carves each pass, there is a fluting effect created where the center of the bit passes over one section to where the center of the bit passes over another section. Some artists find this fluting or stepover pleasing and by designating the toolpath they can make the fluting a part of the design. With some CNC machines, the machinist can minimize the fluting; however, this takes machine time and, again, the greater the machine time, the greater the cost. For the fluting to completely go away, sandblasting and sanding may be necessary.

Another aspect of using a service bureau is that they may not be local. In some instances, such as stone-carving, an artist may live in a small town in the United States but will be sending their stone milling work to Italy or China. As the technology grows and more companies offer services,

Dual 85 percent-scale *Jeanne* portrait. Mexican onyx. Barry X. Ball uses the fluting or scalloping of the CNC milling process as a design element in the sculpture.

an artist will find that finding a local CNC service may not be as great a problem. Search the Appendix or this book's accompanying website for a list of vendors. When estimating the total costs for your job that consists of using a service bureau, there are other costs that an artist must be sure to include. There are no costs in shipping the work to the service bureau because the files are digital. The artist sends these files over the Internet. The shipping of the artwork back to the artist or client is an additional cost. Be sure to include insurance in this shipping. Use a reputable shipping company that is familiar with shipping art. There are shipping companies listed in the Appendix of this book. In your cost estimates, you may also want to include the cost for you to visit the service bureau to approve final designs and/or consult with the machinist and those doing the handwork.

Spend the time and get to know your service bureau. Tell them your needs. Ask questions and don't be afraid to ask them to help you to understand their process. You may even go as far as asking them to show you the way they are going to slice the files. With each piece of art and each step of the project, you will gain experience. As you become familiar with the process, especially as it pertains to your job and the type of work you do, you will get to know what you do or do not require or desire from a service bureau.

Owning Your Own CNC Machine

Studio CNC machines can be quite affordable; they fit nicely in the corner of the workshop and can be a lot of fun to use. They also come in a variety of sizes. Depending on the artist's workflow, and the type of work as well as the frequency of the work, an artist may find that purchasing larger affordable machines is something to consider. Sculptors whose jobs include having to create medallions, signage, and bas-reliefs may find that incorporating digital sculpting and design with CNC milling with a machine in their studio or workshop can be quite profitable. Using CNC technology can, in the long run, save an artist time and money. This book is not a manual on how to run a CNC machine or a CNC shop; there are links to these manuals in the Appendix and on this book's accompanying website. This chapter is an introduction to the process of integrating CNC milling in an artist's workflow and the many creative possibilities.

If you are a tinkerer, you may opt for building your own CNC machine from a kit. There is a host of do-it-yourself (DIY) CNC kits available online. BuildYourCNC.com's small DIY machine has a build area of 12 inches by 36 inches by 3 inches with a price just under $2,000. The larger DIY machine from BuildYourCNC.com has a working area of 4 feet by 8 feet and sells for around $3,000. An artist can find assembled desktop machines at a reasonable price. A purchase of a CarveWright CNC machine will cost approximately $2,000, a ShopBot desktop router is $4,995. If a heavy-duty commercial machine such as a Frogmill is needed in your studio or shop then the investment will be much greater than these desktop CNCs (www.carvewright.com, www.shopbottools.com, www.3dcutting.com).

When purchasing a CNC machine, there are other accessories that you need besides just the machine. Many CNC machines do not come with a vacuum system. To keep your projects running smoothly, and to assure longevity of both your health and the health of your equipment, vacuum systems are a necessary investment that should not be overlooked. You can often find recommendations for vacuum dust and chip collection systems through the company where you purchased your CNC machine.

Putting together a CNC machine from scratch is not for everyone. Some artists may prefer to buy a small shop CNC machine that is already complete. When shopping for CNC machines you will want to consider size, precision, usefulness, and maintenance, along with customer support. Size does not only mean the footprint that the machine will take up in your studio, but also the available build size. Don't let the limited build size of a CNC machine dictate the size of your artistic work. An artist working with CNC may need to change their creative thinking. CNC software can tile designs, and, depending on the material used as stock, an artist can create a large design by milling them in sections and securing the pieces together.

Precision is another consideration when comparing CNC machines. There is nothing more disappointing than going through the process of creating a design, preparing the files, loading valuable stock onto the machine, and then have the machine perform poorly. If a CNC machine has a tendency to be temperamental—and most machinists will tell you that they do—then hours might go into a project, and if it acts up while you are out refilling your coffee, you will have a great loss. You lose the stock and, if this is expensive and rare wood, this could be quite an expense. You will also lose the hours put into the project and if you damage the machine then you lose the time and money it takes to get it repaired.

There are other things to research when considering a purchase of a studio or workshop CNC machine, including performance. Is it loud? How long does it take to carve? An artist can compare the usefulness of a studio machine not only by its performance but also its expandability. Can it do multiple things, such as carve two sides or many different materials? Does it come with proprietary software? How easy is the software to learn? What type of computer will you need to run the machine?

Maintenance is something every operator and owner of a CNC machine should expect. Regular maintenance will consist of cleaning all parts and oiling them. Parts will break. The questions that a consumer needs to consider and research are how often these parts break and how much it costs to replace them.

Makerspace

There are ways of being able to have access to CNC machines other than purchasing your own. Makerspaces or hackerspaces are popping up everywhere. The Appendix has more information on makerspaces and hackerspaces. Through these resources, you may be able to find links to a makerspace near you. A makerspace is a shared shop experience. For a monthly fee, you have access to all of the equipment in the shop. Most makerspaces require you take a class in using the machines. These classes may cost money in addition to your monthly membership fee.

Something that a makerspace can offer that working with a service bureau cannot is an opportunity for experimentation. As you see what the machine can do, you begin to understand how your designs can push the limits. The downside in depending on a makerspace during your creative process is that the machine may not be available when you need it. There may not be a CNC expert around to help with problems, and the learning curve will be steeper when going in this direction. Makerspaces take pride in their machines and try to keep up the maintenance, but with so many new CNC users, the machines may suffer abusive wear and tear.

What Machine to Use?

We categorize CNC machines by the number of axes in which they operate. Remember the Cartesian coordinates that we referred to in Chapter 1? Here is where we begin to see how they apply as we create objects in a physical form. In computer space, we design a part and align it to the origin (0x, 0y, 0z). Then we translate that position to the physical space of the CNC machine by aligning the machine to a similar origin. CAM (computer aided machining) software creates a toolpath for the machine to carve. This toolpath is then translated to G-code, which is a series of coordinates for the tool to follow to cut. The G-code also tells the machine how fast to move through the material and how fast the bit spins. We refer to this as the toolpath.

Artists may feel overwhelmed when thinking about another language that they may need to learn to translate their ideas into art. If you are a person who likes to code, you certainly could learn to create your own G-code. Some artists want nothing to do with the idea of coding, and for those people there is no need to know how to create G-code for milling. If you are using a service bureau, again, there is no need to worry; the G-code is in their operational software. Simply provide the bureau with an appropriate design in the appropriate format and they will take care of the backend work. They create the G-code. If you have a CNC machine, there are software programs that create G-code for you. Some software programs interact more like digital sculpting programs or design programs and take the fear of G-code out of the equation. In these programs, the software creates the code behind the scenes.

How Many Axes is Your Machine?

Let's refer again to Chapter 1 and the right-handed Cartesian coordinates. In this case, the coordinates refer to the motion of the tool. It does not refer to the motion of the table. If you are in the operator position or in front of the machine, the z-axis moves up and down. The y-axis moves away from the operator and the x-axis moves to the right (depending on the machine). Three-axis milling means that the machine will move the tool freely in the x, y, and z axes simultaneously. This type of cutting produces objects that have more of a 3D affect. In 2.5-axis routing, the tool moves freely in x and y, but z will be at a fixed depth. A 2D or 2.5 axis CNC machine creates shapes with no free-form variation. Instead, the designs are perfectly vertical or horizontal as compared to 3D CNC machines that can produce more organic shapes.

2D design, 2.5D design, and 3D. Photograph courtesy of ShopBot.

The limitations in both 2D and 3D CNC milling have to do with undercuts. The spiral router bit on a three-axis machine only goes up and down, side to side, and back and forth. When a design has a void or space under something else, and the artist desires this to be carved, a three-axis machine cannot reach the void to carve it out because the bit does not move in this direction. In this case, the artist will have to do handwork to carve out these voids. However, CNC milling is not limited to three-axis machines. There are multi-axis machines that add more movement of either the carving arm and/or the table. There are also robotic CNC machines where the arm can move organically around the object it is carving, just as a human arm can, but with greater precision and speed. The robotic arms of multi-axis CNC machines move across the surface of an object shaping it with an algorithmic dance.

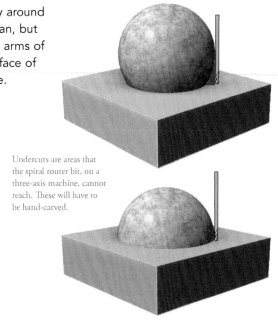

Undercuts are areas that the spiral router bit, on a three-axis machine, cannot reach. These will have to be hand-carved.

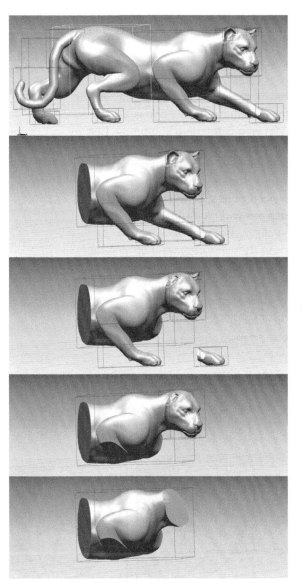

The machinist uses the CNC software program to divide the model into manageable slices for their particular CNC machine. Synappsys Digital Services divides Bridgette Mongeon's Prairie View panther sculpture into multiple sections. The panther is featured in the Gallery section of Chapter 1.

The majority of the CNC machines in use and the most affordable tabletop versions are three-axis machines. Now that we understand undercuts, a three-axis machine can feel limiting in creative possibilities. Moving or carving in only three directions may even feel flat. However, 3D milling offers an endless possibility of exciting forms to create. Due to machine limitations, many artists will have to get creative about how to get those parts off of the machine. It is possible to create 3D pieces by dividing them into sections. The artist or machinist will have to slice the model, cut it into several layers, and then assemble them after milling. Many CAM software packages offer easy ways to slice parts.

Software at a Makerspace/Hackerspace

If you are working with a makerspace or hackerspace, you will have to check with them to see if they provide software. Most makerspaces will probably be working with freeware or shareware. Some may have programs that are more robust. If you are training on a CNC machine then you are likely to begin on an entry-level program. An entry-level software program is good; it will help to introduce you to the processes. If you have software that creates and provides G-code, then you can ask permission to use that software and your computer to run a CNC machine. You may find that in makerspaces there are different people who teach and help to run the CNC equipment; each person most likely has their preference of software. If you do not take the time to investigate different software and see what is available, then most likely the machinist who is teaching you on the CNC equipment will guide you to their preference. As you will see by many of the artists featured in this book, the variety of software applications available is extensive, and some artists prefer one software to another. Some may be useful for creating jewelry and others for creating signage. Working in a makerspace with their machines and their software may have been a very steep learning curve but, until you get to know what the machine can do, you really can't push it to its fullest capacity. Knowing the underlying process helps you to push the limits. You don't know what you can do until you know what you can do. Having access to a makerspace combined with individual exploration of software and processes can open up creative possibilities to which an artist might not otherwise be exposed.

Vector Art

Besides using 3D models in CNC machining, you can also use vector art. You can create vector art by using programs like Adobe Illustrator, Corel Draw, or Freehand (or free programs like SketchUp and the Autodesk 123D Series to name a few). In vector art, the mathematical algorithms preserve the image quality. Because of the math behind the art, an artist or service bureau can resize the art without distortion. The image will be crisp no matter what size. Vector graphics are

Bitmap Graphic   Vector Graphic

You can enlarge vector graphics without any pixilation, unlike bitmap graphics. Logo by Diliberto Photo and Design.

different from raster graphics. Pixels or small dots or squares of color make up raster graphics or bitmap graphics. When you enlarge these graphics, they become pixelated and fuzzy. If you are not sure what type of graphics you have, you can look at the file extension, which is the last three letters after the period. If your file extension is jpeg, png, bmp, gif, psd, tif, pdf, pwt, psd, or doc, it is not vector art. If someone created the art for you, ask him or her if they have a vector file. If all you have is raster art, you can convert the files to vector art. If you prefer not to do this, you can hire a company to create them for you. This is an area where working with a service bureau can be helpful. Consult with your service bureau, tell them your intention and direction, and see if they can help you to figure out how to get there. They want your business, and this is motivation to help.

Types of Files Needed for CNC

The type of file that an artist can provide for CNC machining varies. If you are using a service bureau, it is best to contact them and ask them what type of file they will accept. There are many more options with service bureaus because they have software that can take different file types and translate them to the G-code needed for the CNC machining. If you are creating a file for a service bureau, ask them which file type they prefer and if they can convert the file that you have. They will probably tell you they can work with native CAD files, an STL, or OBJ. You can create these file formats in a variety of software programs on your computer. Refer to the Appendix for suggestions for 3D sculpting programs to create the design and artwork for CNC milling. The 3D sculpting or modeling gives you the geometry. The other software you will need if you are not sending your work to a service bureau is CAM software that will create your toolpaths and convert the file into G-code. This software also tells the machine how to cut and how to move around the stock. If you own your own CNC machine, it may or may not have come with design CAM software that also converts your files to G-code. Vectric Aspire software is a standalone software that allows you to do both the CAD (creating your designs in the computer) and the CAM (creating toolpaths) in one program. Aspire then converts the toolpaths to G-code for a particular CNC machine in a function called post-processing. You can also import many different files from other programs into Vectric Aspire. Typically, most CAD and CAM programs run on Windows platforms, but there are a few programs that will run on a Mac. Vectric Aspire is not cross-platform and runs only on a Windows computer. You might also want to investigate free software programs such as Blender with possible add-ons for CNC. Other software programs that work to create appropriate files are Rhino, Auto CAD, and ArtCAM (www.rhino3d.com, www.autodesk.com, www.artcam.com/pro). For other software suggestions consult the Appendix or visit this book's accompanying website.

Transferring Files

When creating artwork and using a service bureau so that you can incorporate 3D technology in your workflow, it is quite convenient that you don't have to move physical objects or molds across the continent or the world. Instead, you are sending files. The files that you might create in a 3D sculpting program or from a 3D scanner can be enormous. They are much too large to fit in an email. There are other ways to get your large files to a service bureau so that they can recreate your work in a physical form. Many of the service bureaus offer an opportunity to FTP files to them. FTP stands for file transfer protocol and is usually a safe way to send large files over the Internet. Ask the service bureau for the information that you may need to FTP a file. They will send the FTP information to you in an email. The FTP information that you need will consist of four things—the FTP address, username, password, and directory. The FTP address is the IP address or web address, the username is a name that you will use to get into their site. You will also need to have a password to access the FTP folder. Remember that the username and the password are case sensitive. A directory is a file folder that they have made on their server that will hold your job. Save your file without spaces and in a manner that makes sense for them, for example, "Yourname_jobtitle." Having a clear, but short file title as a description, without any spaces, makes it easy for the service bureau to find your files. Ask the vendor if they prefer that you compress the files. You can compress a file quite easily from both a Mac and a PC. On a PC, right-click the file. (To select a few files hold down the ctrl key while selecting.) Go to "Send To" and press "Compress Zipped Folder." On a Mac, right-click while selecting a file and select "Compress." A compressed file will have the same name as the original but will have the extension .zip. Compressing a file does just that, it compress the file to make it faster to transfer and saves space on your service bureau's server. To FTP your file to their server, you will need an FTP client on your computer. There are many FTP clients and several are free such as FileZilla and Cyberduck.

Another option in sharing files is to use a device such as Dropbox or Google Drive. These file-sharing sites are free but do have limitations. The service bureau may offer you another resource for getting your files to them. They may instead have an Internet web interface, a special place on their website where you develop an account and then place the files. You should still compress these files.

Whatever way you choose to transfer your files, you will first want to investigate. You will want to be sure that the FTP sites that you use to send your artwork are safe ways of transferring files. It is important to take precautions so that you do not compromise your vendor's information, your work, or your client's sensitive subject matter.

Before you even begin to send your sensitive information via the Internet—and you should always consider your artwork "sensitive information"—you must familiarize yourself with your service bureau's policies about protecting their client's files. When they complete your job, do they delete the file? How safe is their system? Do they ever reuse a file without the client's permission? It is also recommended that you have them sign a simple "nondisclosure" form that we have provided for you at this book's accompanying website, www.digitalsculpting.net. You can never be too careful. This is your design and may be the culmination of many months of work. You need to protect yourself, the work, and your clients, by making yourself aware of policies and understanding your rights. Visit Chapter 9 for more information on rights and responsibilities.

Fixing Your Files for CNC Machining

Even though your service bureau may be able to convert your file to what you need for CNC, you may not be able to send large files to your service bureau. They may have limitations. If your files are larger than the specifications given by the service bureau, you will need to decimate the files. If you do not have a way to decimate a file, you can ask the service bureau if they can do this for you. When decimating a 3D file you are lowering the polygon count while still preserving the detail. For more information on decimating a file, please refer to Chapters 4 and 7. There are free programs available for 3D decimation. You may also want to review your files to be sure there are no problems with them. There are several ways to review files and free programs listed in other chapters. Additionally, there are service bureaus who prepare files for CNC machining and/or 3D printing. See the Appendix of this book or the book's accompanying website for a list.

FIRST PRESBYTERIAN
CHURCH OF THE COVENANT

First Presbyterian Church of the Covenant, Erie, PA, hired Mezalick Design Studios to redesign the entire sanctuary to create a more efficient use of space and to produce an area for better sound transmission of the choir. The process included adding two new wood window frames, painted to match the surrounding stone, new sound diffusers with matching ornate millwork, and installing stained glass divider panels to restrict the sound of the choir from dissipating.

They created a seamless transition between old and new by using 3D technology. 3D scanning of the original millwork ensured accurate production of the required millwork. IBILD Solutions scanned the trim and Mezalick Design Studios then revised the 3D models (www.IBILD.com). Mezalick Design Studios reports they use a variety of software programs such as Aspire, V-Carve Pro, PhotoVCarve, Modo, DAZ, Sculptris, ZBrush, FaceGen, and Photoshop in their workflow, but the primary software used on this project is from Aspire. Once transferred and modified the designs were then CNC milled on a CAMaster Cobra408 X3. The Cobra408 X3 has a cutting area of 48 × 96 inches and three spindles (routers) so they can use three different cutting bits without stopping the process to change bits (www.camaster.com). The software that controls the machine is WINCNC (www.wincnc.net).

First Presbyterian Church of the Covenant, Erie, PA, before modifications by Mezalick Design Studios.

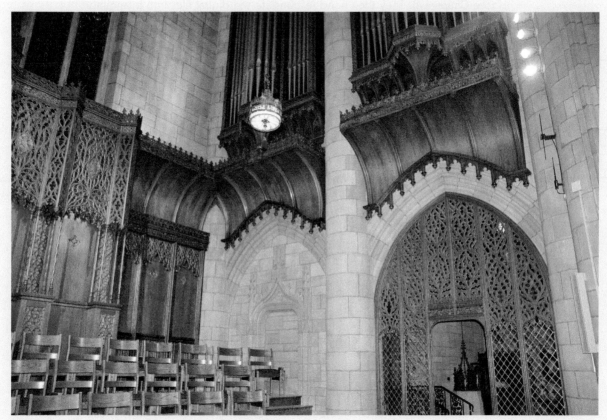

First Presbyterian Church
of the Covenant, Erie,
PA, after modifications by
Mezalick Design Studios.

The Process

Whether you are using a service bureau, your own CNC machine, or a CNC at a makerspace, it will help to understand the process and the terms associated with CNC milling. Of course, the creative process starts with a plan, an inspiration, or a client that has a need. The artist's first challenge is to figure out how to take the creative inspiration and translate it into a digital file. They can do this with digital sculpting software, or CAD software (see Chapter 4). They then need to translate the digital files into a language that the CNC machine will use to make the artwork into a physical form. The final piece of artwork, the material, and what it looks like will depict what CNC machine to use and what programs to use to create the necessary files.

The blue lines in the main window show the actual path the tool will take to "rough" the areas shown.

Let's follow some steps through to see how to create an image for CNC milling using Vectric Aspire, and the continuation of the coffee bean art used to depict the text in the tutorial, "Creating 3D Text For Sculptures," mentioned in Chapter 4 and found on this book's accompanying website. Readers can also find a detailed video tutorial at www.digitalsculpting.net. We have previously referred to Vectric Aspire as software that would fill the gap when trying to create text in the 3D model. Creating text is just one use of the program. In addition to a selection of other drawing and modeling functions, the software will also create the cutting data (the toolpath) that the machinist needs to mill the artwork with a CNC router or engraver. This part of the process is where the artist becomes machinist, takes a virtual model, and creates the data that will make it into a physical form. To make the jump from digital to creating the art in physical form, the operator needs

The completed animation of the "rough" cut.

to make decisions about the material, tooling, cutting speeds, part hold-down, and many other considerations.

Aspire provides a suite of toolpath options depending on the intended shape that the artist needs to cut. Many of these are for production processes such as routing out 2D shapes or engraving text; for 3D carving there are usually two stages. The "rough" cut uses a larger tool to remove as much material as efficiently as possible leaving a facsimile of the finished part with an added skin of material. This operation makes it possible to then "finish" cut with a tool small enough to maximize the detail in the machined part. For each of these stages, the tool typically moves back and forth across the 3D model with overlapping passes. The closer the passes are, the better the finish, but the longer it takes to machine.

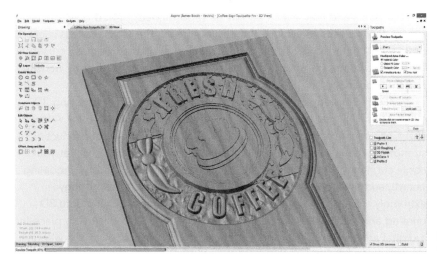

The "finish" cut, partially animated.

To make it easier to select the correct toolpath parameters, the software animates each stage of cutting as it takes into account the tool geometry. The animations allow the user to see the effects of their decisions and, if required, make changes before committing to cutting the part on the machine. If the artist is having the cutting done remotely by the vendor then they can send an image of this "simulation" for approval. Remember, time is money and material is costly.

Completed animation of the "finish" cut.

Once the operator is happy that the preview looks acceptable, they save the toolpaths in a format that is appropriate for the particular CNC they will use. This data known as G-code often uses terms such as "G1," "G2," etc., for different types of commands. Due to the physical limitations of a three-axis (x, y, and z) CNC machine, a part may require more than two toolpaths and may even need to be repositioned, turned over, or cut into multiple pieces to achieve the desired result. The CNC process is not simple, but there is a great deal of information available to a novice user. We will provide many tutorials and information through this book's website and the Appendix.

3D printing does have its merits when it applies to reproducing 3D models into physical form, but CNC milling also has much to offer. A low-cost CNC offers a great deal of flexibility in terms of speed of production, strength and quality of the part, as well as build size. A CNC will let you easily cut hard and soft wood, plastics, composites (MDF, foams, modeling board), and even non-ferrous metals (brass, aluminum), it can achieve extremely small detail and provide an excellent surface quality. Both 3D printing and CNC technologies do have their merits and deserve a place in a digital artist's workshop. It is worth researching them both to see whether one or both would be most beneficial if you want to start realizing your artwork in the physical world.

Materials

There are many different materials that an artist can use with CNC milling. It is difficult to list them all. Each machine may have recommended materials and, as stated before, different machines are usually meant for different projects. For example, if your machine can only carve soft material then you cannot carve stone. Service bureaus that provide CNC milling also specialize. The same service bureau that mills your foam may not mill wood or stone. If an artist works in a variety of materials, they may also have a variety of service bureaus.

When deciding on how to mill or what service bureau or machine to use, you will have to take the end product into consideration. Are you planning to CNC machine foam as a part of a sculpting process? Do you plan to cover the foam in clay and make into a bronze as in Bridgette Mongeon's tiger in Chapter 6? Are you creating detailed foam carvings for outdoors or as an architectural design such as Gary Staab's work? If your work is outdoors, how will the elements affect the choice of wood or product that you are milling? There is a variety of materials and each has its own properties. These properties dictate where an artist can display the art and what type of machine will mill it.

When choosing a material for your studio or shop machine, you will want to check with the manufacturer. Some materials may void your warranty or the manufacturer may have specific suggestions for carving certain materials. If the manufacturer creates a CNC machine for wood and you are carving something harder, then the manufacturer may suggest you monitor the depth of your carve or the speed rate of the machine so that you don't damage the machine. And with each material, the maintenance may change. Also, note that the residual build-up of some materials can damage machines more quickly than others.

There is a vast selection of wood. Each will have individual characteristics when it comes to CNC milling. Top to bottom: honey mahogany, mesquite; zebra; soft maple; Peruvian walnut, white oak; padauk, osage orange; white oak, purple heart; bubinga. Photograph courtesy of Houston Hardwoods Inc.

The Cost of Materials

Finding a dependable distributor for your materials can sometimes be a challenge. If you do not have a distributor that sells in small quantities and you are a small shop only needing a minimal quantity, then you may find some materials harder to come by. For example, some foam companies only ship truckloads of foam. Creating a sort of material co-op with other artists in your area can be a solution. Usually, the larger the quantity that you can purchase, the less expensive your materials will be. Find others who are using your materials and buy the larger quantities to get a better price. You may even ask the manufacturer if there are others in your area that are purchasing material. They might be able to help you find other resources. Find a shop that is doing the work commercially or a makerspace and ask them if you can purchase material from them. If you are buying quantities of material and storing it, you might be cautious as to the emissions of the product. Some individuals are very sensitive to the fumes of certain products.

Sometimes finding materials is a creative process in itself. One woodworker reported that whenever he would see a new building go up he would watch the trash pile. The pieces that the builders cut out of countertops to make room for sinks make a great cutting medium for his CarveWright machine. Another artist waits for wood to come to her. It is the spirit of the adventure of the wood that makes it a viable medium. Pruning her trees, she has her wood planed and uses that for her creations. It helps her to feel connected to the art.

There are many more materials than those we list below. Explore your possibilities as well as your materials. Speak to vendors and visit forums where others are doing what you want to do. Exploring someone else's experience in using a material can go a long way toward educating yourself about the pros and cons. For a list of materials and distributors, as well as a list of forums, consult the Appendix or visit the website at www. digitalsculpting.net.

Soft Materials

WOOD   Wood comes in a variety of hardnesses from soft pine to exotic hardwood. The moisture in wood can play a part in how the CNC machine will work. Some woodworkers claim that the wood that comes from one location may not be the same or carve the same as wood from another location. The drier the wood the better it carves. When considering wood you want to think about the grain direction, tear out from the machine, and how much sanding you will have to do in the finishing process. Other things to take into consideration when it comes to wood are the weight, availability, aesthetics, grain, structural stability, and durability. For example, woodworkers recommend redwood and cedar for outdoors.

- Soft wood: pine, spruce, cedar, fir, hemlock, cypress, redwood, and yew.
- Hardwood: ash, beech, birch, cherry, mahogany, maple, oak, poplar, teak, and walnut.
- Plywood: furniture grade—Baltic birch; cabinet grade—China birch; construction grade—OSB.

PLASTICS   It is important to be careful of some plastic material. The bit generates heat and with some material the melting temperature is lower than the heat generated by the running of the machine. Melted material will clog the machine. These types of plastics might include ABS, extruded acrylic or Plexiglas and nylon, polycarbonate, Corian or styrene. There is also a variety of expanded foams such as sign makers foam boards. Each material has its own unique qualities when it some to cutting. Run a test before committing to the actual materials.

Some artists have reported that casting acrylics such as polycarbonate (Lexan) are useful for CNC machining. Sign makers use plastic, acrylic polymer such as Corian or Staron often found in kitchen countertops. CNC machinists report that these are good CNC materials.

When machining there are safety concerns such as the safety of carving, melting points, toxic dust, and residue that can irritate skin or eyes. You should take precautions, including using the appropriate safety gear, dust collectors, and ventilation.

As with wood, foams also differ with their hardness, quality of carving, and the type of post-processing work. Some foam can be extremely gritty. An artist should take safety precautions and wear safety gear when milling,

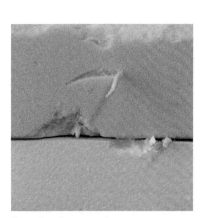

Polyurethane foam-top and polystyrene foam-bottom.

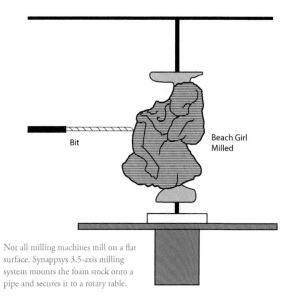

Beach Girl Milled

Bit

Not all milling machines mill on a flat surface. Synappsys 3.5-axis milling system mounts the foam stock onto a pipe and secures it to a rotary table.

hot wiring, or carving foam. No artwork is worth ruining your lungs or eyes. Also, some foam such as polystyrene will react to other materials. They can melt when certain paints or glues come in contact with their surfaces. Test your foam before using the product on your CNC art. If an artist is creating a project for an indoor public building then the building's fire code may play a part in the foam allowed. The fire marshal may also require a fire protective coating.

Artists use foam for many different applications. An artist can apply a variety of artistic treatments to foams to make them weather resistant, fire resistant, and colorful. You can find more tutorials for foam in Chapter 6 and on the book's accompanying website.

RIGID POLYURETHANE FOAM   Most people probably know polyurethane foam as the foam that you buy from the hardware store, spray in cracks, and that expands. Artists have repurposed this spray foam for years spraying it over metal armatures, carving it, and using it as a sculpting medium. Polyurethane foam also comes as manufactured foam for carving. Distributors differentiate types of polyurethane foam by weight. Rigid urethane foam comes in blocks or sheets. If you are working with sheets then the size of sheets that your distributor carries may determine the slicing and tiling process of your milling. The range of density of foam is between 2 and 50 pounds per cubic foot. The higher the density, the harder the foam; for example, a 20-pound piece of foam is like wood. The cost of rigid polyurethane can increase with density. So, 3-pound foam can be twice the cost of 2-pound foam. Typically, the CNC machine can carve greater detail in denser foam, up to a certain point. The machine can only do so much. So, it is up to the service bureau, vendor, or the artist to decide on what foam is the most economical and best product to work with to get the desired results. To save costs, an artist can also mix foam in a project. When sculpting an angel, as in Bridgette Mongeon's sculpture in Chapter 6, delicate wings required stable foam. But she has the torso's basic shape milled in polystyrene.

POLYSTYRENE FOAM   The trade name for polystyrene is Styrofoam. Most artists know it by the trade name, or that restaurants use it for coffee cups or to-go containers. We may also know polystyrene as the item that most recycle plants won't take and is not friendly to the environment.

Manufacturers compress polystyrene pellets together using steam to create solid blocks for carving. It can be CNC milled and is inexpensive to purchase. Even though it consists of small pellets, with the proper tools and some elbow grease, an artist can sand polystyrene to a smooth finish. The downside to creating in polystyrene is that it is not as physically stable as some rigid polyurethane foams and may need more support.

Pointing Up

We have learned quite a bit about the subtractive process and technology of CNC. Before we go into our next feature section of CNC milling in stone, let's first revert to the old ways. Do you remember the pointing up process in Chapter 3? Michael Keropian Sculpture Studio used a 3D pantograph to enlarge and reduce sculpture by Berthold Nebel. Artists used pointing up to enlarge or reproduce their art before 3D scanning and milling, and many still do. The examples in the 3D scanning chapter referred to a sculpture that artists created using an additive process. The artist was adding clay to the armature while they used the pointing up process. But the pointing up process is also done in the subtractive process of sculpting or carving, although this is much trickier.

In this section, stone carver Gilbert E. Barrera shares the age-old process of pointing up as done by sixth-generation sculptor Lucho Carusi of Carrara, Italy.

First, the artist uses the pointing up tool to find three main points that are on the original model of the image he wishes to transfer. Usually, these are the foremost portions of the sculpture as well as the highest point of the head. The artist will move this pointing up tool back and forth between the original and the duplicate. In this example of pointing up, we are not enlarging the sculpture. Instead, this is a one-to-one reproduction. In a traditional sculpting process, an artist may have sculpted the first image in clay and is now reproducing the image in its final material of stone using these same techniques.

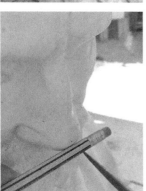

The artist marks the three points on the model with a screw. They use the screws as measuring points. When measuring certain points, the artist needs a little wiggle room in the measurements, so they do not put the screws in all the way. These guides and the extra room will help them to know how much material to remove without accidentally taking off too much.

The second part of the fascinating pointing up tool is a horizontal bar that moves up the first piece of wood. This part of the tool has various measuring mechanisms that swivel with the use of adjustment screws; plus all of the parts twist and turn. With this portion of the pointing up tool, the artist can reach many of the key surface points on the front and sides of the model.

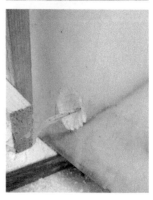

Once the artist has measured all the points on the model and found a suitable piece of stone that they have blocked out they will begin to transport these first three points to the blocked out stone.

Of course, the artist measures many more points on the model and translates them to the stone block over and over again. Each time, they slowly carve away more material. It is a very slow and methodical process and takes an experienced hand to know exactly when to stop carving. If the artist accidentally knocks an ear off or carves too deep

there is no "undo" button as there would be in a digital process. It will take the carver many, many weeks to replicate the sculpture using these old methods. Now, let's take a look at some of the new technology by visiting the stone carving of the Digital Stone Project at Garfagnana Innovazione.

THE DIGITAL STONE PROJECT

In 2013 and 2014, the Digital Stone Project teamed up with the masters of stone carving at Garfagnana Innovazione in the lush hills of Tuscany. The collaboration provided an artist in residency to students, professionals, and educators interested in learning about, and exploring the possibilities of, merging digital technologies with traditional artistry of stone-carving. Over the month-long residency, participants of the Digital Stone Project workshop, along with the craftsmen and robotics engineer Gabriel Ferri from Garfagnana Innovazione, watched as the seven-axis robotic CNC machine helped to release the digital models from stone. Prior to carving in stone, the participants created their models using a combination of 3D modeling and sculpting or programming, scanning, and 3D printing. Each artist created their artwork digitally, in a variety of different software programs. The files were first 3D printed on a MakerBot Replicator 2 desktop 3D printer. The 3D print became their maquette and reference for machining and handwork. Participants then spent many hours incorporating traditional hand tools to finish their designs.

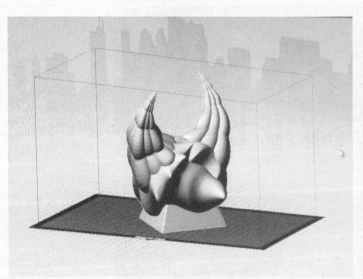

Diploidal Pas de Deux by Robert Michael Smith. Created using Rhino and 3DS Max. © Robert Michael Smith.

Participants spent time learning about the process of CNC milling. This head sculpture is property of Garfagnana Innovazione and is used as an educational tool. It displays the toolpaths and different surface cuts that we have reviewed in this chapter. © Robert Michael Smith.

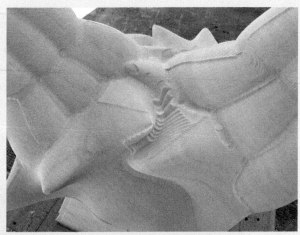

The seven-axis robot makes multiple passes over the marble. The first pass is to rough out the form and then further passes refine details. © Robert Michael Smith.

Robert Michael Smith's sculpture *Diploidal Pas de Deux* after the carving of the Carrara marble by the seven-axis robot at Garfagnana Innovazione. The artists spent many hours doing handwork on their marble pieces. The CNC machine can provide more detail on the marble and make a smoother finish, but as we have learned, machine time costs money. © Robert Michael Smith.

Robert Michael Smith's *Diploidal Pas de Deux.* © Robert Michael Smith.

There is a world of creative possibilities when incorporating CNC in a traditional studio practice. There is an increasing number of vendors and resources available, and the cost of software and machines is decreasing. This chapter has helped you to become familiar with the tools, terms, and trade of CNC. The accompanying online tutorials and links should get you well on your way to investigating and creating. There is more to CNC. Let's look at some more possibilities with CNC as we focus on creating monumental sculptures in Chapter 6 and learn about the influences of CNC on the bronze foundry of the future in Chapter 8.

Akor Restaurant and Bar Walls by Matsys. 2013. Matsys had minimal waste when fabricating this undulating wall. They used parametric modeling to align adjacent ribs. The backside of one rib becomes the front side of the next. Photograph by Andrew Kudless.

CHRIS SCHAIE

Chris designed *Nautilus Door* in Rhino (www.rhino3d.com), toolpathed with Vetric Vcarve Pro (www.vectric.com), cut the door on a Shopbot CNC router model BT48 (www.shopbottools.com). The assembly and finishing is done at Makerplace (www.makerplace.com).

Nautilus Door by Chris Schaie, 2010, wood and brass.

ERIC STANDLEY

There are many different types of CNC art. Not all CNC uses a router or milling machine. A laser cutter is another process that uses CNC. Eric Standley laser cuts vector drawings in paper and stacks the sheets. Some pieces of art are more than 100 sheets high. Standley likes to look at the math behind Gothic and Islamic art for his inspiration. In a video from Virginia Tech Standley states, "Every efficiency that I gain through technology, the void is immediately filled with a question. Can I make it more complex?"

Either/Or Newmarch,
detail by Eric Standley.

Either/Or Newmarch by Eric Standley. Cut paper, 20 × 20 inches, 2013. This work occupies 151 layers of paper.

BROOKE M. DAVIS

Brooke M. Davis creates her designs in Rhino and uses Aspire or Visual Mill as the CAM software. She mills her work using a Shopbot CNC.

Intertwined, detail by Brooke M. Davis.

Ricercar Rocking Chair by Brooke M. Davis. European birch ply, bent plywood seat.

WIM DLVOYE

Twisted Dump Truck (Clockwise), 2013, by Wim Dlvoye. Laser-cut stainless steel, 200 × 83 × 95 cm. © Studio Wim Dlvoye, Belgium. Courtesy Galerie Perrotin.

G. WATSON DESIGN

Watson works on a Laguna 5 × 10 foot CNC router and a Laguna CNC lathe (www.lagunatools.com/cnc). He uses Aspire software from Vectric to generate his G-code. For carvings, he uses the machine to remove as much as 95 percent of material, finishing what remains by hand. While he typically models his carvings in Aspire, Rhino, and AutoCad, he also creates custom designs by modifying existing vector art found at Vectorart3D.com

Leaf Mantle by G. Watson Design. Sculpted in Sapele Hardwood. Watson Design molded the leaves in Vectric Aspire software and produced the lines in AutoCAD

BRIAN COOLEY

Brian Cooley sculpts his work traditionally as an 18-inch maquette. He has his work scanned using the Frogscan™ and Frogscan™ Scanner Table.

The design is processed by Frogware™ and milled on the Frogmill™ in 2-pound density polystyrene. The inside of the foam has an engineered welded steel frame. To finish the work the foam is coated with Frogskin™ 110. And then Cooley adds self-hardening epoxy clay and paint for the final details (www.3dcutting.com).

Albertosaurus exhibit, Royal Tyrrell Museum, by Brian Cooley.

On the book's website at www.digitalsculpting.net you will find:

* Links to further descriptions on the process of creating the artwork featured in the galleries.
* Podcasts with the artists.
* Videos featuring the artists at work.

CHAPTER SIX

3D FOR PRESENTATIONS AND CNC MILLING FOR ENLARGEMENTS

———

"I rarely sketch my ideas on paper. I have been sculpting for so long that my brain automatically thinks in 3D. When I want to create a presentation for a client, I can work through the movement, action pose, and possibilities using 3D tools. The process is fast and enjoyable. In these digital presentations, we can "walk around" virtual models together and see the possibilities."

Bridgette Mongeon

facing page
Jenna by sculptor Bridgette Mongeon

For centuries, artists have been creating miniature maquettes, a smaller version of a life-size or monumental sculpture. The maquettes portray the artist's vision for the look of a life-size or monumental sculpture. Sculptors will also use these small maquettes in the hope of presenting them to a potential client and securing a commission. Once a sculptor has the approval to create a large sculpture, and they have secured their contract, the larger work begins. Before 3D scanning and CNC machining for enlarging, a traditional sculptor would use the painstaking process of "pointing up" to enlarge their creations. Chapter 3 covers the traditional pointing up process. Now, let's see how fine artists are using digital technology for presentations and CNC machining for enlarging.

Presentations

Securing a commission from a client on a proposed project takes a tremendous amount of forethought and work. Often, an artist is bidding against other artists and may not have secured the job or might not have even received any money from a client when they are creating a presentation. The investment of time in creating a presentation is important; after all, a large commission can mean a year's worth of work for the artist. However, spending a week or more creating a small maquette for a job that the sculptor may or may not get may not be the best investment of the artist's time.

Unlike two-dimensional art, such as a painting or a sketch, the sculptor's intent is for the viewer to see the sculpture from multiple directions. Therefore, it is important for the design to look good from all vantage points. Clients may even have specific directional views in mind. For example, on a college campus, the sculpture may face the entrance to the campus, but the client may want to know what it looks like from the student center or the window of the president's office. It is difficult and time-consuming to portray this information in many two-dimensional sketches and just because a sculpture maquette is small does not mean it will take a minimal amount of time to create. Another option is that an artist can create a very rough "quick sketch" in clay for a presentation. This sketch may show the gesture but not the detail; however, clients are visual, and rarely will a "quick sketch" present the true intentions of the artist, in a way that a client can understand. If the client is only seeking work from one particular artist and they are considering no other artists for the commission, a "quick sketch" may be sufficient.

Most artists will spend hours sculpting a maquette in hopes of receiving a larger commission. This labor may not even transition into a commission. Creating designs using 3D programs can help with this. By using a variety of software programs, an artist can use digital presentations to help clients visualize potential jobs. They can present several poses and multiple views, and with the digital technology they can create these in less non-billable time. By working with architectural plans or photographs of the space, they can even place images of the proposed sculpture in its intended environment. Add photographs using photogrammetry to the design process and an artist can create a realistic presentation that just might make their design stand out above the other artists that a potential client is considering.

Sculptor Bridgette Mongeon used DAZ 3D models and Poser, along with Photoshop, to help the parents of Ellie envision her sculpture for Ellie's gravesite. The digital model allows the artists to show the client how personal elements such as Ellie's gift heart drawing, created for MD Anderson Cancer Center, and her stuffed bunny can be used in the design. The sculptor then proceeded to create the sculpture using traditional sculpting processes.

The 3D model helps the client to visualize. However, the digital model is just a representation of an idea. The final sculpture depicts the likeness, emotion, and the essence of the individual. *Ellie* by sculptor Bridgette Mongeon. Left –model and render by Mike de la Flor.

  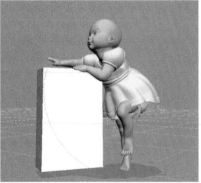

The digital models also help the artist and client to visualize the sculpture's interaction with other elements, as in the case of Jenna Rose Mangini and her headstone. Using a Poser model and a DAZ dress similar to the dress of the client's child, the artist can quickly move through the process of posing an infant in a variety of poses while using primitives to represent a headstone. The client decides on the design with a sign language hand gesture of "I love you," and a butterfly.

Photographic reference, digital model, and clay sculpture. *Jenna* by Bridgette Mongeon.

The client for the sculpture *Ultimate Frisbee* approached sculptor Bridgette Mongeon about creating a sculpture of his son playing Ultimate Frisbee for his college team. The client desired a sculpture featuring a jump, with height. The artist used DAZ models and clothes, Poser, and ZBrush to create a presentation. The digital design provides the artists with a tool to incorporate two figures to present to the client—the main figure of his son jumping, and a fictitious player. Here is a case where physical laws, as well as the engineering laws of the medium, apply. In the computer, two figures can float in the air, but in the real world, the laws of physics take place. For a

Ultimate Frisbee presentation using Poser and ZBrush and traditional figurine created in bronze by sculptor Bridgette Mongeon.

Ultimate Frisbee, bronze by sculptor Bridgette Mongeon.

Grambling State University chose a design of a tiger climbing a rock. It is one of four digital design presentations created by sculptor Bridgette Mongeon. Having poseable 3D designs gives an artist more possibilities while using less time to create a presentation. The digital models not only helped the artist and client visualize the project, they also helped the foundry bid on the job, as well as the landscape architects and designers.

bronze sculpture, especially where one of the figures is in the air, the jumping sculpture should have at least two if not three points of contact. There also needs to be balance in the sculpture. The 3D model allows the artist to work through the design with the foundry to confirm the engineering of the sculpture, as well as to present to the client to be sure the artist does not interpret the action incorrectly and mistakenly portray a foul play. Once the design is approved, the artist creates the tabletop sculpture with the traditional sculpture process and wire armature.

Depending too much on digital models can be an artist's downfall. They need to be able to work from life. Even though they have started with digital presentations, they must now go back and begin their own research into the action and anatomy of a piece. To create the folds for *Ultimate Frisbee*, the artist hires a model to run back and forth and jump while she videotapes the action. She uses still photographs from the video as the reference for folds and action.

CNC Milling for Enlargements: Traditional Armatures

In traditional sculpture, before 3D scanning and CNC machining, once the artist secured the commission they began the long, arduous process of making the enlarged sculpture. First, they built an armature. The artist creates an armature from wood, welded metal, plumbing pipe, chicken wire, PVC pipe—just about anything that will support the clay and hold the weight of the sculpting medium. Armature building is a science and art in itself. It is not the most creative part of the project, but it is a vital part. There is nothing worse for an artist than being in the middle of creating a life-size or monumental sculpture and finding that the clay is sagging, falling off, or—God forbid—the armature breaks from the weight.

Sculptor Bridgette Mongeon created a traditional armature for a seated figure titled *Richard Hathaway* using welded pipe, pieces of urethane foam, and spray foam. Once the sculpture was roughed in with foam, the artist covered the foam with foundry wax and then finished the details in Classic Clay. When a sculpted design needs modification in this traditional armature-building process, the sculptor may take a sledgehammer to the armature to beat it into creative submission or she may have to cut through the rebar with a reciprocating saw and reposition appendages. Once sculpted, the sculpture will go through the traditional process of mold-making for bronze casting.

Now, instead of making difficult and time-consuming traditional armatures with a variety of materials, artists can combine 3D scanning and CNC machining to easily create

A traditional armature for Bridgette Mongeon's sculpture *Richard Hathaway* using rebar, foam, and clay.

an armature—at any size. Many artists embrace this new technology as an extension of their toolset. This process of enlargement may initially add additional cost to the project, but in the long run it saves time. An artist can save more than a quarter of their time on the total project using CNC machining for armature building. The time saved not only adds up to money, but gives the artists more time to create.

In the process of creating an armature using CNC milling, you will need a 3D computer model. A digital 3D model can be obtained in different ways. You can create a sculpture in the computer using a 3D sculpting program or you can make a small maquette in clay and then scan it. For more about scanning models refer to Chapter 3. Those who work in CNC machining that enlarge sculptures on a regular basis suggest a few pointers for artists creating maquettes for scanning.

- For a life-size or monumental sculpture, create a maquette that is at least 18 inches tall or larger. If the maquette is any smaller, it is hard to get good features that will translate when enlarged. An 18-inch sculpture enlarged into a 6-foot sculpture is a 400 percent enlargement. As a CNC machinist enlarges the sculpture, they also enlarge the artist's errors. An error made at a quarter of an inch and enlarged 400 percent will be one inch.
- Take note of the head and the hands of your model when sculpting a maquette. CNC machinists find that some sculptors, when creating maquettes for scanning and then CNC machining, will create hands and heads that are not in proportion to the body. These hands and heads in a smaller sculpture may not look out of proportion but when enlarged they look too large.

Scanning

Refer to Chapter 3 of this book to be sure that you have prepared your maquette properly for scanning. Many CNC machining companies that specialize in enlargement can also provide the scanning process for the artist. You may also find a local scanning company through the Appendix of this book or you can scan with your own dependable scanner. Once you have a scan, it is easy to transport your artwork. An artist can send the scan files to the enlargement company at the push of a button.

There is a computer axiom that states, garbage in and garbage out (GIGO). The data you send limits what the CNC machinist has to work with. If the scanned model is of poor quality or has holes or missing information, then this will affect the outcome of the CNC milled sculpture. In some cases, a bad file will mean that the machinist may also not be able to mill it for you. Good communication with your vendor is essential. Some vendors will fix files; however, every artist should be aware of the possible problems and review how to fix files for 3D printing in Chapter 7. An artist will use the same process for fixing files for CNC milling as they do for 3D printing. There are many free programs that will help you fix your file. If you are sending your file to a service bureau that specializes in CNC machining of foam for sculpture reproductions then they may be able to fix your files for you; however, remember the more time they spend on the files, the more money it may cost.

Real-world Measurements

Software companies have initially created their software programs for computer graphic artists working in animation. When an artist or craftsman is using 3D computer programs to create art for the real world, real-world measurements are necessary. These measurements are often impossible to obtain in the virtual world of many 3D sculpting programs.

In the case of the Grambling State University tiger sculpture, artist Bridgette Mongeon began the sculpting of the Grambling State University tiger in the computer using 3D sculpting software. To obtain real-world precise measurements it was necessary for the artist to take the 3D model back and forth between the 3D sculpting program and a CAD program to work on the design.

Another option to taking the sculpture into an expensive CAD program is to use the measuring tools in the free software—SketchUp. A measuring tape offers accurate measurements of two points. Perhaps, one day, the opportunity for real-world and precise measurements similar to a measuring tape in SketchUp will be part of 3D sculpting programs.

The artist needs measurements to be sure of the design's overall height, width, and depth. However, there is a variety of reasons real-world measurements are important in 3D sculpting programs when creating art for a physical world. What size studio will the artist need? Can the CNC machining slice up the sculpture in the computer to enable the artist to sculpt in a smaller space? If not, what size warehouse will the artist need to accommodate the full height of the monumental sculpture?

How does the sculpture relate to any existing objects that it will surround? In many cases, an artist is placing work in a real-world environment next to objects or in places where other items interact with the sculpture. When creating bronze sculpture there are already variables that affect the outcome of the sculpture, such as shrinkage of the art through the bronze casting process. The artist needs real-world measurements to compare the digital art to the objects that already exist, while keeping in mind other variables, such as shrinkage.

Keeping the client's wishes in mind, Bridgette Mongeon's client expressed excitement that the shape of the rock looks like the state of Louisiana from one vantage point, so the artist was careful to change measurements without sacrificing this design element. The artist takes the work back and forth from sculpting program to CAD program to measure.

While creating, the artist will be thinking forward to the completion and preparation of the art for the delivery. While creating the design in the computer, nearly a year before delivering the monumental bronze, the artist checks with the shipping company to decide the most economical way for the sculpture to ship. Given exact measurements from the shipping company, the artist modifies the design to enable the sculpture to rest on its side in a semi truck upon its completion.

When creating the art in the computer, the artist will also be thinking about the installation. When creating artwork that will be installed and interact with the surroundings, it is necessary to be able to measure parts of the sculpture to accommodate these interactions.

The real-world measurements go beyond design, installation, and delivery. There are many other needs for real-world measurements. For example, the artist gives real-world exact measurements to foundries so they can bid for the job properly. The shipping company that will create the crate for the art will need these measurements to be able to accurately give quotes on shipping. The architects, crane operators, designers, landscapers, and insurance companies will also need these measurements to do their jobs. All of these vendors need measurements. The artist will need these measurements to obtain the appropriate cost estimates from these vendors and the vendors need these measurements for planning their part of the job.

Another form of measurement that is helpful with the 3D design process is the surface volume. This measurement, which will come from the CNC machinist's CAD file, is a measurement that an artist can give a bronze foundry. Should you want to get this measurement on your own, MeshMixer from Autodesk is a free tool that will give you the measurements of surface volume. The foundry will use these measurements to bid on the job. When estimating the prices for bronze, providing the foundry with surface volume instead of just height, weight, and depth will ensure accurate pricing. The foundry will appreciate this added bonus of working with a fine artist who has digital tools at their disposal.

There are several CNC milling companies that CNC mill foam. Check the Appendix or this book's accompanying website. Luckily, foam is light, and ships easily. The CNC milled foam does not come to the artist as one complete sculpture. It can come in boxes or crates. Be sure to budget the delivery of the foam in your total expenses on monumental or even life-size sculpture projects.

CNC milled foam ships to the artist in pieces.

The Sculpting Process

The sculptures that are CNC milled in foam are not complete. More often than not, artists will add something to the foam. For a bronze sculpture, the artist applies clay to the foam to add detail before preparing the sculpture to go through the mold-making process for bronze casting. Not all artists enlarge and CNC mill foam just for bronze casting. In other instances, for example, in interior or exterior scenery or a themed environment, a sculptor may decide to modify the foam, add more detail, and then coat the CNC foam with another material. There is a great number of materials that an artist can use on foam. If the reader has an interest in creating a themed environment, check this book's accompanying website for providers of materials to coat foam.

Steven Ramirez of Smash Design in Houston, Texas, creates themed designs using digital sculpting, CNC foam, and a variety of materials over the CNC foam (www. smashthedesign.com).

There are several different types of foam for CNC milling. The foam used for the Grambling State University tiger is urethane foam. Urethane foam is easy to carve and the artist can use traditional sculpting tools to shape the foam. The use of urethane foam should come with a warning—it is gritty. Some artists prefer working outside with a fan blowing away the grit. The alternative is to have a vacuum handy to vacuum the surface often—but be careful with the vacuum hose, as it can dent the surface of the foam if it accidentally scrapes it. Taping a large painter's brush to the end of the hose helps to brush the surface without causing damage. When carving urethane foam we recommend using a facemask and goggles for safety. After sculpting on the CNC foam of the tiger, it was necessary to vacuum the surface before adding a coating of paint or foundry wax to seal the foam and keep pieces of urethane foam from entering the clay and leaving an unwanted texture. After a layer of foundry wax, the tiger received multiple layers of clay, some as thin as ¼ inch and others several inches thick, depending on how the artist modified the design.

If an artist is going to apply clay to CNC milled foam, as is the case with Bridgette Mongeon's tiger sculpture, the clay will need to be a wax-based or oil-based clay such as Classic Clay, and not water-based clay. A water-based clay will dry, crack, and fall off. The artist will want to notify the CNC enlarging company prior to milling to ask them to provide a clay allowance. The milling company will then reduce the surface of the sculpture to allow room for the artist to add clay. It is important to note that, depending on the size of the clay allowance offset, some features may disappear. For example, a nose or ear will morph into a basic shape instead of carved detail. The lack of shape is not a problem for some, as many artists prefer to sculpt these details using the traditional process and only use the foam as a basic armature.

Across the Board Creations milled the foam for Bridgette Mongeon's Tiger Project. (www.acrosstheboardcreations.com/)

Hand-carving the Foam

We have already learned about the limits of three-axis CNC machining. Unless the machinist uses a CNC machine with a robotic arm and gradually decreases the bits, which adds up to a considerable amount of costly machine time, the sculpted foam will not have the deep recesses that bring contrast. For a sculpture to have movement and to feel lifelike, it must have undercuts and deep crevices. Without it, CNC machined foam of a figure looks flat and lifeless. There is just no substitution for handwork. Sculptor Bridgette Mongeon continues the sculpting process by carving and sanding the foam. Before the artist applies clay to the foam, she first adds a thin layer of foundry wax.

An artist may also discover that some parts of a design do not translate well into an enlarged milled object. Seeing a 15-foot tiger and a

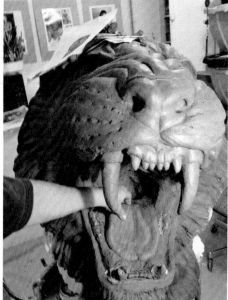

virtual tiger are two totally different things. The ease of the process might lull an artist into a false sense of completion. Just because the artist spent hours on the computer looking at a reference, and comparing that to a digital design, the sculpture is not complete. Once the CNC milled foam arrives at the artist's studio, the sculpting process begins all over again. They compare the reference material to the CNC foam at this machined size. The foam is easy to modify with clay tools. In some cases, taking into consideration weight and the structural engineering, an artist can cut sections apart and reposition them. A 2- or 3-pound foam will allow the artist to carve into it with sculpting tools, and the consistency will be like a gritty butter. Light sanding or even a washing of the foam is also possible.

Internal Armatures

High-density rigid urethane foam is pretty firm and often will stand on its own. From time to time, as in the example of a large mass on thin legs, the sculpture will need some additional support. The artist glues PVC or metal pipe into the foam with spray foam and secures the armature to a

Across the Board Creations builds an internal armature in the tiger. Square tubes in the legs of the tiger nest inside a larger square tube in the torso. Bolts secure the pieces in place.

wooden base. However, in monumental armatures it is good to consult an engineer. Some CNC machining companies will put an internal armature within the sculpture. In the case of the foam for the Grambling State University tiger sculpture, the CNC machining company Across the Board Creations created an internal metal armature with nesting structural square tubing that bolted one inside the other. The torso pieces bolted together, as did the head to the torso. The process allowed the artist to sculpt each appendage separately prior to putting the tiger together. Upon completion, the artist then bolted the appendages to the main body. The milling company welded an eyebolt in the tiger's back for raising the tiger onto the enormous rock. The artist raises the monumental sculpture and secures the pieces together with bolts to finish sculpting the entire tiger, and then she can lower it to take the sculpture apart for mold-making.

The artist could have chosen to hand-carve the rock base out of a large block of foam instead of having it milled. It was tempting, especially with the enormous cost of CNC milling of the rock. Milling companies estimate an additional $7,000 just for the milling of the rock. There are hundreds of pounds of clay on the foam torso and legs of the tiger. That means lifting a very large, very heavy tiger and placing it onto the carved rock. Having a milled rock with additional armature support, as provided by Across the Board Creations, the sculpture can be easily raised on top of the milled rock for final sculpting. It will not stay on top of the rock long, just long enough to obtain a client approval. Then the entire sculpture will be disassembled. It is important, for the safety of the art and all of the workers, to have a stable foundation. The milled rock with internal armature allowed the artist to raise the tiger so that it fit exactly in place. The mass of foam and clay did not have to hang and swing precariously or rest on something that might be unstable, even it if was only temporary.

The foam pieces can be worked on individually and later bolted onto the tiger's torso.

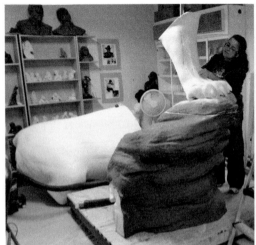
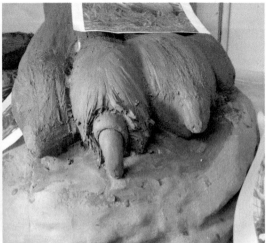

With an eyebolt securely welded to the inside armature of the tiger, the tiger can be raised onto the rock and lowered again.

Creating the design of the tiger climbing the rock in 3D also offers the artist other creative opportunities. The foam is designed at the perfect height as a stone shelf to accommodate the seating of a few students. The artist takes time to modify the design in the foam to be sure that there are no indents or large concave surfaces in the rock where water would pool. These areas will later cause rust in a monumental outdoor sculpture.

Putting Together the Foam

In other CNC milled artwork, there may be no internal armature. In these cases, the artist attaches the foam pieces, one to the other, with non-expansive spray insulation foam from the hardware store. Wooden dowels help to secure the pieces together.

A quick spritz of water on each piece after applying spray foam will assist in the curing of the spray foam. The artist takes care not to bring the spray foam to the edge where it will leak out. When carving and sanding on the foam, the spray foam has a different consistency than the milled foam. If it is close to the edge, it makes it difficult to use sculpting tools. The foam causes the tools to catch and drag instead of moving smoothly across the surface.

Spraying the foam with water will help to cure the foam.

Spray foam that leaks out between pieces of foam can cause havoc when trying to smoothly sculpt with sculpting tools. Sometimes it is better to carve these areas away and then fill them with clay.

Even if the artist does not plan on creating pieces that must glue together, the CNC milling and enlargement company may be gluing pieces together to obtain the size needed. The urethane foam, depending on the density, comes in sheets and not blocks. If an artist plans to do a lot of carving on the sculpture, he or she might ask their CNC milling company to glue their pieces together using this same process of staying away from the edges. Otherwise, the artist will have to cut out the foam in channels, leaving a visual disturbance. Then the artist must decide which is more important to them, the feel and ease as they move their tools over the surface or the visual disturbance of carved lines between sections of foam. If the artist chooses the smooth carving and sanding over the visual disturbance they can easily fill the crevices with clay after carving.

CNC milling for sculpture enlargement offers more benefits in production. A clay sculpture that is created using CNC milling for bronze casting is much lighter than it would be if the artist created it in the traditional old fashioned way of rebar, chicken wire, wood, etc. That means if an artist needs to transport it to the foundry it is easier to do so. The CNC milled foam is also easier to section; this is necessary for the foundry production of the sculpture, which we will cover in Chapter 8.

(top) Carving on foam that the artist or CNC company have pieced together can be frustrating. The glued areas cause the tool to catch and drag over the surface.

(bottom) To smoothly shape the tiger with sculpting tools, Mongeon carves out the glued channels. In the next step, she and her interns will fill these channels with wax and clay. The arrows in this picture are for her interns to understand the flow of the tiger's hair. They will add the wax and clay following these directions.

The use of 3D sculpting, modeling, and posing programs assist fine artists with their presentations. Incorporating digital tools to create presentations helps clients to begin to view the intended art from all angles. Digital presentations save the artist time and may just help to place their artwork above the presentations of their competition.

The use of scanning and/or sculpting combined with CNC milling can shave hours of time off of the production of life-size or monumental artwork created in a fine-art studio. Time saved means the artist has made room for more work, increasing their income and giving them more time for further creative exploration.

Once the clay sculpture is complete, the artist sends the sculpture to the foundry to be cast into bronze. Chapter 8 documents the tiger's travel through the traditional foundry as we compare the steps of creating a bronze and how the digital technology is slowly infiltrating this process. Before we will be able to recognize these digital processes, we have one more place of investigation—3D printing.

"LONDON INK"

The Discovery Channel London created two public pieces to initiate an interest in a show titled "London Ink." The marketing team at Discovery combined forces with Asylum Models & Effects to fabricate these public installation pieces. The gigantic figures were CNC milled in foam, painted and then clothed. For more information on this process, listen to the online podcast interview at www.digitalsculpting.net.

As an interesting marketing technique created by Mother UK in 2007, the Discovery Channel created *Victoria* with her head in a photo booth for the Victoria Station.

The sculpture called *The Swimmer* swims in the grass along the River Thames near the Tower Bridge. Tattoos by Louis Molloy display the date and time of the London Ink television show featured on the Discovery Channel. Photograph used with the permission of photographer Mike Marsland.

3D FOR PRESENTATIONS AND CNC MILLING FOR ENLARGEMENTS

GARY STAAB

Gary Staab of Staab Studios combines science, history, art, and technology to reproduce some pretty incredible sculptures.

Brachiosaurus Mother and Baby by Gary Staab, Indianapolis Children's Museum.

Allosaurus by Gary Staab, Tabiat Tarihi Muzesi: National Museum of Natural History, Ankara, Turkey.

On the book's website at www.digitalsculpting.net you will find:

* Links to further descriptions on the process of creating the artwork featured in the galleries.
* Podcasts with the artists.
* Videos featuring the artists at work.

CHAPTER SEVEN

3D PRINTING

———

"Because he's an artist, he's pushing the envelope further than an industry would. An artist just has a creative vision and they kind of ignore what the tools are supposed to be able to do and they realize their creative vision."

Autodesk director **Maurice Conti** speaks about the work of Joris Laarman

facing page
Dragon Bench by Joris Laarman Lab.

3D Printing—Rapid Prototyping

This book has taught us quite a bit about 3D technology and how it is influencing the arts and how artists can use this technology to create some very inspirational work. You may even begin to feel more comfortable with the virtual world in which artists create these masterpieces. We have looked at how computer numerically controlled (CNC) milling subtracts material, carving it away as it makes the physical object. In contrast, let's now take a look at additive fabrication. Additive fabrication adds material layer by layer to create a physical object. Industry and artists refer to additive fabrication technology by many different names—3D printing, rapid prototyping, solid freeform fabrication, layered manufacturing, and others. The name "3D printing" seems to be the term most commonly used. Artists, craftsmen, engineers, architects, and scientists, as well as many others, use 3D printing. The wide use of 3D printing in many different applications has contributed to it evolving. The hacker community is very excited about the idea that a 3D printer is evolutionary. In other words, it can print its parts for other 3D printers or offspring. The interdisciplinary nature of the medium and the great amount of materials available to print, combined with the decreasing cost and the inspiration and influence of hackers and open source, brings an incredible toolset to any creative person's studio.

As with CNC milling, 3D printing was produced for manufacturing, but the interest in the technology, outdated patents, and a strong hacker community has influenced the technology, making it more available for the mainstream user. Now, artists, hobbyists, and people working in crafts are using 3D printing, and they are printing in a variety of materials from chocolate to bronze. The cost of owning a 3D printer has also changed. In 2009, a 3D printer might cost $20,000–30,000 or more. Now you can go to Office Depot and pick up a desktop printer for $1,300 or you can become a part of the hacker DIY community and build a 3D printer for a few hundred dollars. It is no wonder that the technology has spread. With the understanding of the possibilities of this new technology, artists and craftspeople find their creative and inspirational process expanded. Understanding the process helps an artist imagine what they can create.

> You just don't know what you can do, until you know what you can do.
>
> Sculptor and author Bridgette Mongeon

With 3D printing, artists can create pieces inside of pieces, voids with objects in them, intricate detail, complex sculptures with interconnecting articulating parts, and much more. Artists are creating and manufacturing objects so intricate that they were not even possible to create before 3D technology.

Types of 3D Printing

3D printing is a large and broad category that consists of not only many different materials, but also many different processes. Understanding the manufacturing and the processes of creating in 3D will help the artist to know the best process for their work. Within additive manufacturing there are several processes to choose from and many are readily available to the average consumer. In this chapter, we will look at some of the most common—fused deposition modeling (FDM), selective laser sintering (SLS), and stereolithography (SL/SLA), as well as a few others. It can be a bit confusing to understand the nuances of each process at first, but understanding the details of each of these forms of output will help to determine the best output for your art.

Fused Deposition Modeling (FDM)

In fused deposition modeling, a machine prints small layers by extrusion. Most familiar to individuals is the extrusion of plastic filament through a heated nozzle. Building from the bottom up, the art emerges with layers—each layer bonded to the other as they harden. The nozzle moves over the object as it deposits the material.

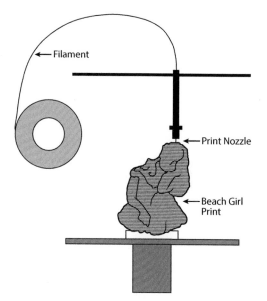

Fused deposition modeling (FDM).

In some cases, there are fragile overhangs in a design that will not print without assistance. It is important to add support structures to these areas when 3D printing weak parts using FDM. The artist can remove the support structures after printing. You or your service bureau may add these structures in the pre-fab process. Support structures are common in many types of 3D printing; for example, SLA will also require support structures. In 3D printing, some support structures are water-soluble. Removing these is as simple as washing them away. A breakaway material is another type of a support structure; however, plastic pieces can fly off, and many artists recommend wearing safety glasses when breaking these off. However, even if a sculpture makes it through the process of 3D printing, please remember that protruding parts still may be fragile or they may not ship well.

Most of the low-cost desktop 3D printers that are available on the market today use the fused deposition modeling process of 3D printing. FDM 3D printing is affordable and is easy to come by. Examples of 3D

printers are the RepRapPro Ormerod 2 Kit at $747 (www.reprappro.com), the MakerBot Replicator at $2,899 (www.makerbot.com), and the Cube X Duo at $2,999 (www.3dsystems.com). However, the detail and resolution of images printed with FDM are often not as good as other 3D printing processes.

Selective Laser Sintering (SLS)

In selective laser sintering, a laser passes over a bed of deposited powder. This powder can be plastic, metal, even glass or ceramic. The laser fuses the powdered material together. After one layer is complete, the build bed lowers, and the machine adds another layer of powder on top. The process continues through the building of the product. Once it is printed, the operator brushes the powder off the object revealing the art as an archeologist would reveal an artifact among the dirt. Some applications and materials may require additional steps that consist of firing or curing.

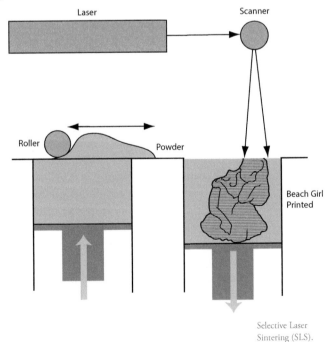

Selective Laser
Sintering (SLS).

The advantage of SLS 3D printing and a few others is that the support structure is within the material. The powder that creates the object during printings supports the object as well as any of the overhangs that may be in the design. And as long as the powder has a way to escape, it is feasible to print an object inside of an object. Creating objects inside of objects is very difficult in traditional processes such as ceramic or bronze casting. SLS holds wonderful possibilities for artists.

When can you purchase a home SLS 3D printer? There was a surge in desktop models of FDM 3D printers available to the public when patents for that process expired in 2009. The key patent for SLS machines expired in 2014. But SLS technology is a bit more detailed; the SLS process means fusing metals and the laser used in SLS compared to SLA is different and not as safe. Also, there are still many patents that are in effect that are a part of the SLS process. So SLS home 3D printers are not yet available; however, consumers have access to all of the 3D printing processes through online service bureaus.

Artists can create intricate intertwining or nesting shapes with 3D printing. *Tentacon Fork* by Bathsheba Grossman.

Stereolithography (SL/SLA)

Stereolithography also works with divided layers. In SLA, a laser beam passes over a photocurable liquid resin. Just as in SLS, an SLA machine adds layers as the table lowers; but instead of adding a fine layer of powder, the lowering of the build table allows a fine layer of resin to accumulate over the top of the object. The laser cures the resin. The artist may still need to incorporate support structures for overhangs as in the FDM process. Watching the SLA process, one feels eerily like a mad scientist with their creation emerging out of the liquid resin on a rising platform. Removal of support structures is all that is necessary to reveal the finished 3D product.

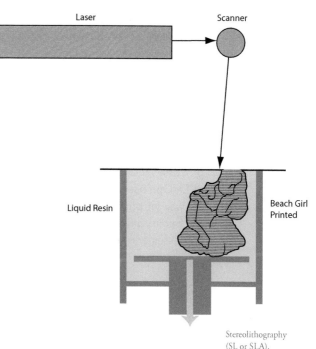

Stereolithography (SL or SLA).

There are desktop SLA printers coming onto the market, sparked by the expiration of some of the patents in the process. Individuals see the necessity of creating an affordable 3D SLA printer, as this is one of the processes of 3D printing that holds the most detail. Formlabs put together a kickstarter that closed October 6, 2012, and raised $2,945,885. To see such funding happen so quickly, it becomes apparent that others have a desire to see SLA made available to the general public at a reasonable cost. However, the large 3D printing companies are watching and they are filing lawsuits.

A few of the SLA printers on the market are the Form 1 3D Printer at $3,299 (www.formlabs.com) and the 3D Systems Pro Jet at $4,900 (www.3dsystems.com).

Autodesk, a leading software company, announced in 2014 that they plan on getting into the 3D printing industry on the hardware side. In a Bloomberg TV interview, CEO Carl Bass states that he was, like many, "fascinated by the promise but frustrated by the reality." There are a lot of steps involved in 3D printing, and Bass believes that it needs to be simpler. The interesting concept is that this large company will be creating an open source SLA 3D printer. Bass understands the concept of how the input of others can play a role in the evolution of the product. As the product evolves so will the creative thinking: "Things you design should be different" (http://spark.autodesk.com).

Other Types of 3D Printing

Fused deposition modeling, selective laser sintering, and stereolithography are not the only types of 3D printing processes available. There are others. Some of the processes are not known by a single name or are proprietary to the manufactures. One example is the process of ExOne used by Bathsheba Grossman. We will look at another in the feature section of 3D printing of jewelry by Krikawa Jewelry Design. The amount and types of 3D printing available is no doubt confusing, but if you can familiarize yourself with these processes (FDM, SLS, SLA, the proprietary process of Ex One used by Bathsheba Grossman, and the 3D wax jet printing used by Krikawa Designs), you will begin to have a base understanding about the processes and the possibilities.

Get Off My Yard by Mathieu Aerni. Created in ZBrush and printed through Mold3D (www.mold3d.com).

Brian Chan creates his articulated (moving) sculpture inspired by the ancient Japanese decorative art called *jizai okimono*. With *jizai okimono* the intricate metal art moves freely. Chan models in Wings3D, creates individual joints and copies and pastes them in the correct positions. He prints his pieces with Shapeways that are either sintered nylon or investment cast in metal from 3D printed wax.

Metal Bowls by Carl Bass of Autodesk, printed in 420SS/Bronze, ExOne. Photograph courtesy of ExOne.

3D Printers for the Home/Studio

There is a variety of 3D printers available for the home. As we said, most of the 3D printing technology standard for home use incorporates fused deposition modeling (FDM), but more options are becoming available such as stereolithography (SLA). The difference between the detail and resolution of SLA compared to FDM is drastic. Although the build envelope on many home machines, especially SLA, is rather small at 4.9 × 4.9 × 6.5 inches, the detail is quite good. Some SLA providers are even working on a resin that will easily burn out for investment casting. It will not be long before we begin to see other types of 3D printing processes made more accessible through home 3D printers and, in turn, the cost of 3D printers will decrease.

There are many online sites that review and compare 3D printers. There is also a special annual issue of *Make* magazine: "Ultimate Guide to 3D Printing $300–$3000: Which Printer is Right for You? 3D Printers Buyers' Guide With 23 Printer Reviews." Not only does it review printers, it inspires and makes the reader think of the possibilities. If you want to purchase a home 3D printer, it is a good idea to take some time to research and compare the different machines. Technology changes quickly, and suggestions mentioned in this book could become obsolete before the book goes to print. The book's accompanying website contains additional links to sites that review printers.

There are several things to consider when purchasing a home 3D printer.

Printing or Tinkering

Some people like the experience of building and tinkering with their 3D printer. If you are not a tinkerer and only want to print, then be sure that your 3D printer review criteria factors in the temperamental nature of home 3D printers. If you do prefer to tinker, then you might want to purchase a 3D printer that is hackable, extending or modifying the machine's capabilities. For example, a hacker can add an extruder to a RepRapPro machine and, instead of printing out filament, the 3D printer can extrude clay slip.

Build Envelope

What size item would you like to print? Be sure to check the build envelope or build size in comparison with the type of material you are seeking to print. Many home printers print small pieces 5 inches by 5 inches, while the Cubify reaches a build envelope of nearly 10 inches. Some artists slice their designs in the computer and then print them in multiple parts. Understanding how you will use your home printer and the maximum size 3D print you will need will help to determine the best 3D printer for you.

Detail-resolution

At first, understanding and comparing what some refer to as resolution of 3D printing machines can be confusing. One could go into a great extent talking about all aspects of the detail such as the axis, thickness, and even dots per inch (DPI), but let's simplify this. We can see the many layers of 3D printing in the close-up photographs of the baby and the tiger. Whether FDM, SLS, or SLA, they all work in layers. It makes sense that the detail of the 3D print is in the layers. The layer height determines the resolution. 3D printing manufacturers measure layer height in millimeters: 0.1 mm is approximately the thickness of a piece of paper. The 3D printing machines that print in thicker layers often will leave a noticeable "stair-stepping" effect in the finished piece. As the layers get thinner, the stair-stepping effect is less noticeable and, in some cases, post-processing can help to eliminate layers. Some artists embrace the machines' limitations and use the stair-stepping effect as a part of their art. They incorporate it into their design.

A close-up of the layering in the 3D printing from Captured Dimensions in Chapter 3.

Even though you may get very good print results from a specific 3D printing machine, it will be important to research how consistent the machine is. If, for example, every third print is considered usable, then it might be worth looking elsewhere. Users of printers will talk about the consistency of various 3D printers openly on user forums.

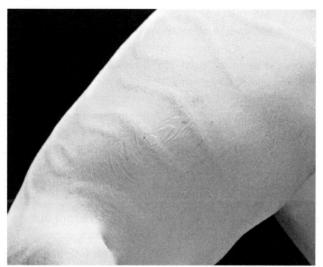

A close-up of Bridgette Mongeon's tiger printed in SLS displays the layering of this process of 3D printing. The layering is not as noticeable and the direction of the layering seems to give movement to the fur.

Print Material

What does the 3D printer print? There are two primary sources of printing material for FDM printers, ABS and PLA. When you buy your printer, you will be printing with this "thermoplastic filament" to create your excellent 3D designs. The term thermoplastic means that it becomes soft when heated and hardens when cooled. Take note—the spools of 1.75 mm and 3 mm thick thermoplastic products are a usable product. You will have to replace and purchase filament for a 3D printer just as you would paper for your copier. Understanding the pros and cons of each of the plastics is important.

ABS stands for acrylonitrile butadiene styrene. ABS is petroleum-based thermoplastic. There are both positive and negative aspects of ABS. It is more flexible, which makes it a good choice when creating interlocking parts. It is also easier to sand than PLA. However, humidity can affect ABS during long-term storage. ABS can warp and requires a heated bed for better performance. Unlike PLA, it is not biodegradable and smells like burning plastic when it comes out of the machine.

The other thermoplastic used in the FDM 3D home printers is PLA—polylactic acid or polylactide. PLA is a plant starch base made from corn, beets, or sugar; therefore, it is biodegradable. Print a shoe for your child on your 3D printer and, when it no longer fits, simply toss it in the compost and print another. The smell, when extruding at 180–200 degrees, is more like burning cooking oil. PLA is strong and rigid and is less prone to warping during printing, but you would not want to leave a printed piece in a car in the Texas heat.

Many arts and crafts people are experimenting with using their PLA and ABS 3D printed pieces as a positive burnout design for a mold. Instead of using the lost wax method of casting featured in Chapter 8, you could say they are using the "lost PLA" and "lost ABS" methods of casting. Although SLS printing brings better detail, the incorporating of the technology in art and craft is often about experimentation. There are more details on this process in the next chapter. Because of the toxic fumes of ABS, it appears the preferred plastic for burnout is PLA. If you are planning on experimenting with this, you should note that the chemical makeup of each filament is different, and so is the melting temperature.

Filament can be costly, which is important to remember, especially when it is a consumable resource—3D printed practice pieces pile up. A spool of filament can run anywhere from $35 to $100, depending on the type, manufacturer, and machine. Plans are already underway for recycling machines that take your old PLA or ABS, grind it up, and melt it into new filament. It is important to note that, when choosing a 3D printer, some companies will not allow the use of anyone else's filament but theirs. Their filament can cost nearly three times the amount of buying filament elsewhere. Being bound to one supplier for filament is limiting. Having to stay with one company's filament may also leave you with fewer choices in printing colors and price.

When purchasing filament from a supplier, check on the grade of the filament. Standard grade for PLA is 4043D, and the standard for ABS is PA-747. While comparing and deciding on what material to print in, it might also be necessary to look at the price per roll of filament as well as the price to print each piece. Many comparison charts will have this information in them.

Varieties of Printing Colors

Some FDM machines have multiple extruders and print multiple colors at the same time. Most have just one extruder head and print in one color. Filament does come in different colors. Different filaments have variations even if they are the same material and color.

There are also specialty filaments. Form Futura offers a variety of filaments such as Laywood D-3, which is a 40 percent recycled wood with a binding polymer. This wood filament can change color depending on the temperature upon extrusion. There is no doubt there will be many other filaments available for FDM. Anything you can mix with the plastic and extrude with precision is a candidate for new FDM filament.

Using 100 percent natural Timberfill material from Fillamentum, Akemake created a wooden speaker. Ondra Chotovinsky designed *Spirula 4.0*. Chotovinsky uses a variety of CAD software to create his 3D designs and Martin Hreben prepares the files for 3D printing. *Spirula 4.0* was printed on a highly modified Leapfrog 3D printer re-engineered by Hreben. The design is currently available for free download and can be found at www.akemake. com. You can print it out on your own 3D printer but be prepared; it may take up to 36 hours to print one pair.

Speed of a Print

If you are printing a 3D print on a home 3D printer you can specify if you want a quick print that will take less time. Time and resolution work hand in hand. Less time means you will sacrifice resolution. A higher resolution print will take more time to generate on the 3D printer. For example, one 3D printer may take 15 minutes to print a cell phone case and another printer may take three hours. Time is money, so when weighing the many criteria of buying a 3D printer be sure to take print time into consideration.

Software

With the many varieties of printers on the market, it makes sense that some will be easier to operate than others. When considering operating a 3D printer it is necessary to consider the software. Does the software come with the machine? Is it a plug and play? Is the software designed for engineers or the general consumer? These are all things to look at when considering the purchase of home 3D printing systems and software.

Operating System

Most printers use both Windows and Mac operating systems, a few do not. If a Mac operating system is important, be sure to look for this aspect of a 3D printer in your review process.

Other Considerations

Accuracy of print, warranty, ease of use, and customer support are all important considerations with a temperamental piece of equipment like a 3D printer.

There are many criteria to consider when purchasing a home printer. With a little exploration and out of pocket cash, an artist or craftsperson will be up and running, creating new designs while friends and family look on in amazement, but that is not the only way to print your art.

Accessible Technology and the Possibilities

It was not long ago that if you wanted to have something printed using 3D printing you had to invest in to some expensive equipment. Now, there are many alternatives. Just as with the use of both scanners and CNC equipment there are options to investing into your own equipment. There are 3D printing service bureaus. Service bureaus are both national and local. Many makerspaces and hackerspaces also have at least FDM 3D printing machines.

Service Bureaus

There is an ever-increasing community of online service bureaus now available to the consumer. The artist creates a model in a 3D program and then logs onto the service bureau website. Prepare a file for printing, upload the file, pick the material, and then print. The service bureau will then send the printed item to your home or studio. The nice part about the service bureaus is that it gives artists and craftspeople a variety of materials and processes from which to choose. Without the 3D service bureau, the artist might not be able to have their work recreated on such expensive machines, and artists might not have access to such expanding possibilities in the 3D printing process. An artist can easily have something printed in plastic, glass, metal, ceramic, and much more. The variety of materials and the cost of 3D printing can be quite reasonable. With so many national service bureaus to choose from you can even compare prices. Many have a strong community where you can seek answers to your questions. The disadvantages to using these national service bureaus is that you may not get the one-on-one service that a local company can offer. Working out design problems can be costly if you have to print the product out multiple times before you work out the problem.

There are websites that are taking the search for price comparison between national service bureaus out of the equation. An example is http://3dprintingpricecheck.com: upload your file and they will check the prices of several 3D printing service bureaus such as Ponoko, Shapeways, Sculpteo, i.materialise, and Kraftwurx. The website Supply Better offers quotes from vendors on your specific projects. So, if your goal is either a "one off" or many pieces of one design, consider providing specs to a website such as Supply Better and let different companies bid on your project. Prior to uploading files to these sites, it is advisable to read the chapter on intellectual property rights, as well as their terms of service. Always check into the standards of each website and company where you submit your work. It is necessary to protect your intellectual property rights wherever you are submitting your files.

Some Staples office supply stores and UPS stores around the world are offering FDM 3D printing services, although it will be interesting to see how stores train the employees that will be printing your pieces. Depending on where you live, there may be local vendors or individuals who own expensive equipment that will print your work for you. No matter what type of 3D printer it is, all 3D printers have moving parts. The owner of the machine needs to use it on a regular basis. Working with a local vendor, you have the luxury of asking questions and, if you have a good relationship, the vendor can even help you to push the limits of the process. It is often advantageous to scout out a smaller local company that can offer you the kind of 3D printing that you need and with whom you can develop a relationship. Even if a local service bureau is more expensive, in the long run, the one-on-one time will pay for itself.

Working with the Service Bureau

Companies like Shapeways, i.materialise, Sculpteo, Ponoko, and Kraftwurx are the most recognized names in full service, online, multi-material 3D printing service bureaus. See the Appendix and website for a list of service providers, and special offers.

These personal service bureaus cater to the novices, hobbyists, and small entrepreneurs that wish to use 3D printing as part of their production, but who don't want to invest in a 3D printer. They are a bit different from the commercial companies that specialize in creating prototypes for manufacturing, industry, and the sciences such as RedEye (www. redeyeondemand.com). Although the technology in the personal service bureaus is not any different than the commercial, the personal service bureaus target their marketing strategies and price points to the general consumer. These service bureaus have certainly helped to make 3D printing more accessible. Before we look at some of the many elements of a service bureau, let's take a closer look at how many service bureaus are helping artists sell their work through 3D printing storefronts.

Some service bureaus offer storefronts for artists to sell their designs. Featured artist Bathsheba Grossman uses storefronts at Shapeways and i.materialise websites, but states that her primary sales venue is still her own website at www.bathsehba.com.

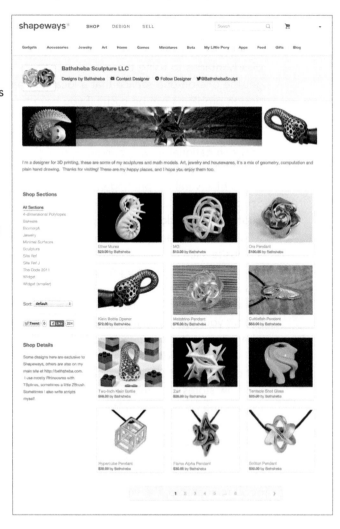

3D Printing Storefronts

Some of the personal service bureaus also make selling 3D products easy by offering storefronts to their customers. Storefronts at i.materialise, Sculpteo, and Shapeways offer not only printing services that print in a variety of materials, but also the opportunity for designers to set up a shopping cart and create a place to market their work. It is very similar to Etsy, but with 3D printed products and a built-in manufacturer. Artists create their designs, pick their materials, and then set their retail prices. Shoppers come to their storefronts, pick an item, and order a 3D print. The service bureau manufactures and prints the design. The artist's account grows with the deposits made by the service bureau shopping cart. Some shops also offer individualized products, such as a bracelet created with your child's name. Many designers love the ease of having an online storefront through these websites. It relieves them from marketing, sales, and even shipping. They can simply sit back and create, and they don't have to pay attention to the business side of things. However, before we look at the service of the personal service bureau, let's take a look at the storefront option. There are some things to note when weighing the option of a storefront for your 3D printed arts and crafts.

OVERWHELMED BUYERS One of the online shopping cart sites states that they have "Over one million objects" in their storefront. Can the buyer easily navigate the website? For example, can I search "necklaces," and then navigate to necklaces of a particular material or the best sellers? If not, then your work may be harder to find. Also, what are the demographics of the storefront? Who is coming to Shapeways, i.materialise, or Sculpteo to buy these things? It is safe to say that the majority of people floating through the websites are those who are themselves creating items using the 3D printing. This may not be the demographic that is the best for purchasing your gifts.

Many artists have reported regular substantial income through their storefront. This type of "easy" revenue has an appeal. As these storefronts become more known by the general consumer they may increase the profits of small artists, offering them income with little overhead. There are other things to watch out for with these online 3D printing shopping sites if you decide to go that route.

THIS DESIGN CANNOT PRINT When you upload a design to the sites, you are sure it can print because it goes through a review process. On occasion, artists have reported that the design has printed with no problems, but then a client orders it and the client receives a message that the design is not printable. The service bureau notifies the artist, but the sale is hardly redeemable. Buyers just move on to an item that is printable. So, why would a piece print one time, but not all of the time? There are several reasons why your previously reviewed design might not print and cause your client to receive this error in their order. Perhaps someone else reviewed the printing file or the post-processing requires more work. 3D printing is rarely just a push of a button, there are many steps in creating a 3D print. The service bureaus are friendly and work with you to solve this issue; however, there is no recouping the damage to that sale. The client only sees that it is unprintable and may wonder why a professional artist has put an unprintable design on the site. The artist's reputation is at stake. The sale is lost.

No matter what storefront you decide to try, it is important that you first create your designs and have them shipped to you. Designs are rarely created perfectly the first time. Modifications mean multiple prints with tweaking of the design between printings. Any manufacturer knows that periodically you have to check what is coming off the assembly line. Quality control means that the product meets the design standards of the designer. Materials can change, employees can change, and even machines can change. The quality can change from order to order. Does the product that is going to your customer meet your standards? If the service bureau creates and ships it to the customer, you may never know if it did. It is important to monitor your work. After all, it is your name on the product. For this reason, even if it is more convenient to have the service bureau print and ship your item to the end-user, it is advisable to revise that process. Sending designs directly to your client from these service bureaus means you are blindly trusting that the quality is to your standards.

SPEED OF SERVICE The complaints about turnaround time are consistent in the world of designers concerning personal service bureaus. The Shapeways website states an order can take between one and three weeks or more, while Sculpteo and i.materialise both give a range of between one day and 21 days. When a customer orders a product from you, they are anxious. They want to receive what they have purchased and would prefer not to wait. Investing into purchasing a few of your products is a viable business alternative. Build a little inventory, and then ship from your studio. With the build envelope or build size available for 3D printing, the products will take little room to store, and shipping, although inconvenient, is possible.

CLIENT RELATIONSHIP Knowing your customer or those purchasing from your store is important. If you are an artist or craftsmen and are trying to make a living by the labor of your hands, then studying a bit about marketing and applying that to your business is important. As the saying goes, "You don't get a second chance to make a first impression." With e-tailing, selling retail in an online space, the artist makes that impression in moments. When another person has control of the website and the manufacturing then you are giving up control of an important element of business. Placing your work on an online store means an artist does not have to worry about sales, shipping, and many other things, but you may also give up the client contact. The information collected by the shopping carts on 3D printing websites is owned by the service bureau and often is not shared with the storefront owner. If you created a new design and felt that those people who purchased a similar previous design might like it, you may have no way of letting them know.

There is a marketing saying that states, "It is all in the list." Collecting data, such as name, email, and phone number from your clients is crucial. At the time of writing this book, many of the 3D printing service bureaus do not pass the client information on to the artist.

MARKETING AND BRANDING YOUR PRODUCT   When you use a storefront, the products ship from the company that makes them. In other words, i.materialise will ship your designs in i.materialise's packaging, and with any marketing material that i.materialise decides they would like to put into a shipping box. It would be far better to have your packaging, created with your labels. Marketing of this sort does not have to be expensive. A designer selling only a few products can easily purchase quality packaging and print their marketing material on their home inkjet printer.

Using a Personal Service Bureau

Many people make online storefronts work for their business, and have fun doing so. Even if you are not going to get a storefront at a personal online service bureau, they have so much else to offer. Let's look at what else these personal service bureaus have to offer and the things to consider when working with the service bureaus.

THE TYPE OF 3D PRINTING PROCESSES   In the many online service bureaus, you will find all types of 3D printing at your fingertips. However, whether it is SLS, SLA, FDM, or others, how do you know what is the right type of printing for your design? There are several factors that you will want to consider. What is it used for? What detail or resolution do you require? What size do you require? Can the object be printed in the size you require with the process and in a material that you need? What is the desired texture or finish of the print? How strong does your print need to be? What is the cost of the 3D print?

Scanning a sculpture or object and modeling or designing it in the computer are some of the ways to obtain an object for print. You can also find free 3D models at such places as Thingiverse (www.thingiverse.com). Some processes, such as scanning and sculpting, can provide very detailed 3D images. If the specific 3D printing processes, and the material and resolution available for those processes, cannot preserve and print the detail, then modifications need to be made. An artist can choose to change the type of printing process, choose a different 3D material, or modify the design.

The cost of the many different materials varies greatly. The service bureau websites are becoming increasingly helpful in aiding the consumer in deciding the best material and cost.

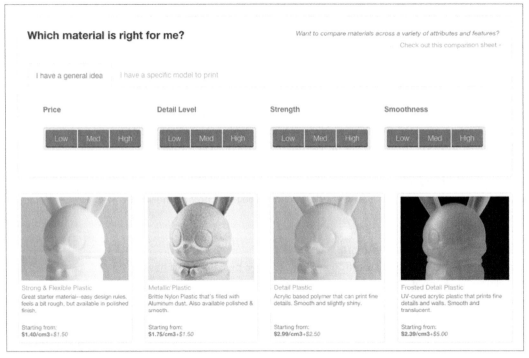

Searching the service bureau's sites you can get a better understanding of material prices and characteristics. Photograph courtesy of Shapeways.

COST   When considering the cost of a 3D print, it is important to understand that the cost may change depending on a few criteria: the material, the size, and the mass or volume of your piece. If your art is difficult to print then this will also affect the cost. Costs also vary between vendors, so you should compare service bureaus. There is another aspect of the designing and printing in the 3D process that most artists beginning to 3D print do not realize. It is important to take into consideration how many test prints and revisions you will need to print before a 3D piece of art is correct. Many of those designing and printing in 3D find that 3D prints rarely come out correct the first time. Sometimes a design needs modification for the material and size. An artist may find that they need to thicken, thin, or change certain elements of design for aesthetic or manufacturing reasons. If that is the case, it might be advisable to do a test print or two in the appropriate size and in a less expensive material before creating something in, say, gold or bronze.

Does the price of your sculpture come down per centimeter? If there is more volume in the sculpture, is it cheaper? Can you gang up some pieces; for example, print four on a plate and bring the cost down per piece?

Sometimes the direction of the build axis may need changing. The placing of a design on the build box in the 3D printer will affect the layering, and if there is stair-stepping, this may change the look of a piece. The 3D printer prints from the bottom up. Sometimes turning the 3D design in the computer as it sits on the build table, so that the 3D printer builds layers from another direction, say on its side instead of standing, can make a difference. If there is no desire for a finished polish on the piece, then the print orientation and the stair-stepping effect could be essential to the design process. This is something that cannot be seen without a test print.

SIZE   The build size or build envelope available in 3D printing changes depending on the material and the machine. The service bureaus list the build envelope for each of their materials. Although there was a time when the build envelope was very small, you could say technology is really pushing the envelope on this, no pun intended. Artists and hobbyists might be limited to what they can get out of their own home printer or the service bureaus. Keep an eye on the technology. Artists are pushing the technology to accommodate their needs, and it might just feed your need as well.

SHIPPING   What is the cost for shipping compared to the price? Where is the service bureau located and how much will it cost to receive your items from them?

Materials

The service bureaus have a variety of materials available, and they present them in different ways. It is worth visiting the websites of these service bureaus regularly as new materials are added. i.materialise has a periodical table of materials (www. materialise.com).

The types of material that are 3D printed are expanding every day. The i.materialise screen shot on this page depicts the table of their materials that are readily available to the average consumer through 3D printing at just one service bureau. Many of the service bureaus have a tremendous amount of information on their websites concerning the properties of each material and suggestions for their use.

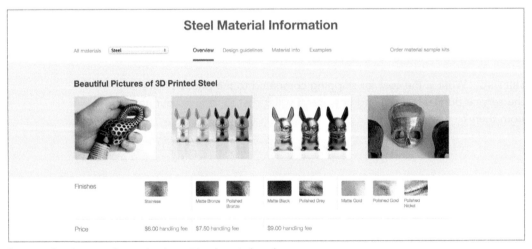

It is not until you begin to really research each material on the service bureau's website, that you will see the creative possibilities. Be sure to explore deeper into the materials to find specific design guidelines for each material in which you are interested. From the Shapeways website.

METALS Aerospace, the automotive industry, medical fields, jewelers, artists, and many more are 3D printing in metal. The applications of 3D printing in metal are growing daily. There is a variety of metals listed on the service bureau websites including stainless steel, alumide, titanium, brass, bronze, and gold.

Not all of the metals listed are directly printed using the 3D printing process. Alumide 3D printing uses the SLS printing process but is really nylon plastic mixed with aluminum powder. 3D printing service bureaus offer some metals such as bronze cast, sterling silver, and gold that uses 3D printing but in a different way. These 3D printed materials use the lost wax method of casting. The process begins with a wax 3D print. This wax can retain great detail. Gating up the wax helps the metal to flow and the gases to escape. Just like the traditional lost wax method of bronze casting detailed in Chapter 8, a mold or the vestment holds all of the details of the original wax after the foundry burns out the wax. Pouring molten metal in the mold cavity, and breaking away the mold reveals the final cast metal. The finishing process will consist of grinding off supports and gates just as in the investment casting of a bronze in a foundry. There is no need for artists to worry about the entire mold-making process and cost when working with a service bureau. They include these costs in the total cost of printing 3D metal using these processes. However, it is important to note how the service bureau will print your 3D model in metal. They can make the metal using the lost wax method or by 3D printing using ExOne's process of printing in metal. The process may influence how you design.

It is convenient to be able to order these lost wax metal 3D printed materials through online service bureaus. Or you can have the wax pieces go through the investment casting process right through the service bureau. Some service bureaus print metal using selective laser sintering (SLS) or a process referred to as direct metal laser sintering (DMLS). Others use ExOne's process of a bonding agent to sinter the metal. Then they cure the (stainless steel) metal with heat. In both processes of 3D printing, whether using a bonding agent or sintering, removing the excess build powder is necessary for the next step to take place (see page 206).

3D PRINTING OF JEWELRY
BY LISA KRIKAWA,
KRIKAWA JEWELRY DESIGN

Lisa Krikawa has been using 3D technology, CAD design, and 3D printing at Krikawa Jewelry Design, since 2003. She shares much more in her interview with the author on the *Art and Technology* podcast found on the book's accompanying website. Krikawa's primary software is Rhino. She also likes the organic feel of ZBrush; however, there are no measuring tools.

Krikawa Jewelry Design owns both a T66 Solidscape and a T76 Solidscape 3D printer that prints in a workable but brittle wax that is good for burnout (www.solid-scape.com). These Solidscape printers are different types of printers. It is like an inkjet printer along with CNC milling. The printer is precise, but 3D printing can take a long time; one ring may take 8–12 hours to print. They also explored the purchase of a Viper (www.3dsystems.com). A Viper is a resin printer, which is good quality and prints many rings in a short amount of time. However, Krikawa favored the burnout of wax and preferred not to have to deal with the residue left from resin. These are all commercial level printers that begin at $40,000. If an individual wanted to use a service bureau to 3D print their ring, it would cost approximately $50–$150 depending on the design. This price is just for the wax.

Krikawa states that incorporating 3D technology in her workflow has expanded her creative process. In traditional design, you don't always know if things are going to line up, but in 3D design the modeler can check in with the designer to see if what is on the screen is their vision. Of course, they are zooming into rings that are a foot across on the screen. It looks great on the screen, but there is always some change, even if they measure. After all, they work with a tenth of a millimeter as their smallest unit of measurement. Other hints from Krikawa:

- Measure, and if possible put the sprues for gating right into the wax.
- On designs that are more complex, they will create nubs where the foundry can add the wax sprues.
- Remember that files always have problems. It behooves the designer to know what makes a good file for printing and make that a part of your modeling.
- Make sure you allow a tenth of a millimeter for clean-up on all sides.
- Finally, don't do everything digitally. Leave space for handwork.

The detail in the 3D print is exquisite. Krikawa suggests adding nubs or pouring sprues in the wax to help facilitate casting.

Krikawa Jewelry Design print their jewelry using a Solidscape T76 3D printer that uses a "drop-on-demand (DoD) thermoplastic ink-jetting technology and high-precision milling of each layer with the company's proprietary graphical front-end software, 3Z®Works."

Krikawa says it is important to leave some room for handwork in your digital creations.

3D PRINTING IN METAL WITH BATHSHEBA GROSSMAN

Bathsheba Grossman began as a math major that moved into creating sculpture and 3D technology in 1997. A pioneer in the industry, she was one of the first artists to create art using ExOne's process of 3D printing using a binder powder and sintering (www.exone.com). In the *Art and Technology* podcast at www.digitalsculpting.net, Grossman and the author talk in detail about 3D printing in metal.

For the same reason that Krikawa Jewelry Design creates nubs for spurring the jewelry line, Grossman prefers to incorporate the infiltration stilts into her 3D designs. Just as the foundry has to cut the metal sprues in the lost wax method of casting, so does the 3D service provider have to cut off the infiltrate stilts in the 3D print. The cutting produces a break in the surface texture, which the artist then needs to match by hand.

Hyperwine by Bathsheba Grossman.

Grossman describes the finish on a piece that has not been post-processed as, "So toothy you don't want to even touch them… They are super repulsive." Shapeways and i.materialise do the post-processing on the smaller pieces, and Grossman does her post-processing on her larger pieces of art. Post-processing consists of tumbling the pieces in a ceramic cut-down medium and then also with a stainless steel burnishing medium. Some pieces of art are also hand-buffed and hand-polished.

Grossman is in transition with her software. She has been working in Rhinoceros 3D, combined with some Pearl coding and uses T- Splines with a Rhino plug-in. Rhino has been her chosen software for 15 years, but she has a desire to transition to a mesh modeling software that is more organic, instead of NURBS modeler that models with splines. She uses Magics Materialise to condition meshes for 3D printing, although she suggests Netfabb and MeshLab for those on a budget (www.software. materialise.com/magics, www.netfabb.com, www. meshlab.sourceforge.net). Grossman has storefronts on both the i.materialise and Shapeways websites and sells her lighting and home designs through .mgx as well as on her own website (www.bathsheba.com). You will find these links along with math resources that Grossman shared in the Appendix.

Grossman has had a long relationship with .mgx that sells her lighting designs. *Quin*, MGX by Materialise

Her newest piece *Tetrabox* also contain magnets. The pulling apart and putting together of these designs is meditative.

INFILTRATES Several types of 3D printing processes use infiltrates. An infiltrate is a powder or liquid that a 3D print absorbs. Infiltrates then change the make up of the final product. In the case of 3D printing in metal, the infiltrate is bronze powder. The 3D print has infiltration stilts, similar to the sprues we have seen in other processes; however, these sprues or flutes will absorb the metal and infuse it into the 3D printed piece. The 3D print is fragile and porous when first printed in steel. A 2,000-degree oven heats the 3D print. As the bronze powder melts and turns to liquid, the 3D print absorbs the bronze as it wicks up throughout the infiltration stilts in to the 3D print.

The vendor then gradually cools the art. The gradual cooling anneals and strengthens the piece.

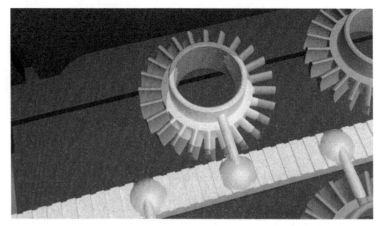

The bronze wicks into the metal. Photograph courtesy of ExOne.

In traditional casting processes at an art foundry, the castings are usually done with one of the two combinations of metals. Everdur Bronze contains 95 percent copper, 4 percent silicone, and 1 percent manganese. Another combination of traditional fine art foundry casting is 85-5-5-5 and consists of 85 percent copper, 5 percent zinc, 5 percent lead, and 5 percent tin. However, the pieces created with a bonding agent or sintered have entirely different metals and properties. The ExOne website does state that artists can weld or solder a 3D printed piece printed with their process.

In traditional sculpture, a foundry creates a patina by putting chemicals on the sculpture. These chemicals interact with the metal. We talk more about this in Chapter 8. As far as patina or the coloring of the metal art, it would take some trial and error for an expert in patina to see if they can match patina on digital prints.

There is a variety of surface finishes available. The metal can be sandblasted, bead-blasted or polished, plated, and have color added with patination. Check back with the service bureaus often as they seem to be adding more finishes all the time.

CERAMICS   3D printing of ceramics is also available from the service bureaus. The 3D printing of ceramics with the service bureaus uses powder fused with an organic binder. Once the part comes off the 3D printer it is like a traditional piece of greenware pottery and very fragile. The service bureau must then fire the piece in a kiln, glaze it, and fire it again. Remember, when creating art using a powder process, printing the powder offers a support structure, and this enables artists to create intricate shapes. If you are creating for this process of ceramic 3D printing, just be sure to provide places for the powder to escape.

This is not the only type of 3D printing of ceramics that is available. Artists and universities all over the world have been exploring many possibilities of 3D printing and ceramics. Many of these individuals are documenting their processes on the Internet; each building upon the success and failure of the next. 3D printing in ceramic offers artists an opportunity to explore the detail and precision of 3D printing while easily incorporating post-processing handwork.

Unfold Design Studio creates intricate designs using a process similar to FDM, but with an extrusion of clay instead of filament. The exploration of 3D printing of ceramics is extremely exciting.

Various single wall ceramic prints created using the G-code Stacker software tool developed in collaboration with Tim Knapen. © Unfold, photograph by Kristof Vrancken.

As in traditional firing of ceramics, there is shrinkage when drying and firing 3D printed ceramic. With the high temperatures used in creating ceramic 3D art, warping can also be a problem. Just as in traditional pottery, glazing can fill in the detail that an artist creates. 3D printed ceramics do not necessarily have to be fired. Solheim Additive Manufacturing Laboratories and others are using all sorts of infiltrates with their 3D printing of ceramics. Infiltrates added to ceramic include waxes, glues, polyurethanes, and epoxies. These products supplement the 3D ceramic powder and give it strength.

Solheim Additive Manufacturing Laboratories (SAML)

Solheim Additive Manufacturing Laboratories, Mechanical Engineering Department at the University of Washington, is one of several universities conducting 3D printing research in ceramics (and the first to publish information on 3D printing glass). They began by taking an old Z Corp Machine that creates 3D prints with inkjet binding. The laboratory forfeited the warranty by using "dirt" (really any one of 50 art ceramic or cement mixtures) as their 3D printing powder. A 2009 *Ceramics Arts Daily* magazine article ("The Printed Pot") printed a workable recipe for the ceramic powder used in SAML's machine. As a matter of fact, if you check out their blog (http://open3dp.e.washington.edu) you will find recipes for 3D printing for such things as printing in glass, salt, bone, and even cookie dough and other materials. Making their ceramic and glass recipes public is just a sample of how Open3DP shares information. They encourage collaboration and open sharing of the experiments and technology that pertains to 3D printing in ceramics and glass, and their website holds a wealth of information.

Center for Fine Printing Research

Stephen Hoskins is working as the director of the Center for Fine Printing Research at the University of West England in Bristol. Through grants, the university is setting out to research how to use 3D printing technology to make advances in 3D printing for artists and craftsmen, and 3D printing of ceramics for industry. They are also working on an ancient Egyptian recipe of self-glazing 3D printing. They are another resource to watch concerning 3D printing of ceramics (http://uwe.ac.uk/sca/research/cfpr/research/3D/index.html).

Jonathan Keep

"As difficult as it is to pull all the technology and computerization together I suggest it is even more difficult to do something creative, fresh and meaningful with this technology."

Although Jonathan Keep considers his homebuilt 3D clay printer primitive by 3D printing standards, he feels it offers an accessible way to a new and creative process of working in clay (Jonathan's work and printer are featured in Chapter 1). Keep was inspired by Unfold-fab and continues with the sharing of information on 3D printing in ceramic (www.keep-art.co.uk/Self_build.html). He uses open source software, developing digital code in the Processing 2 environment (http://processing.org). He edits his models in Blender and creates G-code for printing with Repetier-Host (www.blender.org, www.repetier.com).

This work is about the beauty to be found in apparently random natural form. The algorithm used to generate these forms has a built-in randomness set within natural parameters as with the formation of icebergs (see page 5). The DIY studio based 3D printing technique offers a timeless sense of layering while the porcelain echoes the translucency of ice.

Ceramic Printing by Jonathan Keep.

UNFOLD

In 2010 Unfold celebrated their first successfully printed ceramic vessel. Unfold-fab, a Belgian design studio, decided to be both tinkerer and artist. They took an open source 3D printer called the RepRap and modified it for clay. The RepRap uses fused deposition modeling; however, it has been modified by adding an extruder. The RepRap now extrudes porcelain clay instead of plastic filament. Unfold have documented their entire process on their blog (http://unfoldfab.blogspot.com). The prints are intricate and combine technology and craft perfectly. They display how impossible these pieces would be to make using traditional processes, but are now possible with this marriage of technology and art. Their documentation is also influencing others.

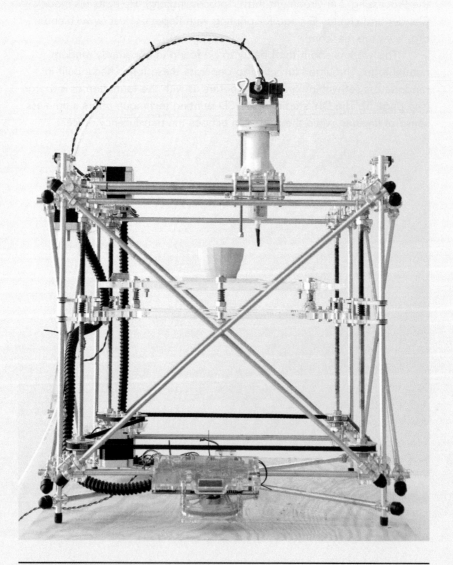

Ceramic 3D printer as seen in the l'Artisan Électronique installation (2010). ©Z33, photo by Kristof Vrancken.

Unfold creates intricate designs using a process similar to FDM, but with an extrusion of clay instead of filament. The exploration of 3D printing of ceramics is extremely exciting.

Experiment with self-intersecting single line printing. ©Unfold, photo by Unfold.

OLIVIER VAN HERPT

Olivier van Herpt wants to push the limits and also wants the limits to push back. He has created his own 3D printer and clay extruder. With this 3D printer van Herpt can 3D print clay objects that are as tall as 80 centimeters and as wide as 42 centimeters. van Herpt not only creates large pieces, but he is also interested in the failures and limitations, and what those look like.

"At the time of my first 3D printed ceramics project there were a lot of random process events occurring naturally. I had to account for these and try to limit them to improve the output. Simultaneously I did realize I was surprised by these events sometimes and there are some failed and collapsed pots that are stunning failures. This made me experiment with a deliberate introduction to random events in the 3D printing process.

We are in a world where machines surround us. In such a world when making a machine one is confronted with the search for perfection and also the coldness of a repeatable manufacturing process. You strive hard for repeatability and good results, but then miss the human element. In a 2D printing scenario the paper output of graphic design is "perfect" but when we move into 3D manufacturing, there are a lot more variables and process constraints. Also, with 3D printing each object can be unique. You don't have to, as in mass manufacturing, have everything looking exactly the same. So, it would be a shame not to use this capability, a shame to have identical things all the time. So, I'm looking to "bake in" the randomness, uniqueness into the process in order to every time get a truly unique piece."

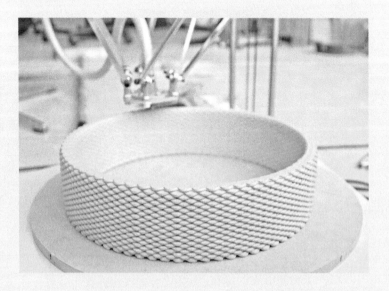

Color

The 3D printing service bureaus offer other materials for 3D printing, including sandstone, and plastics. There are limited options if a 3D full color print is desired—i.materialise offers 3D printing in full color using a binder and powder process of printing. 3D printing companies geared toward commercial and manufacturing have a wider variety of material. At this time, there are only a few methods of 3D printing in color.

3D color printing of sandstone leaves a soft sugary color on the 3D print. This material is fine in certain designs but may detract from others. When printing a picture from your computer on paper with your inkjet printer, the colors can be different than those on the screen—so it is with 3D printing in color. When creating your sculpture in the computer and then translating it to a 3D print, the colors may vary. Shading does not work well with the 3D printing of sandstone, and an artist may find that using solid colors with hard edges is better. As with four-color printing on a press or your inkjet printer, the mixing of cyan, magenta, yellow, and black (CMYK) creates all of the color. Some colors that are a blend of colors, such as brown or those used in flesh tones, are harder to print in 3D. It is important to note that, when printing in color, the color in sandstone does not permeate the entire sculpture but instead is only on the surface. If you are hollowing out your object then wall thickness can affect the saturation of the color applied to the surface. It is advisable to keep wall thickness the same throughout the piece. Also note that, although the 3D printed resolution of your design may be high, the actual resolution of the color on the surface is not that high (see Eric van Straaten's examples on page 217).

Z Corp prints color 3D prints that can be purchased through i.materialise and Shapeways. The process of 3D printing for these full color sandstone/gypsum shapes is with a binder material, but color ink is incorporated in the process. This is an economical material for color, but the Z Corp material is not the strongest. The 3D print does go through post-processing to make it stronger.

Another form of full color printing that is less expensive than traditional printing is Mcor's 3D color printing in paper. (Some people in the

3D printing in color using paper by Mcor Technologies.

industry hesitate to call this 3D printing.) It offers creative possibilities and it will be interesting to see what artists do with this process. In 3D printing in paper, the thickness of the paper determines the thickness of the layers. Glue adheres the paper, attaching each layer to the next. A 3D laser cuts each layer in the shape of the 3D object before applying another layer of paper. What is incredibly spectacular about this process is that the object can be created using full vibrant color. Once again, the artist must keep the printing process in mind when they create using this process. The paper, once cut, must be removed. This makes creating designs with objects inside of objects difficult if not impossible, unless the artwork is first sliced. This technology is available through Mcor machines that print in more than one million colors.

Interior Journey by Assa Ashuach. Image by Assa Ashuach Studio. Ashuach used mixed techniques (NURBS and poly modeling) as platforms for scripting and coding. Color multi-material printing. Printed on an Objet500 Connex3. Photograph courtesy of Stratasys.

Another 3D printing of color that is new to the market as of the writing of this book is Stratasys' new Objet500 3D printer. This printer not only prints in full CMYK, opaque and transparent, but also in a variety of materials—some rigid and others flexible like rubber. The creative possibilities continue to grow with the technology.

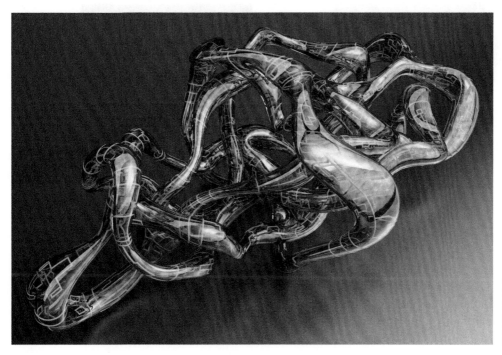

Gnilicer by Nick Ervinck. Created with 3ds Max. Photograph courtesy of Stratasys. Color multi-material 3D printing. Printed on an Objet500 Connex3.

3D PRINTING IN COLOR
BY ERIC VAN STRAATEN

Eric van Straaten 3D prints his piece as fine art. His process consists of using DAZ 3D as template designs, ZBrush to deform the templates, and Magics Materialise to prepare his files. If he needs to change the file format he uses AcuTrans 3D Object Conversion (www.micromouse.ca). He takes the objects into Photoshop to adjust the saturation—it takes some trial and error to get the correct color. He prints his 3D printed art pieces at i.materialise in color on a Z Corp machine (3D Systems purchased Z Corp in 2012). He describes the product as a gypsum product that when printed resembles sugar or marzipan. This is a material that lends itself to the subject of children that is key in van Straaten's work. The strength of the material is comparable to ceramics/baked clay, but a bit flexible because of the glue.

PiezaH by Eric van Straaten, 2014, 100 × 37 × 25 cm.

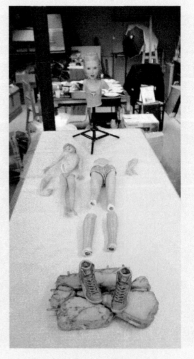

When asking van Straaten for tips on 3D printing in color he states that skin tones are hard to get and black is a problem because it comes out grey. He suggests that when you are using red, use less, and notes that the 3D process of printing is not consistent in the color. The process is all about experimentation. Generally, he says to keep the colors lighter than you think. In the process, the binder changes the color. An artist cannot do much post-processing on the pieces because when you sand the art you may hit the glue and it changes the color. It creates white spots. If you try to paint it, the paint stays on the translucent portion.

He has pushed the build envelope by creating a large print measuring 3 feet 7 inches. He designed it in individual parts and took advantage of the seams of the clothing such as a sock to hide the seams in the leg. The sculpture consists of ten different hollow pieces that he strengthened inside with a two-part component resin and a rod.

Wasp by Eric van Straaten, 2013, 55 × 20 × 20 cm

van Straaten has also set himself up as a middle man between artists and vendors to help them to achieve what they want without having to concern themselves with fixing files for 3D printing. This is a new area of service. He realizes that some artists just want to create but don't want to have to worry about fixing files. To hear more about Eric van Straaten's process concerning 3D printing in color, listen to the *Art and Technology* podcasts.

Permanence?

Let's talk about permanence with art. First let's look at some traditional art examples that are less than permanent.

The intent of some artists when creating their artwork is not permanence. Andrew Goldsworthy balances ice upon ice upon ice, or he strings maple leaves together that float in a stream. The photograph that he takes of the art documents the moment. Descriptions of the art are included with the image. For example, for the artwork *Ice Arch* Goldsworthy comments, "Left to freeze overnight before supporting pile of stone removed. (Made in a field of cows—tense wait.) Pissed on stone too frozen to come out."

Some artwork is a combination of art and performance. Brazilian artist Néle Azevedo created 5,000 figurative miniature ice sculptures for people to place on the steps of Birmingham's Chamberlain Square in August 2014. She created this collaborative art in remembrance of the soldiers and the lives affected by WWI. The action of "melting" infused even more meaning and thought to the art. These are examples of fine art that is temporary or "in the moment."

Many artists are not looking for transience in their work. In fact, having unstable mediums such as the colors that have faded in van Gogh's paintings, is far from desirable. With the deterioration, the paintings no longer depict the true intent of the artists. Manufacturers of paint categorize pigments with their permanence or light fastness. Many artists, collectors, and galleries want to be sure that their investment of time and money will appreciate and not disintegrate.

For those of us using digital technology in fine art and realizing our artwork in a physical form, we must ask, "If I 3D print a piece of fine art, how permanent is the material?" Collectors collect bronzes because they know that it is a proven material. The metallurgy of bronze has changed very little over hundreds of years. But how permanent will a mixture of materials be? How permanent will a powder and binder be over time?

Other Types of Printing

Sweet Idea

The material and printer list grows. If you have a sweet tooth or are into confections, then it might be good to know that people have been printing in sugar for a while. Some hackers have used the MakerBot to print sugar in 3D, but 3D Systems offers ChefJet™, a home printer on the expensive side, advertised at around $10,000, which prints in edible materials. But, as with all aspects of the technology, by the time this book is in print, many other sweet 3D printers will follow, and hackers will push the limits to bring more affordable technology to the average consumer.

3D printed cake stand and cake topper. ChefJet by 3D Systems.

Biology

It appears that it is all about what you can push through a printer. We have seen this as experimenters have pushed such things as sugar, wood pulp, and even dirt through a 3D printer. As science asks the question, "What can be shoved through a 3D printer?", we enter bioprinting and regenerative medicine. Scientists are printing bone, skin, and will eventually move to printing organs. In the future, if you need a kidney, instead of getting a donor kidney from someone and taking anti-rejection drugs the rest of your life, you will simply be wheeled into surgery and a 3D printer will print you a new kidney with your own biomass.

In Chapter 1, we mentioned the combination of hackerspace and science to create a vascular system for living tissue using a RepRap printer. Artists are not the only ones pushing the limits of technology. Photograph from the University of Pennsylvania, printed with permission of Jordan Miller.

Victimless Leather, a prototype of a stitch-less jacket grown in a techno-scientific "body." The Tissue Culture and Art Project (Oron Catts and Ionat Zurr). Medium: biodegradable polymer connective and bone cells. Dimension of original: variable, 2004.

Art and Biomass?

Oron Catts with the Tissue Culture and Art Project (TC&A) uses "living tissue to create/ grow semi-living object/sculptures and to research the technologies involved in such a task." There are several projects at TC&A that are using 3D printing. Oron's art titled *Victimless Leather*, which is skin that is kept alive in a biosphere, feels almost Frankenstein-like. After the exhibition is over, the coat of skin is "killed" by opening the biosphere. *Victimless Leather* does not incorporate 3D printing but does bring attention to how we are removed from what is happening in the lab. As the TC&A

website states, TC&A examines, "the gap between the fast pace of development in science and technology and the slower pace of cultural understanding and adaptation." They are indeed pushing the limits of acceptance both socially and culturally. They hope that the term "semi living object/products and sculptures" will make the art more palatable. "Our art challenges many people to examine their perception of the boundary between the living and the inanimate." With bioprinting comes responsibility. Just because we will one day be able to replace our kidneys, does that mean we have the right to abuse our bodies? Through his art, Catts hopes to bring attention to what is happening in the laboratories. He takes the distance and the impersonal aspect of this science and makes it gut-turningly personal. More about this topic is found on the *Art and Technology* podcasts.

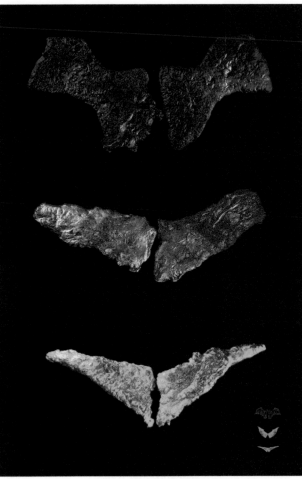

Pig Wings. The Tissue Culture and Art Project. Medium: pig mesenchymal cells (bone marrow stem cells) and biodegradable/bioabsorbable polymers (PGA, P4HB), 4 × 2 × 0.5 cm each, 2000–2001. While critically engaging in the hype surrounding the human genome project, *Pig Wings* became a political science project. TC&A creates art that tends to poke, provoke, and disturb. They bring to light in an artistic way the issues surrounding tissue engineering and what is happening in the lab. *Pig Wings* is grown on a 3D printed scaffolding.

The type of materials being 3D printed grows daily. Scientists print bone, skin, and one day will print human organs from a patient's own biomass. New filaments for 3D printing are being created out of wood, tie-dyed nylon, seaweed, glass, rubber, and many more. Some of these are filaments that an individual can experiment with in their own home printer, other materials are available through local and regional 3D printing companies and service bureaus. The question "what can I shove through a 3D printer?" continues to intrigue the scientists and hobbyist alike. Now that we have looked at what can be printed, let's look closer at how to print.

Getting Your Model Ready for Print

An artist does not create a 3D printed object at the push of a button. There is much more to it, and there is a learning curve in preparing files and using the service bureaus. Leave plenty of room for deadlines when working with these companies. Feeling overwhelmed when considering 3D printing is natural, but this book will help. Many of the service bureaus also have online tutorials to assist in this process, and be sure to check this book's online support documentation and resources. Once you get past these hurdles, then the creative opportunities are vast. Creating something in a virtual world is pretty amazing. Holding your 3D printed artwork in the palm of your hand, artwork that, at one point, was just an image in the computer, is a type of "birthing." How do you get it into the physical world? How do you create it so that it is sturdy? We could feature many more processes and incredible artists who are pushing their limits, but in the remaining portion of this chapter, let's focus on the "how to" of 3D printing.

Steps for 3D Printing—Design

A sculpture or design that comfortably exists in a virtual world, with no gravity or pressure, may not be easily reproduced for the real world. That is why the first consideration of 3D printing must begin with the design. It is important to look at the design of the piece while understanding both the qualities and downfalls of the 3D printed material and the 3D printing process in which you desire to print your art. You must be sure that the design prints well.

A Poor Design

The 3D model of this dodo is a poor design for many 3D printing materials. Its thin legs hold up a large body mass. If the dodo were 3D printed in metal, then the sculpture might stand up on its own. However, some 3D printing processes that print in metal first create a fragile piece before the post-processing strengthens it. Therefore, it might still make it difficult to print. When printing in sandstone, ceramic, or some plastics—that are much weaker materials—breakage will occur or it may not print at all. A good suggestion

is to change the design to incorporate thicker legs. If your design does not have a solid mass and has weak sections to it, then having three points of contact will help distribute the weight. A suggestion would be to add a base to the dodo, and maybe a rock or some foliage that touches or presses against the bird will help. Large masses attached to small pieces create pressure on certain areas of a 3D print. Modifying the design by thickening weight-bearing areas to accommodate that stress or provide support may help. Even so, some 3D printing materials are not suited for some designs. We will say it again; in many 3D sculpting programs, you can create a tremendous amount of detail. It takes a trained eye to know how much of that detail will print in the 3D printing process you choose, and in the material and the size in which you wish to print. Also, a designer will need to modify some designs. For example, in the design of Bridgette Mongeon's monumental tiger, what works as a 15-foot tiger may not work as a 7-inch or smaller 3D print. Depending on the medium, teeth and claws might disappear. It takes experience to realize how much detail is necessary and what will translate into a 3D print at what size.

Stability

If you feel you want to push the limitations, this can cause creative headaches. Fragile pieces in manufacturing mean fragility in shipping. This is where having a good relationship with your service bureau is important. In traditional manufacturing, the artist/designer works closely with the manufacturer reviewing the proposed design. The design must fit the process of manufacturing. The manufacturer, with their years of wisdom, can offer suggestions for changes. These simple changes may not affect the overall design. That is where working with a local company is helpful. The large service bureaus will answer your questions —in time. Solutions will come through many emails or online forums. A small local or regional vendor can offer face-to-face or over the phone service in a timelier manner. Working with the different 3D printing processes, the materials and the vendors will bring experience and a bit of expertise that an artist may not have in the beginning. Over time, an artist develops confidence and becomes familiar with the 3D printing process and the materials. Until then, it is advisable to contact the vendor and forums for their suggestions on such things as design modification and maximum and minimum wall thickness that will best accommodate your design and the material.

We mentioned stability as it pertains to being able to hold up or withstand the mass of other parts, like the dodo. Stability of a design with the intended material is important; however, for those interested in pushing the limits, you might want to check out Make it Stand (http://igl.ethz.ch/projects/make-it-stand). The Interactive Geometry Lab is a research group within the Institute of Visual Computing of ETH Zurich.

They continue to work on code that helps dictate how to make 3D prints stand in challenging poses. For example, is it possible to make a 3D horse stand on one leg?

When trying to figure out all the ins and outs of 3D printing materials and the processes of 3D printing it can, at first, feel overwhelming. The service bureaus have gone to great lengths to offer online tutorials to educate the consumer. For example, if you go to the Shapeways' website, click on "Design," and then on "Materials," you will see some of their materials. The properties of the material are important to any designer. Strength, detail, smoothness, flexibility, glossiness, and transparency are all depicted on the site, in an easy-to-understand visual chart.

On this same website, when you decide on the material, be sure to look at the "Design Guide" for each material. The Design Guide gives designers some clear hard facts about the product and the capabilities. Be sure to scroll down on this page, as the "Design Tips" found under "Design Guide" will help you to perceive what problems you may come up with and how to avoid them. Don't feel like you are sacrificing design to manufacture to the specifications of materials and process. All areas of manufacturing need design modifications from time to time, not just 3D printing. Modifying designs for the least amount of material usage and little or no breakage during shipping is part of good business.

You will also want to note which 3D printing process that the 3D printing company uses for each of the materials in which you want to print. For example, the bronze casting process shown on the Shapeways website is not done with the powder and binder and infiltrate as Bathsheba's work is printed, it is instead printed in wax and then goes through a traditional casting process. The process of printing will play a big role in how you create your art as well as what limits you can push.

Thin Walls

As with fragile connections on a design, support pieces, and sections that protrude, another area to watch is thin walls. If you are printing in ABS and PLA plastic material, some parts may print fine, but some thin areas of plastic may warp during shipping. This means both the shipping to you from your service bureau and from you to your client.

Thickness and Hollowing Out

When you create your work using a 3D sculpting program, there is no thickness. You are working with the surface area of the geometry. As you consider which material to print, you must also give your 3D model thickness. You can, of course, make your artwork solid, but the more material used in a sculpture, the more money you will pay for printing. It may feel a little daunting, at first, to balance the minimum thickness of a sculpture against the necessary requirements for strength and durability while also considering the material properties and warping. The savings in material when hollowing out a sculpture can be substantial—sometimes you can save up to 80 percent of the cost. Once you have chosen a service bureau, note their minimum thickness requirement for the material for which you wish to print.

Besides accommodating and making a hollow object, there are cases where escape holes will be needed. Once again, depending on the 3D printing process, excess material will need to escape. These holes will give the material a place to exit the design. Selective laser sintering, stereolithography, and powder fused with a binder will need holes for the liquid or powder to escape in post-processing. It is often best to have more than one hole in case one hole gets clogged during post-processing. A minimum of 4 mm diameters is good for one hole. Another option is to create a plug in an area where the material can escape; you can then attach the plug after post-processing.

The tiger, upon a rock, has a lot of weight. Printed with selective laser sintering the material in the belly will need to escape. The only place this can happen, without a plug, is through the legs or possibly the ears. Now the question is, at 7 inches, can holes fit in the center of the legs and will these allow material to escape in post-processing? Will this make the legs considerably weaker when someone lifts the entire sculpture while holding only the tiger? It is also interesting to note, if the sculpture is to go smaller, how much smaller can the design be to accommodate the minimum amount of hole thickness needed for the material to escape from the stomach? Also, if the artist wishes to create the tiger in other processes, how do escape holes differ in size between materials and processes? The artist may also find that, as she reduces the tiger's size, she will need to make it a solid object.

All of these considerations and hollowing out are done as an artist prepares the file for print. An artist can do many of

3D print of Bridgette Mongeon's tiger printed by 3D Rapid Prototyping, http://3drp.com. Photograph by Christina Sizemore.

these processes themselves with free software such as MeshLab, Netfabb, and MeshMixer. If you do not want to do this step, contact a 3D printing product design liaison to prepare your files for printing. Bridgette Mongeon contacted Dotsan (www.dotsan.com). Dotsan recorded the many steps of preparing Mongeon's tiger file. Communication is the key with any company. Files are easy to transport; it does not matter if your service bureau liaison is in another state or another country, although you should always take precautions to protect your intellectual copyrights. Visit the book's accompanying website for full tutorials on these processes and a list of design liaisons.

File Size

The more detail that you have, the larger the file. You should check with your service provider to see the maximum file size they allow. For example, Sculpteo has a maximum size of 50 MB, Shapeways 64 MB or 1,000,000 polygons, and i.materialise 100 MB. Remember the larger the file, the longer it will take to upload.

How do you change the file size, if your file is too big, without sacrificing the detail or quality of the design? You will need to decimate the file. Decimation reduces the polygons without sacrificing detail.

Many of the graphics programs offer a decimation tool, but if you don't have one, MeshLab will decimate the file for you. However, be careful. If you decimate the file and then try to decimate it again, MeshLab may crash. So, save your incremental files.

The original tiger created in ZBrush is 560 MB and 16,500 faces. The file was first decimated and sized using MeshLab. Then Mongeon's tiger is imported by Dotsan into Netfabb Cloud. Netfabb reviews several of the possible errors, such as reversed or missing normals, and fixes them providing a watertight shell.

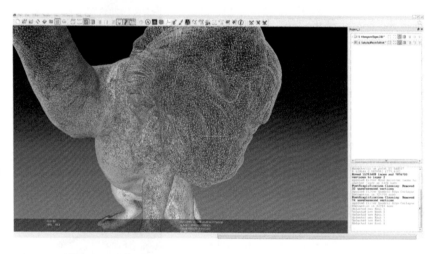

Hollowing Out the Sculpture

It would be nice if there were a free 3D printing program, for which you could upload your sculpture file, press a button, and watch the magic of hollowing out a sculpture. It would be a bonus if the program were sensitive enough to tell you where the problems of the design might occur. As of the printing of this book, the technology does not offer one single, free, computer program that does these things at the push of a button. Some computer graphics or sculpting programs can help you to hollow out your model. As with many other areas of this book and this technology, what is available changes often. For complete tutorials on hollowing out models using other software programs for 3D printing please visit the book's accompanying website.

At this time, the service bureaus do not provide hollowing out of the model. Dealing with a local supplier or regional 3D printing company may offer you more service in this area. Of course, their time is money. They may charge you a fee for hollowing out your design. If you are 3D printing more than one copy of the design, then it will be worth it for you to have a hollow model for further prints. Even if it is just one print, the cost of paying a technician to hollow out a design as compared to the extra cost in the material is worth exploring. If you do it yourself and end up having to print a few to "master" the process, then you would be better off having paid someone else. Service bureaus may not offer all the personal interaction needed to relieve the stress of preparing files. It would be nice if they could remedy the fears of those artists who just want to create and don't want to learn software to prepare their files. Vendors do need to step up to the plate. Software companies need to find a solution to making this process of preparing files easier. 3D printing liaisons who fix files and offer suggestions to artists for modifications may soon be a booming intermediary business. Of course, the person running such a business would need to be dependable, and also be willing to respect the intellectual property rights of their clientele.

Back into MeshLab, Dotsan creates a duplicate layer and once again decimates that layer. This second layer is an offset to create an internal wall. Photographs by Vijay Paul from Dotsan.

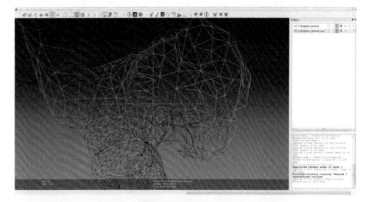

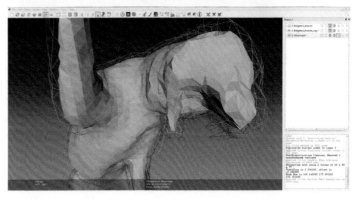

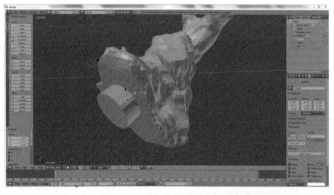

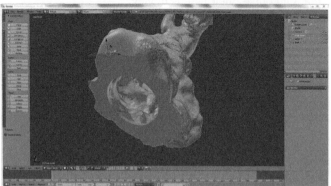

The cost for printing Mongeon's 7-inch high tiger as a solid sculpture at a smaller local company was $468 solid and $370 hollow. Machine time, set up, and material is what determines the cost of the print. The less material you use, the less you will pay for your 3D print. Uploading the same file to Shapeways, the cost states it is $89.44, which is considerably less. There are advantages to going with the larger service bureaus. A professional has prepared the tiger files, but there is no telling if it will take multiple prints from the larger service bureaus to get the print correct. They may get it correct on the first try. Other than pressing a button to send your file, there is little interaction with a larger service bureau as compared to the smaller local companies. It may take several prints and many weeks at a large service bureau. An artist must consider all of these things when considering the appropriate vendor for their work.

The leg is now hollow. The hollow legs give a place for material to escape from the torso of the tiger. Photograph by Vijay Paul from Dotsan.

File Format

To print something in 3D, you will need to have a file with the proper supported file format. As we have seen in our previous chapters, you can make a 3D file in many ways. Your design software may have its own proprietary format for saving files. The program may also give you the option to export the file in different formats. A standard file format for creating 3D printed pieces is STL (stereolithography). However, many of the 3D printing service bureaus will accept other files, as well. It is best to contact your 3D printing service to see what file you need. Here again, the file type may depend on the 3D printing machine. If you are using FDM, SLS, or SLA, the file type may be different. The material can play a role in the file that you will need, as well. If you are printing in full color, then an STL file is not a file format you want because this file does not save the color information. You will have to use a VRML, PLY, 3DS, or ZPR. You may also be able to send the service bureau a couple of files together. For example, send an OBJ file that will give the machine the shape of the 3D model. Along with that file, include a materials (mtl) and a texture file, to indicate color. Some companies may charge extra for applying the material and texture to your file. Communication with your 3D printing company will help to understand these factors. Printing in color is another beast to tame. There are many tutorials on the service bureau websites to walk you through the process and additional support material and videos on this book's accompanying website. If you need to convert your working file to an acceptable file format and your software program does not allow you to export it in another way, MeshLab will convert files.

Physical Size

The build envelope or the maximum physical size that the 3D printer can print is different for each machine and process. For example, Sculpteo reports their maximum build envelopes are: for white plastic, 26.7 × 14.5 × 22 inches; for alumide, 12.2 × 12.2 × 23.6 inches; and for sterling silver, 2.3 × 3.15 × 3.15 inches.

Of course, the larger the build envelope, the larger the file size. If it is a very detailed model or sculpture, the artist will have to weigh this against the maximum poly count allowed by the vendor.

There may be problems with the geometry in your model or, as mentioned before, parts of the design may be too thin or protrude. Some of the service bureaus will fix your files for you. For example, Mesh Medic provided by Netfabb analyzes your files and, according to the Netfabb website, it fixes 95 percent of the files that come through Shapeways. There is also a free version of Netfabb. Sculpteo and i.materialise both state that their websites will fix some files. However, they don't fix all files. Adobe Photoshop CC offers a 3D printing add-on to their Photoshop program.

Photoshop designed this program to take the guessing out of preparing files for print. It is not a free program, and monthly membership is $49.99. You can also purchase a single app for $19.99.

If you own a 3D printer, a software program may have come with the purchase, making file preparation easier. The accompanying 3D printer software is something worth looking into when purchasing a 3D printer. Keep a watch on the technology. It won't be long before a software company offers free or affordable software for consumers that integrates well with the service bureaus and printers.

Even though you might be able to fix some of your problems through the service bureau websites it is good to know some of the potential problems found in files, so that you can avoid them. If a service bureau puts your file through a check, it may send you an error message. You will have to fix that error and resubmit. It may then send you a different error message. It is a process. If you do not want to fix files, you can hire an intermediary company to do this as Mongeon did with the tiger.

Watch for These Errors

Watertight and Non-manifold Edges

A watertight file is one that has no holes (see Chapter 1). A 3D model might look solid as you are working on it in the computer, but non-manifold edges or places where the geometry does not come together can play havoc when 3D printing. Non-manifold errors indicate that the model may have additional faces or edges that may go undetected. There may also be overlapping vertices.

Extruded Planes

Everything in your design must have a thickness. For example, a flat plane will not print until it has a thickness. Extrude the plane to at least the minimum amount of thickness needed for your material.

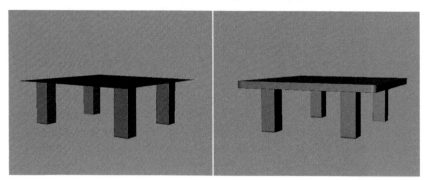

Remove Unnecessary Geometry

Another obstacle in the printing is unnecessary geometry that may go unnoticed while it is in your computer, but makes the 3D print impossible or difficult to print, and of course, more geometry means more cost.

No Reversed Normals

A normal is a vector perpendicular to the surface of a polygon. A reversed normal in 3D printing means that the normal points inside the model.

More Exploration

Postproduction or Post-processing

Postproduction/processing is the work done on the sculpture after the 3D printing has taken place. These steps are as vast as the materials and 3D printing processes. Those 3D prints using selective laser sintering will have to have the powder removed from the piece. Post-processing may also consist of firing or curing the 3D print. To be able to handle and prevent breakage, some materials require a postproduction process of the 3D print. Many of the postproduction processes happen before the artist even receives the 3D printed piece from the service bureau. However, many artists are experimenting with their own post-processing. The book's accompanying website has tutorials on post-processing and the experiments of other artists.

Articulation of a Model

It is possible to create articulation or movement of the 3D printed model. For example, you can create joints that will print together. The joints will never need assembly, and they will move after printing. Articulation is a bit tricky. When creating articulated 3D designs, be sure to leave a 0.5 mm gap. For further hints on creating articulated 3D prints, visit the book's accompanying website.

———————————

Before we finish out this book, there are just a few more things to discuss. We have learned so much, and seen examples of how 3D technology is changing the way some people create and offering them many more opportunities and ways to create than they ever had before. Now let's look at one more change. The bronze casting process has changed very little over hundreds of years, until now. In Chapter 8, we will see how some of these processes are affecting the way some artists make fine art—processes that may just introduce us to the foundry of the future.

JOSHUA HARKER

Many of the pioneers or those working in the 3D industry are doing so because they had access to 3D printing machines as they worked in universities or in industry. Joshua Harker was one of those. Harker entered 3D technology by first creating action figures. The 3D printing machines created the prototypes. Harker felt stifled by the traditional methods of creating, feeling that no process could express what he was after—until he found 3D printing. Voxeljet 3D printed his intricate designs with a material that would burn out with no ash content. As is the case with many in the field of 3D printing, Harker had to wait for the technology, costs, and resolution to come to a point where he could use the technology in his studio.

Harker finds a satisfaction in 3D technology. It allows him to finally create designs that he has wanted to create, but was unable to until this technology evolved.

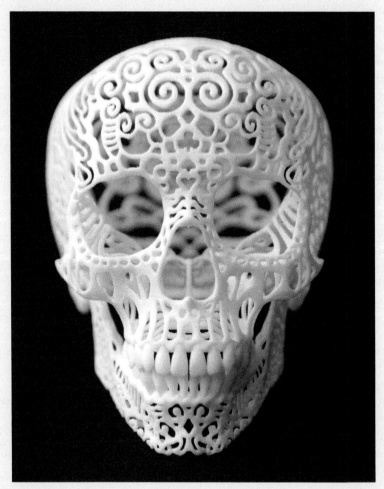

Joshua Harker facilitated a very successful kickstarter campaign back in 2011 to create his *Crania Anatomica Filigre*.

The author interviewed Harker for an *Art and Technology* podcast. There she inquired about his secrets of 3D printing pieces that articulate. Harker states:

> *"As much as anything, it is experience, working in product development and toys, working on the mechanics of things… gears, clothes… When you are designing it, mechanical engineering and physics apply, and as you scale things up, things change as well. Intuition is a bit of it… form follows function. Mechanical things have to happen; you work back and forth between the aesthetics and the functionality."*

Permutation Prime by Joshua Harker.

Harker uses Blender, ZBrush, and Solid Works, but in the beginning he used many more types of software just to be able to get his work to the printers, which he described as tedious and frustrating. His vendor list consists of Paradigm development group (www.pardev.com), Voxeljet (www.voxeljet.de/en), and eos (www.eos.info/en). He also uses Shapeways, Sculpteo, and Ponoko.

Harker likes articulation, as is apparent in his sculpture *Anatomica di Revolutis*.

CHRISTIAN LAVIGNE

A pioneer in 3D, Lavigne has been working in 3D technology since 1981. His work experimented with both virtual and physical art as well as a variety of tools including water jet cutting, machining, electronic installations, laser cutting, laser engraving, and more. He is also the cofounder of ARS Mathématica (www.arsmathematica.org).

L'Age Du Fer by Christian Lavigne, France 1999–2010. Created with a Minolta 3D scanner, CAD and SLS metal by GM PROD.

EYAL GEVER

Eyal Gever has spent 18 years developing 3D technologies. His art is about freezing time and creating an emotional situation. Gever has an extensive knowledge of art and technology that he uses to develop computer simulations of extreme events. He 3D prints some pinnacle moments from his simulations and transforms them into cutting-edge physical sculptures.

Gever works with math, physics, animation, code, and modeling to create simulated physics as art.

> "We will see a lot more artists who will be breaking down the boundaries of art and looking outside of traditional art to incorporate other aspects into their work. Less about the static work and more time-based, live experiences. The genres will be getting blurred and new vocabulary within the art world of how we define different media will be developed."

Waterfall Gallery Room.
Render/printed on Object
200 vera by Eyal Gever.
© 2011/14,
www.eyalgever.com.

LIA

Lia has gone on a deep exploration of FDM 3D printing and its filament. She did not want to just print things to print them she wanted to know "what can be achieved with the actual properties of filament and the movements of the print head." She discovered that, "surfaces can be continuous or chaotic; lines can be rigid or organic, and filament can be closely controlled or let free to find its own form."

The speed and movement of the extrusion, as well as the location of the print head, are all a part of her process. She achieves this by writing her own code and documents the entire process on her blog where she features the fluid pieces of filament that seem to dance (www.liaworks.com).

> "I actually quite like the fact, that small errors become bigger and bigger with each layer."

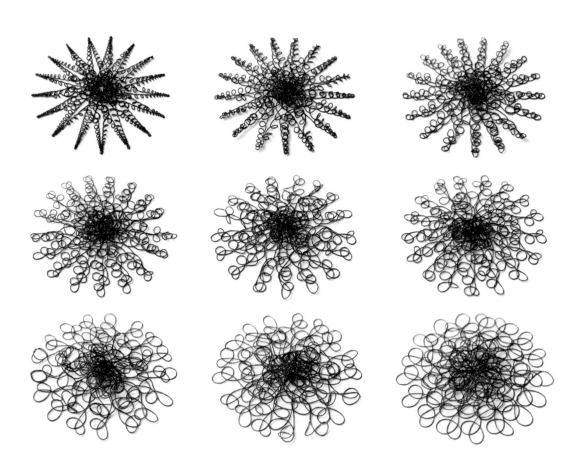

JORIS LAARMAN LAB

The project team at Joris Laarman Lab developed the MX3D-metal
3D printer. The MX3D is part robot and part welding machine. It allows
the design team, with the help of Acotech, HAL robotic programming
and control, to 3D print metal without the need for support structures.
They can print with metals, such as steel, stainless steel, aluminum,
bronze, or copper. By adding small amounts of molten metal at a time,
they print lines of metal in mid air. The sculpture *Dragon Bench* was
one of the first objects created with the MX3. Once again, the software
company Autodesk steps in with support for the project. Working with
Joris Laarman Lab is allowing Autodesk to explore the limits of its digital
design tools. They are working together to create the new tools necessary
to achieve Laarman's creative vision.

"Autodesk is particularly interested in collaborating with artists
because they are focused on realizing their creative visions, as
opposed to a more traditional engineering approach, which is to
solve problems within a given context with the tools available.

These new digital manufacturing techniques are having a profound
effect on creativity, for two reasons: First, they disassociate handcraft
from the creative vision. A designer or artist no longer needs the
skills to make what they imagine, because that intelligence and
skill is built into the automated system. Second, the artist/designer
is able to instantiate ideas that previously simply could not be
manufactured. With additive and robotic processes we can achieve
forms that are otherwise impossible to fabricate."

Maurice Conti,
director of strategic innovation,
Autodesk

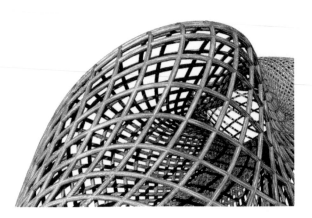

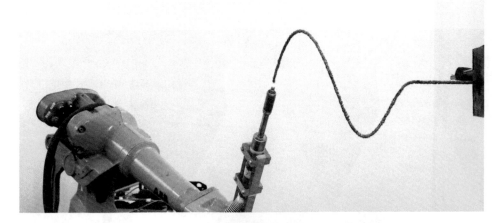

NERVOUS SYSTEM STUDIO

Nervous System Studio create their designs using computer simulations.
They write computer programs that mimic nature and patterns in nature
to create their incredible art, jewelry, and housewares.

The website of Nervous System offers a variety of ways for visitors to
be a part of the design process. They offer their work as interactive web
applications (programs that take visitors' input and react to them visually).
Visitors can design their own jewelry and art objects using the Kinematics,
Cell Cycle, Radiolaria and Dendrite software at http://n-e-r-v-o-u-s.com/
tools.

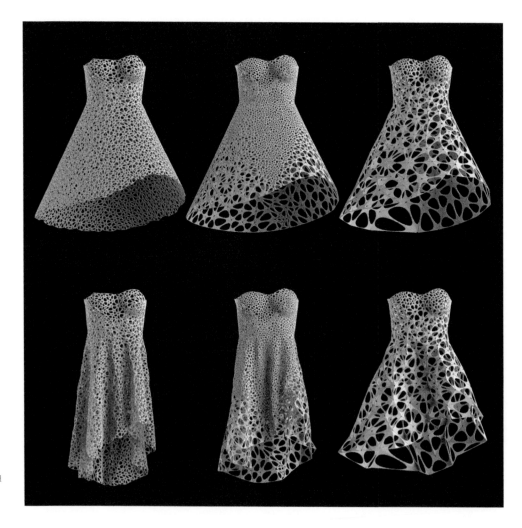

*Kinematics Concept
Dress—Variations* by
Jessica Rosenkrantz and
Jesse Louis-Rosenberg,
Nervous System.

Hyphae Lamps by Jessica Rosenkrantz and Jesse Louis-Rosenberg, Nervous System.

On the book's website at www.digitalsculpting.net you will find:

* Links to further descriptions on the process of creating the artwork featured in the galleries.
* Podcasts with the artists.
* Videos featuring the artists at work.

Colony 3D prints. Meshes generated by processing. 3D-printed by Shapeways by Jessica Rosenkrantz and Jesse Louis-Rosenberg, Nervous System.

CHAPTER EIGHT

THE FOUNDRY OF THE FUTURE?

———

"Digital tools incorporated in my process save me time and money. These digital tools also relieve me from the monumental tasks that are the least creative—armature building. In the long run, this gives me more time to create. When it comes to bronze—one day the build size, cost, and resolution of 3D technology will catch up to a fine artist's needs. I don't expect that will be too far in the future."

Sculptor **Bridgette Mongeon**

facing page
Grambling Tiger, mascot by Bridgette Mongeon.

Bronze casting has been in existence for thousands of years. In that time, the process of casting a bronze has changed very little. We have already seen the possibilities of creating in metal through 3D printing. However, with 3D printing of metal, the build envelope or size, the cost, and the resolution at this time leave larger sculptures or even monumental sculptures impossible to create at an affordable cost. However, new 3D technology strives to infiltrate the bronze casting process and is doing so in a variety of different ways and stages. Let's walk through the traditional process of bronze casting and see how the new technology is influencing the processes. These influences may change the way we make fine art bronzes in the future.

Limited Editions

When an artist decides a sculpture is a limited edition, they reserve the right to pour a designated number of bronze copies of that same sculpture. Collectors often seek out numbered limited editions. Because the artist may have a mold for a long time, and the mold may deteriorate, many collectors feel that the lower the number in the bronze edition, the more detail it will retain and the more valuable the sculpture. Artists reserve rights to pour multiples, up to a certain number, and will label the artwork indicating the number in the edition during the casting process. At times, the sculptor may mark the art with "AP." An AP means that the foundry poured this bronze first in the edition, and it is an Artist Proof.

If the artist or foundry places a mark of 1/20 on a bronze, it means that the individual bronze is the first copy in an edition of 20. There may be one original of the artwork, one mold of the artwork, but there will be 20 waxes made from the mold in the lost wax method of bronze casting. The foundry makes one wax for each number in the bronze edition. They are not made at the same time. The artist will have the waxes poured from the molds as needed. That means a seasoned sculptor may have a large repository of molds. When they sell out the edition, they destroy the mold. Of course, some editions sell out fast, others may take the artist's lifetime or even the lifetime of their heirs before the artist or their heirs sell out the edition and destroy the mold. Rubber does deteriorate over time. That is why early numbers, as well as smaller numbered editions, are more desirable to fine art collectors. Art collectors believe that a sculpture that has an earlier mark of perhaps 10/100 (ten of an edition of 100) will hold the original detail and intent of the art, as compared to 80/100 (80 in the edition of 100). The artist and their foundry use the mold made of the original art prepared for the lost wax method of bronze casting to reproduce multiple pieces. They do this for either the life of the mold or the amount in a limited edition. Because the artist has accrued a great deal of time and expense when creating the first piece of art, producing multiples is where the artist and their heirs can see additional rewards of their labor—financially.

The process of bronze casting is thousands of years old and has changed little, until now.

Traditional Casting in Bronze— Investment and Sand Casting

There are two types of bronze casting. Each bronze casting process will require several steps. When we are talking about the casting process, it is important to think in both a positive and negative. The positive refers to the art, or something that looks like the art. The negative is usually the mold, the reverse image of the art or a mold that is used to create the positive. "Positive" and "negative" will become clearer with the examples in this chapter.

The first type of bronze casting is sand casting. Sand casting uses a temporary mold—the negative. Once the foundry uses this mold they cannot use it again. The foundry will need to make another sand mold for additional bronzes. Another process of bronze casting and the most-used process is the lost wax method of bronze casting, or investment casting. In the lost wax method of bronze casting, the foundry requires a rubber mold or plaster mold (negative) to create a wax (positive). There are many steps to the lost wax method of bronze casting and many ways that 3D technology is influencing this age-old process, but first let's look at the influences on sand casting.

When talking about casting we refer to the negative and the positive. In this lost wax example, the sculpture is a positive image, a mold is the negative of the sculpture and a wax created from this mold is another positive.

Sand Casting

A foundry may choose to use the process of sand casting for an object that does not contain undercuts. A low relief medallion or machine parts can easily be sand cast. In sand casting, the foundry uses a flask or box to hold the sand.

They place the object in the flask and cover it with a fine release powder and sand.

It is important to tamp and vibrate the sand firmly into the drag of the flask.

They then flip the flask over and sprinkle separating powder over the top of the part.

The foundry adds a pouring channel so that they can pour the molten bronze into the flask. Then, the foundry continues to add the second part of the flask, the cope. They pack the sand into the cope.

At this point, the part is now captured within the two halves of the sand casting flask. Before they can pour metal, they separate the flask, and the part is carefully removed, leaving the top and the bottom impression of the part.

Once the foundry secures the flask together again, they heat the metal and pour it into the pouring cup or pour channel of the flask. Once cast, they simply break away the sand from the metal.

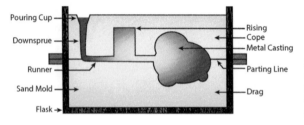

In sand casting, the foundry presses and vibrates molding sand around the art. The art is in a multi-part box called the casting flask. The art is removed and the bronze is poured into the cavity of pressed sand.

The process of sand casting is inexpensive and takes less material and time than the lost wax method of bronze casting. It is primarily used on simple pieces of art with no undercuts and where the artist only needs one part.

In several instances, the new 3D technology is borrowing from the old processes of sand casting and pushing the limits of possibility. In Chapter 7, we learned a great deal about printing objects in different materials. We have seen the detail and intricacy that is available with many types of 3D printing. Now, let's think a little differently, let's think about 3D printing the negative, the mold of an object. In this process, the CAD (computer-aided design) file will print not the positive (the art), but the negative (the mold section). That is exactly what Martin Dirker did in his experiment. Dirker wanted to push the limits of the 3D technology to see if it were possible to create a piece of art with many undercuts, something that could not be

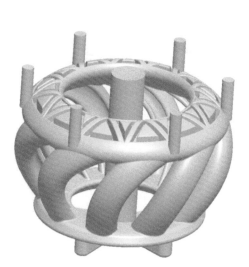

Dirker's *Aztec* 3D model depicts the difficulty of the cast. The pouring sprues and gates were a part of the digital design and were later cut off of the sculpture, just as they would be in traditional bronze casting.

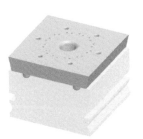

Dirker prints the 3D molds in sections with sprues, gates, and vents incorporated in the design.

sand cast traditionally. He desired to create a mold using a 3D printer that prints sand. The undercuts and intricate design of Dirker's *Aztec* art would be a challenge for any foundry working with a lost wax method and impossible with sand casting. Dirker creates the mold in the computer and even includes the sprues or gates, a pour cup, and vents all with the final production of the pouring in mind. He creates his designs using Wildfire CAD from PTC.com. Then Dirker 3D prints the mold using the services of Hoosier Pattern Inc. on an S-Max made by ExOne. The S-Max prints the sand mold set and leaves the void of the art where the metal foundry pours the metal. The total time to 3D print the mold set is one day. The sand mold is then sandblasted away from the metal after pouring.

Once again, the build envelope or size limitations of this 3D printing process are strong considerations. The size of the next example of 3D printing compared to the traditional process may just surprise you.

Another example of 3D printing and sand is Peter Donders' *Batoidea or Stingray* aluminum chair created with Voxeljet. Donders created the chair in the software Rhino 3D. The sculpture *Stingray* required five 3D printed mold parts all 3D printed to fit together perfectly as designed in the computer. The largest sand part was 1,105 × 713 × 382 mm (approximately 3 feet 7 inches × 2 feet 4 inches × 1 foot 3 inches). This was easily achieved with the Voxeljet machines that have a build size of 4,000 × 2,000 × 1,000 mm.

Voxeljet creates and 3D prints using methods pulled from sand casting. They 3D print the negative or mold for Peter Donders' chair titled *Batoidea* or *Stingray*.

Lost Wax Method of Bronze Casting or Investment Casting

We have taken a look at sand casting, and how the digital processes are beginning to influence this type of bronze casting. Let's now take a look at the traditional process of investment casting or the lost wax method of bronze casting and compare how 3D technology is influencing these ancient processes. There are many steps involved in the lost wax method of bronze casting. We will examine each as we travel through the foundry with the *Grambling Tiger* created by Bridgette Mongeon from Chapter 6. The first step in this long process is mold-making.

Mold-making

If a sculpture has many intricate pieces with many undercuts, and an artist wants to create it in bronze, then they will use the lost wax method or the investment process of bronze casting. When an artist completes a job, whether small, life-size, or monumental, they send the art to the foundry to begin the process of bronze casting, or they do the first stage of the foundry process themselves, the mold-making. This mold-making process has a few steps. In the first step, the artist divides up the sculpture. They then seam up the sculpture to prepare it for rubber. The rubber process consists of coating the sculpture with mold release, painting rubber, and making a mother mold. Perhaps examples of this process will help to make it clearer. Let's go back to the tiger.

DIVIDING THE SCULPTURE With the first part of the mold-making process, the artist or the foundry determines how to divide up the sculpture. They must create pieces that are manageable and that can pour properly. If the sculpture is a life-size or monumental sculpture, they divide up the sculpture using whatever cutting device will work, such as knives or even reciprocating saws. It does seem a shame to have to destroy the work of art to make it into bronze. But this is all a part of the process. When dividing up the sculpture, they are cutting through not just clay, but also the armature. As we have already learned, armatures may consist of a variety of materials such as rebar, chicken wire, foam, plumbing pipe, or other products that will support the clay as the artist works. If the artist has used the CNC milling process to create their

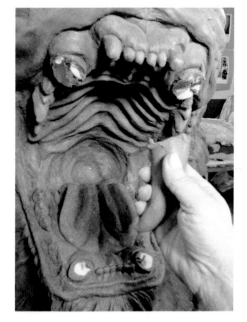

The artist separates the tiger into many pieces. The individual pieces may be both large and small. The artist determines where to cut the sculpture by what they need to obtain a good mold and what will facilitate the bronze casting process. Here the artist removes the tiger's fangs to create a separate mold.

armature, then cutting apart and even moving a sculpture to a foundry is a lot easier. Sculptures created using armatures made of CNC foam are much lighter to handle and easier to slice.

On large sections, the mold maker divides up the mold by creating seams. They can section off the sculpture by either using shims or claying-up the seams. With shims, the mold-maker paints rubber over the shims. This allows them to make both sides of the mold at one time. The mold-maker can also clay up a seam using clay, but this takes a bit more time as they can prepare and paint rubber over only one side at a time. When claying-up one side, the mold-maker paints rubber and then, after making the mother mold, the mold-maker removes the clay wall and repeats the process on the other side.

The artist creates seams by claying-up or using shims. The mold-maker uses playing cards that are taped up and stuck into the clay. These edges create the shims on the tiger's torso.

There are more than 30 mold pieces to the tiger, and each of these pieces has multiple sections or seams. After the artist divides up the sculpture, she prepares each section. She sprays a releasing agent on the clay surface, so the rubber will peel off later, and then paints or pours several layers of rubber over the artwork and seams to reach the correct thickness. The rubber must be flexible enough to allow the wax to release, but strong enough to take the wear and tear of pouring multiple waxes for each number in the edition.

Once the artist makes the rubber mold, it is necessary to contain that rubber mold in something. If it is not contained, the rubber will lose its shape when it is taken off the sculpture. The artist makes a "mother mold" from fiberglass or plaster.

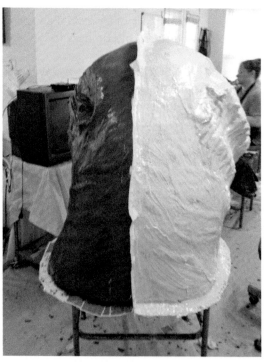

The artist paints multiple layers of rubber over each section of the tiger.

She covers the entire rubber area. She may section the mother mold further so that it can release from the art. The mother mold holds the rubber in place during the next part of the process when the foundry pours or paints in the wax. Once the artist creates the mother mold over the rubber she takes off both the mother mold and rubber from the original art. The pieces are then cleaned and prepared for the next step—the wax. The process of mold making does destroy the original, though the artist may be able to salvage the clay for the next job.

The mold-making process is time-consuming and costly. Usually the mold costs about half to two-thirds the cost of casting the art. For example, if a sculpture costs $7,000 to cast at a bronze foundry, it is safe to estimate the mold will be an additional $5,000–$6,000, and can take a considerable amount of time to create. The mold for the tiger took a team of seven people approximately five weeks to complete.

Mother molds made from plaster or fiberglass resin hold the rubber in place.

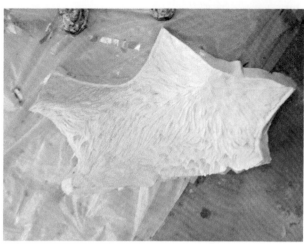

The clean molds hold the detail of the original art and are ready for the next step—the wax.

The Influences of the Digital Processes

Individuals who work in 3D technology continuously develop new materials. It is only a matter of time before we may begin to see the possibility of rubber molds for investment casting printed from a 3D printer. However, digital technology is already entering the next step of the traditional process of investment casting, the creating of the wax. In fact, there are several types of digital technology that are making their way into the bronze process from this step forward. That means that any 3D process that we talk about from here forward, if used, can do away with all of the steps that we have already discussed in the traditional investment process of casting. It may even do away with the physical sculpting if it can be created in the computer. However, we still need to look at the big three criteria—build size, resolution, and cost. A new technology that can provide a large build size, with good detail—including the artist's desired texture and undercuts, and do so at low or comparable cost to the traditional process of bronze casting will become a viable part of the process in the foundry of the future. These processes will be practical and important alternatives in future bronze casting and will eliminate the laborious step of mold making altogether.

We have already seen how the process of 3D printing of sand casting is outshining the traditional sand casting method, although even that process must measure up to the big three criteria. The 3D sand printing must be comparable in build size, have good detail, and comparable cost before it will be a true alternative to traditional sand casting. Let's take a look at the rest of the process of investment casting—the wax, shell, and burnout.

The Wax, Shell, and Burnout

When you look at a life-size bronze sculpture figure on the street or in a museum, they are not solid bronze. The bronze is only a shell of bronze. The next step of the foundry process, the wax pour, determines the thickness of this bronze shell.

In each of the rubber molds, tucked securely and held in position by their mother mold, the foundry will either pour or paint several coats of foundry wax. The wax, when it reaches the appropriate thickness, is a replica (positive) of the original sculpture. The thickness of the wax varies with each piece, with a minimum thickness of 1/8 of an inch.

The foundry paints layers of wax in each shell to create a wax positive of the original art. Photograph courtesy of Shidoni Foundry, NM.

Once the waxes are cool, the wax worker cleans and chases them. They work on cleaning up the many parting lines from the mold and other imperfections that are in the wax. The foundry men and women work tirelessly to make the art perfect, while still retaining the integrity of the artist's work. The artist may even work the waxes to create even more detail. The foundry process of working in wax is just one more area of the traditional process that is hands-on. It can influence how each bronze sculpture in the edition is different from the next. If you remember the Remington bronzes mentioned in Chapter 2, you can now begin to see why each of the pieces in the Remington edition might not look exactly alike; so many hands had to touch and work the waxes to get to the finished bronze. In each step there are nuances of the process and the hands of each foundry worker that works on them affecting the look of each piece. Each set of hands leaves their mark on the art. At this point, in the foundry process of the tiger, whatever is in the wax will show up in metal.

Once the wax worker cleans the wax, it is then sprued or gated up. They place wax gates or rods strategically on the wax positive. Gates are a series of tubes or branches that allow gases to escape and provide a smooth pour. The wax worker also adds wax sprue cups. The cups will give a channel for the wax to exit and a place for the foundry to pour the metal. We will see this in the future steps, but before this can happen, each of the molds must once again enter a new stage of the foundry process—creating the ceramic shell.

As we have already seen in Chapter 7, jewelers have been using the 3D technology to their advantage by having their designs 3D printed in wax for casting. These wax castings hold an incredible amount of detail. Once again, if the build envelope or size of 3D prints can increase, and do so without costing more than the traditional process of bronze casting, it is feasible that 3D printing in wax will be a very viable resource, and probably the best, for eliminating the step of a rubber mold altogether.

The foundry adds sprue cups and gates to the waxes to help the metal to flow into the investment casting and for the gases to escape. Photograph courtesy of Shidoni Foundry, NM.

Some artists create their original sculpture in foundry wax. When providing this to the foundry, unless the foundry makes a rubber mold from the provided wax it is then just a one-up process. The foundry will gate up the wax, adding sprue cups just as in the tiger sculpture. The foundry will burnout the provided wax. When an artist creates a sculpture this way, they can only make one bronze from one wax. Without a mold, they cannot make multiple pieces.

The foundry creates a ceramic shell by dipping each wax into slurry and then covering the sculpture with fine sand. Photographs courtesy of Shidoni Foundry, NM.

The Shell

In this part of the process, the foundry creates another mold of each piece. This time they make a mold from the wax. They call this the investment or ceramic shell, though it is not made out of ceramic. The foundry first dips the wax pieces into a silica slurry and then covers it in sand or dry silica. The foundry repeats the dipping and covering process until they have covered the entire wax with the appropriate amount of shell. Shidoni Foundry in New Mexico transfers the pieces on pulleys throughout the dip room. The pulley system allows them to work on very large sections.

The burnout removes the wax, leaving a cavity in which the foundry will pour bronze. Photograph courtesy of Shidoni Foundry, NM.

In the traditional process of bronze casting, the foundry puts the ceramic shells into the burnout oven, upside down, and heats them up very slowly to prevent cracking of the shells. The foundry captures the melted wax for recycling. They lose the wax in the casting. This is why the process is often referred to as "the lost wax method of bronze casting." The cavity that once held the wax is now a negative space reflecting all of the detail of the original artwork found in the wax. The burnout temperature of a typical investment mold is around 1,300–1,500 degrees Fahrenheit. The heat in a burnout not only melts the wax, but the high temperature also vitrifies or solidifies the shell.

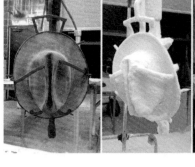

The foundry uses wax for investment or lost wax method of bronze casting because it is inexpensive, it burns away at a low temperature nicely, and it has little to no toxic fumes. Sculptors have been using other objects, besides wax, to create artwork. An artist can use anything that they can dip in a slurry mixture, and that will burn away clean.

An artist can use anything that can burnout clean in an investment cast. Cindee Travis Klement takes an old derby, sprues it up, dips it, and burns it out, pouring bronze into the investment to create *Heritage*.

Artist Cindee Travis Klement's work *Heritage* is an example of using other items in investment casting. Cindee dipped her grandfather's hat and made the investment casting right around the original object instead of going through the mold and wax process. Of course, Cindee sacrifices the original hat that she burns away. As long as the object can burn away clean and leave no residue or ash, an artist can use it in investment casting. Unlike when an artist makes a mold of an object, this artwork becomes one-of-a-kind. To make additional hats, Cindee will have to make rubber molds with mother molds from the bronze that she cast. Each rubber mold would

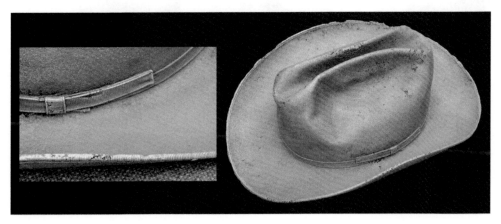

Investment casting can retain great detail. *Heritage* by Cindee Travis Klement. From the Houston, Texas, George Bush International Airport "Portable Works Collection," Permanent Collection 2014.

provide waxes of *Heritage* to cast further pieces in the edition. Let's follow the rest of the process of traditional bronze casting and then review some of the other things that are being 3D printed and burned out.

The ceramic shell, once it comes out of the furnace and is now void of wax, is hollow, heated, glowing, and ready for metal. In the crucible, the bronze ingots melt to about 2,000 degrees. It is quite something to see as workers in the foundry don their fireproof suits, the furnaces roaring in the background. The workmen place the ceramic shells in the sandpit and then, with the help of an electronic crane, the suited foundry men pick up the crucible filled with the molten bronze and pour the bronze in each warm investment. It has been an extremely long journey, from sculpting, mold-making, wax, and metal, but we are still not done with this foundry process. Before we read about more ways that 3D technology is entering these age-old processes, let's complete this bronze process on the tiger.

Shidoni Foundry pours molten bronze in the ceramic shells.

Divesting and Metal Chasing

The foundry must remove the ceramic shell to reveal the art. This process is called divesting. They carefully use hammers, chisels, and sandblasting machines to break away the investment shell from the metal, revealing the detailed tiger. The result of all of this labor is a pile of bronze casted tiger pieces. The sprues, gates, and pouring cups that were once in wax are now extremities cast in metal. They must be carefully cut off of the sculpture. The foundry cast the sculpture in many pieces. Now they must weld all of the pieces together. Welded seams must be flawless. The foundry men "chase" the metal using hand-tools that will blend the welded seams, matching the artist's textures and hand-strokes.

After the long laborious process of bronze casting, the foundry welds the pieces together. They go to great lengths to match the style of the artist as they pull the massive metal sculpture together.

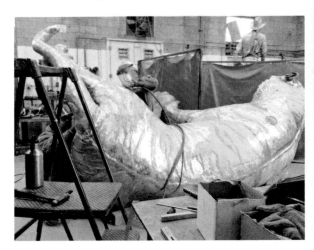

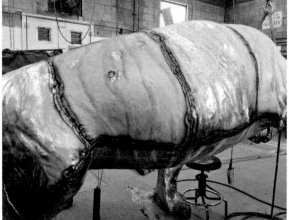

Patination

In our bronze process, the patina is a coloration of a metal surface made by time or a chemical process. However, metal is not the only thing that has a patina. A wooden dresser darkens with age and usage. The brilliant green color of the Statue of Liberty is there because of the chemical reaction on the copper. All of these are examples of coloration of a surface by time and/or chemicals. Poet and architect John Ruskin called patination "the golden stains of time." The foundry's final process before shipping the sculpture is the patina.

Creating a good patina is an art in itself. The person who creates the patina in the foundry is a sort of chemist. He creates a patina on bronze by exposing the bronze to chemicals that cause the metal to react. He knows just when and how to apply, dilute, and mix his pallet to create the effects he is after. He may mix ferric nitrate with distilled water and sulfurated potash to get a blackish brown, or sodium thiosulfate, ferric nitrate, and distilled water to obtain a blue-green. He knows what chemicals to apply and at what temperatures to apply them to get the look the artist desires while enhancing the details of the metal. As a final application, the foundry applies either a wax or plastic coating to protect the precious metal.

A patina is a chemical reaction to metal. The person who creates patinas in the foundry must be a great artist and a type of chemist.

We have talked a bit about patinas used with 3D printed objects in Chapter 7. It will be interesting to see how artists experiment with the patinas of 3D printed metal objects using chemical processes. Will the reaction in the metal be the same as in traditional processes? The author, at the writing of this book, has not found anyone who is documenting their process of exploring traditional patinas created by different chemical reactions with 3D printed metal. Of course, any artist desiring to explore the traditional patination process on 3D printed metal will have to investigate the metallurgy of each 3D printed piece. As we have seen in Chapter 7, 3D printed metal is not always done with the same combination of metals as in the traditional process of bronze casting. Such is the case with the "bronzes" that 3D printing companies create through an infiltration process as described in Bathsheba Grossman's sculpture in Chapter 7. In this process, the 3D print is porous and absorbs the infiltrate. An artist applying a traditional chemical patina to 3D printed art may not have the same control over the application and may not be able to create consistent color over the entire piece of art. Although, as is often the case with art, maybe the lack of control and randomness of traditional patina on 3D prints will become a part of the art.

As you can see, the steps to create a traditional bronze sculpture are laborious and costly. 3D technology is making great advancements, and if the big three criteria—build envelope, detail, and cost—can begin to match the traditional process then we may be on our way to creating the foundry of the future. Now that we are familiar with the traditional processes let's take a look at a few more ways that 3D technology and the experiments of others are pushing the limits.

Investment Casting of Other Materials

Burnout of 3D Print Created in PLA Plastic

Brussels-based artist Haseeb Ahmed (USA) worked in collaboration with Kunstgiesserei St. Gallen while at a residency at Sitterwerk in Switzerland. There he explored the possibilities of 3D printing and investment bronze casting. It is always a creative adventure when vendors work with artists who want to explore the possibilities of technology. Together Sitterwerk (www.sitterwerk.ch) and Haseeb collaborated in taking a 3D model printed in the fused deposition processes of 3D printing from his open source RepRap Mendel Prusa 3D printer using PLA plastic (www.reprap.org). Haseeb also owns a Cartesio by Mauk CC for its large build envelope (www.mauk.cc). What Haseeb wanted to do was use the 3D printed part as others would use the wax in the lost wax method of bronze casting. He wanted to see how this 3D print would react as the burnout substance instead of wax in bronze casting.

In the *Art and Technology* podcast with the author, Haseeb states:

> It was interesting to see how it wasn't exactly the same object. On the one hand, it was very similar and very high resolution. You can see all of the traces

of the 3D print itself, like moving layer by layer, but at the same time there were new artifacts that were present with this form of transformation.

The idea of having an object that is at first a virtual object, then is a physical object in PLA bio-plastic, and then develops real permanence by making it into bronze, was a transition that the artist found interesting.

In another experiment, Haseeb explored the limitations of the 3D process and used them to his advantage by taking the exactness of the 3D printer and using it to the point of failure. His hourglass piece entitled *Stern*, which he cast in bronze, left things to chance. "A new type of materiality. The limitations are what defines it as a unique form of production," states Haseeb. The art clearly exhibits the layering of the PLA plastic created with a low-resolution 3D printer, but as the model builds, and the artist pushes it to the limits, the pieces collapse. The result is a fragile art that resembles a bird's nest.

The foundry gates up Haseeb's 3D print. Photograph courtesy of Haseeb Ahmed and Tim Buechel.

Haseeb's bronze sculpture after pour and before chasing. Photograph courtesy of Haseeb Ahmed and Tim Buechel.

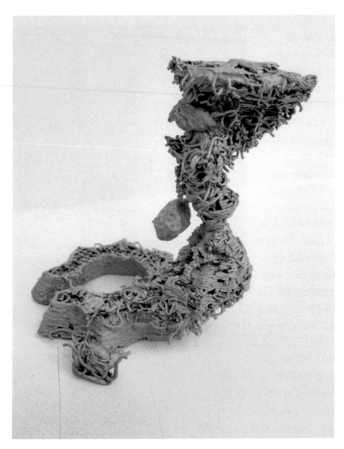

Haseeb Ahmed *Stern Trio series—OCT_Star_783.stl*. Photograph courtesy of Haseeb Ahmed and Tim Buechel.

It is well known that other types of 3D printing such as stereolithography create higher resolution models, but Haseeb wanted to use fused deposition 3D printing, as it is more available to artists. What interested Haseeb was exploring randomness and chance while combining it into something highly controlled.

Haseeb notes that in the experiment, the PLA burned clean and didn't interfere with the bronze pour. It is, after all, thermoform plastic and melts at a lower temperature. An artist should use precautions when burning out any plastics.

Haseeb's future experiments will include 3D printing the sprues for the print with the 3D art. His list of vendors and software are as follows: he has been using Rhino software and claims, "It is the most intuitive and is the closest to drawing" (www.rhino3d.com). He is thinking of moving to Blender because of the large toolset for 3D printing and the fact that it is open source (www.blender.org). He cleans up his files using Netfabb (www.netfabb.com) and for a G-code generator he uses the open source software Slicer (www.slicer.org).

Paper

Artists are always experimenting. Many desire the opportunity to shorten the time that it takes to create a bronze with the lost wax method of bronze casting, as well as decrease the cost. Paul Effinger of Effinger Design and Foundry has been one of those experimenters (www.effinger.us). In 2009, Paul spoke with AGS 3D and together they collaborated on taking Paul's digital design *Artifice*, created in ZBrush, and 3D printing the sculpture.

Paul Effinger created *Artifice* in ZBrush. He had the sculpture printed on a ZCorp 510 in ceramic powder and then proceeded with a cellulose (paper) print. He used this cellulose print as the investment cast to create a bronze of the art.

They first printed *Artifice* in ceramic and then experimented with paper cellulose printing with a wax infiltrate.

The cellulose piece went through the traditional investment casting process at Michael Hall's foundry (www.studiofoundry.com). Effinger abandoned this particular process because he felt that he wanted a smoother finish on the art. The pattern in the surface of the art created by the 3D printer's paper layering process transferred to the bronze. The chasing on the bronze to reduce or eliminate these lines would be laborious and costly.

The layering of the papers shows in the 3D print.

There are others who are promoting the use of paper as investment casting for machine parts. An artist can embrace the nuances of the machining layering process of 3D printed paper and make the lines a part of the art. Unless there is a process to remove these lines before investment casting, it might be better to use other options such as 3D printing using SLA and resin for investment casting and burnout.

Wings of *Artifice*, direct cast bronze from 3D printed medium, produced at Michael Hall's Studio Foundry, Driftwood, Texas.

FACTUM ARTE MERGES FINE ART AND TECHNOLOGY

From a print in Diverse Maniere d'adornare i cammini ed ogni altra parte degli edifizi desunte dall'architettura Egizia, Etrusca, e Greca con un Ragionamento Apologetico in defesa dell'Architettura Egizia, e Toscana, opera del Cavaliere Giambattista Piranesi Architetto, Rome 1769, Wilton-Ely 878 (Factum Arte, www. factum-arte.com).

Factum Arte located in Madrid, Spain, is a combination of artists, technicians, coders, conservationists, and more (www.factum-arte. com). The many creative people at Factum Arte have done what so many artists featured in this book have done. They have combined art and technology, and pushed the limits to find "original solutions to specific artistic and cultural challenges."

In 2011, Factum Arte assisted in creating an exhibition of work by Italian artist Giovanni Battista Piranesi (1720–1778). Piranesi designed works of art on paper around 250 years ago. Factum Arte merged the technologies and the art and craft mentioned in this book and were able to make the Piranesi sketches into a real object of art in 3D physical form.

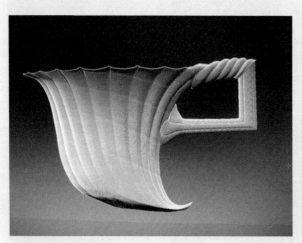

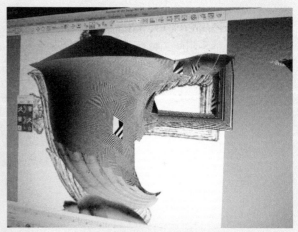

A 3D computer render placed over the sketch of Piranesi's coffee pot created at Voxelstudios, Madrid (www. voxelstudios.es).

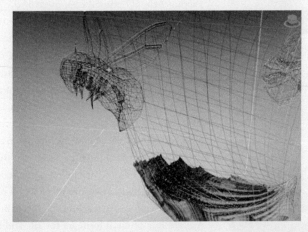

A screenshot of the geometry of Piranesi's coffee pot from Voxelstudios, Madrid.

A render of the 3D model.

Recreating works of art from a sketch takes a bit more thought than just copying a design in 3D and printing it out. Factum Arte wanted the art to fulfill its original intention. A coffee pot had to look and feel like a coffee pot. They could not know when they copied the sketches that the weight of the coffee pot would be too much for the size and the position of the handle. Touching and holding the object is a vital part of the 3D design process. It is possible, had Piranesi had access to this modern technology, that he would have discovered the same thing. Factum Arte experimented with the thickness, along with paying attention to directions from the silversmith and the foundry limitations. They adjusted the weight so that the coffee pot would feel comfortable in the hands of the user.

Materialise, in Belgium, joins the team of craftsmen on the Piranesi project (www.materialise.com). Materialise makes these prototypes using the stereolithography (SLA) process of 3D printing (see Chapter 7).

Factum Arte 3D printed each piece of the Piranesi coffee pot using the company Materialise and SLA prototypes. These were not created for direct burnout. The SLA prototype still went through the traditional process of lost wax casting with a mold created from the SLA 3D print and a wax created from the mold. Besides the complications with the thickness, Factum Arte found that the traditional lost wax process allowed them to put handwork into the piece and detail that they would not get from lost SLA. They recreated *Helix Tripod* (see following pages) using the same methods, as well as other works of Piranesi using other processes. Each of the pieces made and realized in a physical form are for sale and fund further exhibitions at Fonaione Giorgio Cini. Visit the Factum Arte website for more details on their process.

> *"Indeed the results may be seen as being much more faithful to Piranesi's intentions than if they had been made by craftsmen in his own day. This operation is the practical proof that the ideas of the past can travel through time to blend and interweave with those of the present, driven by today's desires and expectations. Through new technologies, Piranesi's ideas have finally 'materialised' in pleasurable new works of art. At the same time, the process has provided remarkable insight into Piranesi's mind, practice and works in a way that could not have been possible in the past."*
>
> **Pasquale Gagliardi**
> Secretary General of the Cini Foundation,
> Factum Arte website
> (www.factum-arte.com/piranesi)

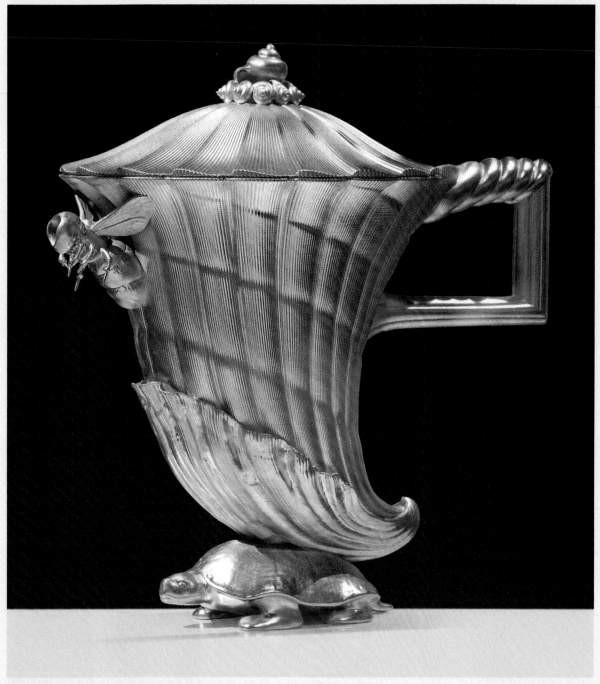

Piranesi Coffee Pot. Edition of 9,
sterling silver, 25 cm high,
www.factum-arte.com.

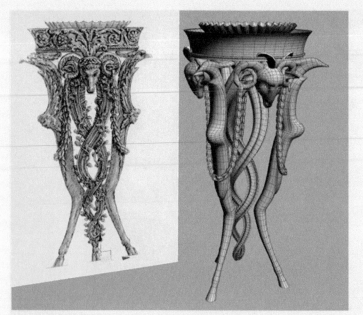

Helix Tripod, digital
design and original sketch.
ZBrush model compared
to the Piranesi sketch.

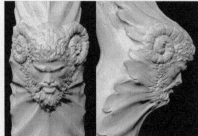

Helix Tripod, details of the ZBrush model
created by Voxelstudios—figures, leaves, and
details in the ram's horns.

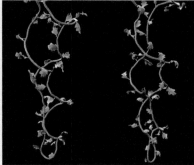

3D printed
resin model by
Materialise.

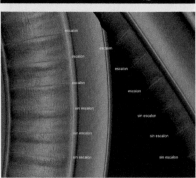

Helix Tripod.
The render by Voxelstudios
is on the left. The completed
design is on the right.

Burnout of SLA for Large Sculpture

We have examined 3D printing in detail in Chapter 7. Many consumers are becoming aware of 3D printing through their exposure to fused deposition modeling (FDM) consumer 3D printers. We have explored how jewelers have led the way with casting metal by creating detailed 3D printing using 3D printing of wax, which they then cast into metal. Jewelers have been using 3D technology this way for years. However, the build envelope or sizes that are available for wax printing is small and the cost per inch is high. We have also explored how stereolithography (SLA) offers good detail for 3D printing as seen in the examples of the Piranesi project with Factum Arte. There are even some affordable consumer SLA machines that print very detailed objects, again with a small build envelope.

What about the possibility of the lost SLA process of bronze casting? There are a few foundries in the world who are working with investment casting and burnout of large SLA 3D printed pieces; three such companies are Polich Tallix (USA, www.polichtallix.com), Pangolin Editions (UK, www.pangolin-editions.com), or Fademesa Bronze Art Foundry (Spain, www.fademesa.com).

To burnout large SLA pieces in investment casting you first need to have large SLA printed pieces. These printed pieces come from Materialise in Belgium. The Mammoth SLA 3D printer at Materialise has a build envelope of 2,100 × 700 × 800 mm. In a 2010 *Art and Technology* podcast, Joris Debois from Materialise in Belgium, expressed an interest in finding foundries in the US that might like to work with the lost SLA process of investment casting. He did say that a foundry would have to modify their casting process a bit.

The printing of the *Areion* by Formula Group on the Mammoth SLA 3D printer.

We can't expect the foundries now casting in SLA to give up their secrets. Knowing what we do about both 3D printing, and now the lost wax method of bronze casting, we can assume there are several problem areas that a foundry of the future will need to address when trying to use SLA as a burnout material. The following are only suggestions and are not meant as guidelines for burnout process of SLA or other materials. A foundry interested in modifying their processes to include burnout of SLA should contact Materialise or 3D Systems for recommendations and suggestions.

We have already seen how creating a monumental sculpture in the traditional process of bronze casting, as with Bridgette Mongeon's tiger sculpture, has its challenges. Let's examine the foundry steps again and consider what modifications might be necessary to create a monumental sculpture using the lost SLA process with large 3D prints.

How thick is the print? The traditional foundry process is, of course, much more involved than what we describe in this chapter. We could go deeper into the process when we talk about how thick a wax needs to be in the lost wax method of bronze casting to accommodate the welding, or metalwork, even the engineering, installation, and safety of the art are considerations. Or, as in the case of the Piranesi coffee pot, the thickness of the walls will affect the usability of the object. The foundry takes all of these factors into consideration when creating the wax in the lost wax method of bronze casting. It makes sense then that the same thoughts will have to translate to the 3D print in a possible lost SLA process. That means that instead of thickening up a wax or a portion of a wax in a mold with a few additional coats of wax brushed on by hand, the designer will need to consult with the foundry to adjust for these considerations within the computer, long before they make a 3D print. They will have to take into account the thickness of each SLA piece, including a variation of thickness in one SLA print or model section. Will the metal department need to weld an area and therefore do they need more or less mass to provide for this? Will the heat from one area in the pour affect another area? Where is the best place to join a seam in the sculpture? These are all things that the foundry will consider. Remember, SLA 3D printing using laser and resin to capture great detail is costly. Materialise bases the cost of the project on four factors. The first factor is the machine time. The second factor is the amount of resin used and the amount of the supports needed. The third is the complexity of the file. For example, if the laser has to jump from one detail to the other it will take longer to build the part. The fourth consideration is the size of the object. The size affects pricing, especially in the z-axis. The higher the object, the more time that it will take on the machine.

Thickening areas in an SLA 3D model for printing will add mass, and mass means expense. However, if the lost SLA process is viable, we could weigh it against the costs of parts of the lost wax method of casting that we no longer need. SLA investment casting means no rubber mold, no mother mold, no wax, and no wax clean up. The lost SLA investment casting offers a tremendous amount of design opportunities, especially for complex geometries that would be difficult to create in a traditional process. It would also serve a purpose for large sculptures. At this date, even with the considerations of what the foundry no longer requires, like wax and mold with a lost SLA investment, the costs of SLA far exceed the costs of the traditional process.

Foundries who work with casting monumental sculptures are set up to produce molds, pour waxes, create investments, and pour metal in larger sections. They have modified their process to be able to accommodate larger pieces—right down to cranes and track systems throughout the foundry. These extras assist them with the dip and transfer of heavy investments. They also have larger crucibles and cranes in the pouring room. Large molds and large waxes have a tendency to bend out of shape. Deformation of pieces can become a nightmare down the road when the sections are no longer in wax but are instead in metal. There are many pieces of a sculpture that need to fit together. Flexible SLA parts might be a bit of a challenge. If they warp then they will not fit together when they are in metal.

Cleaning the SLA

There is less of a chance of marring or damaging a 3D print created for the lost SLA for investment as compared to having to clean up wax made from a rubber mold. However, the artist or foundry may still desire to change, modify, or clean-up areas of the SLA. When working in the traditional foundry process and wax, the wax worker will use a soldering iron, hot tools, buffing cloths, and wax polish to clean up the wax before it goes into the slurry to create the investment. The softness of the wax is good quality to work in. When working with SLA, the foundry worker or artist may still want to add or change elements by hand. The SLA 3D print is made with resin. The cleaning is different and will consist of using an X-Acto knife, foam sanding block, sandpaper, nail files, and possibly chemicals.

Gating Up

Before the foundry can make the investment, they will need to gate up the SLA pieces just as in the lost wax method of bronze casting. Remember the gates help gases to escape and the metal to flow. One option is to create the gates in the computer and have them printed out in the SLA along with the art. Printing the gates with the sculpture may assist in keeping the large sections from warping; however, the cost of using printed gates or sprues can add substantial expense to the project.

We have seen how jewelers are using 3D printing of wax and burnout on a small scale. In Chapter 7 and the corresponding *Art and Technology* podcast, Lisa Krikawa of Krikawa Jewelry Design discusses how her company will often incorporate nubs into the design of her jewelry for sprues. Creating nubs and adding wax gates for the lost SLA process of casting can give the artist more control over the work. They can choose the best place for them. But, of course, the artist must educate themselves to know exactly where to put such extensions so as not to interfere with the foundry process. It would also make sense to remember that the vestment will now contain two materials—the SLA resin piece and the gates made of wax. Each will need to burnout and not interfere with each other. For example, how does the wax affect the resin when the foundry tries to burn it out at a high temperature? Does it make a cleaner mold or cause problems?

Investment and Burnout

Materialise is not the only company exploring 3D printing and the lost SLA method of casting metal. Many other 3D printing companies support investment casting for a variety of applications including the automotive, marine, and defense industries.

The biggest change in the casting process using SLA appears to be in the investment and burnout. We have looked at how artists are burning objects other than wax out of an investment, such as Cindee Travis Klement's sculpture *Heritage*. The foundry and the artist must take two things into consideration during a burnout. The first is how clean is the object as it burns away? Does it leave behind a lot of ash or residue that will change the surface detail of a fine art bronze? The other element to consider is the expansion on the investment during burnout. If the object is solid instead of hollow and there is no place for the object to expand inside the investment during burnout, then the shell may crack. There are two options during the lost SLA process; one is a stronger investment. Indeed some companies are making investment products just for 3D printing burnout. The other is to 3D print a collapsible interior wall, such as QuickCast™ by 3D Systems or TetraShell by Materialise. These hexagonal support structures, printed within the 3D piece, allow the 3D print to collapse inwardly when burned away. Be careful when using these hollow support structures: if there is a hole in the surface, then slurry mixture will enter the top layer. Also, having a thicker cast wall may not be suitable for the design. A thicker casting adds weight and, as with the Piranesi coffee pot, the "feel" of this end product may not be a part of the artistic intention. Also, using a collapsible 3D interior may make dipping the pieces more difficult. The trapped air may make dipping in the dip room like trying to push a ball under water.

Tom Mueller, the author of the *Guide to Casting Using QuickCast™ Patterns* by 3D Systems, Inc. talks about the trend to "over gate" a sculpture when using QuickCast™ and SLA. Gates not only allow the gases to escape but also help with the oxygen flow. Oxygen is necessary because, unlike wax, which melts and flows out of the sculpture during the burnout, many stereolithography resins must burn away. If they do not burn clean then the foundry will need to clean the shells. If it is necessary to cool down a shell to clean out residue before pouring the bronze then the shell becomes weaker.

In the traditional processes, foundries gate up the pieces using as many gates as necessary. Remember that gates turn into metal that the metal workers will have to grind off. They will also need to add detail back to the surface.

These are only a few considerations for a foundry of the future using the lost SLA process of casting. Of course, there are many more factors such as the air emissions and safety of using these processes in a foundry, and the shrinkage of the metal. Still, artists and vendors continue to combine talents, technology, and curiosity to meet the possibilities.

DIGITAL DIRECT TO MOLD

When it comes to digital processes making an impact on the creation of a piece of artwork, there is no bigger impact than the influences that 3D technology will be playing in the creation of a monumental sculpture called *The American*. The sculptor, Shan Gray, has big ideas for the bronze sculpture of a Native American with a bald eagle resting on his right arm. The height of the 217-foot sculpture scheduled for installation in Sand Springs, Oklahoma, is 100 feet taller than the Statue of Liberty. Visitors can enter the sculpture, travel up the cloak and leg to see a panoramic view of the Oklahoma area's pioneer days, projected on screens at about the height of the Native American's belly.

Gray was like many artists and created bronze sculptures the traditional way for years. To create *The American* in the traditional lost wax method of bronze casting would mean a great deal of time and material. Even if the artist had the sculpture milled in foam for enlargement, like Bridgette Mongeon's tiger sculpture, and it traveled through the lost wax method of bronze casting, the use of foam, rubber, wax, and investment would require a great deal of time and disposable material. Synappsys Digital Services in Norman, Oklahoma, developed Digital Direct to Mold (DDTM) with *The American* sculpture in mind (www.synappsys.com). The new process will save millions of dollars on the entire project.

Artist Shan Gray makes monumental achievements in alternative processes of bronze casting that incorporates 3D technology and casting of the sculpture *The American*.

The development of Digital Direct to Mold (DDTM) and the experimental process of *The American* began with CNC milling the mold of Kevin Box's sculpture *Folded Paper* out of resin-bonded sand mixture.

The milled resin-bonded sand becomes the refractory mold for the bronze casting process.

The foundry releases the sculpture from the CNC mold. It then travels through the traditional chasing process.

Synappsys Digital Services debuted their first DDTM bronze molds and casting process on Kevin Box's sculpture of *Folded Paper* in 2007. Synappsys created a 3D scan of *Folded Paper* just as if they were to enlarge it and cut it out in foam. Instead of carving a positive of the art or in this case "the paper," the computer carves a two-piece mold out of a hardened mixture of resin-bonded sand. This carving leaves a ¼-inch cavity for bronze pouring. Once poured, the foundry releases the art from the sand resin mixture, chases the metal, and adds a patina to the sculpture.

For the DDTM process of *The American*, Synappsys Digital Services will divide up the sculpture into 4-foot sections horizontally and then again vertically to create 4 × 5 foot manageable pieces. They will make these divisions within the computer graphics image of *The American*, exhibiting a perfect match piece to piece. This is something that is difficult to obtain in traditional casting using shims or claying up, because each section is a two-piece mold created with DDTM. They can even print information on the inside of the cast to manage the organization and facilitate putting the sculpture together. If they choose, they can honor those who are contributing to the project by engraving their names on the backside of the mold. A foundry will be working in conjunction with Synappsys, to create the 3,600 panels; a process that they expect will take two and a half years. A foundry will pour the bronze pieces working with Leidos Engineering for the added steel substructure.

Folded Paper by Kevin Box.

Working with a combination of traditional sculpting and digital modeling has several advantages in the design process. The digital image offers the artist an opportunity to view the project from many vantage points, including the way a viewer could see the sculpture from the ground. The engineers at Leidos Engineering, the project manager on *The American*, used these same images to view the inside of the sculpture. This inside view was a crucial element in the planning stages because an elevator and stairs had to fit in the left leg of the Native American. With the 3D model, the engineers could anticipate difficulties with allotment of space within the sculpture,

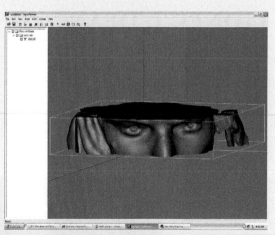

The American team will create a monumental sculpture, in the same process as Kevin Box's *Folded Paper*. Synappsys Digital Services will mill the mold's 3,600 panels for casting. Synappsys will divide this 4-foot tall section further.

which gave the artist an opportunity to modify the design of the left leg and drapery to accommodate the engineer's needs. The architects may change the sculpture again as they finalize the design of the gallery area located on the inside of the sculpture at approximately 78 feet, about the navel height in the sculpture. In the gallery, viewers will see real time, closed-circuit panoramic views of the Tulsa Oklahoma area displayed on high-definition plasma screens. Periodically the scene will change to another period as visitors view the Oklahoma settlers complete with buffalo roaming the surrounding hills. Viewers may continue their journey in the sculpture taking the flights of stairs to the observation deck at approximately 156 feet where they can observe Tulsa from behind *The American*'s hair.

In the planning process of *The American* sculpture, the technology continues as *The American* team meets new challenges. For example, engineers will have to find ways to prevent clouds and condensation from forming inside. They will also need to find a way to change the 50-pound light bulb needed in the wing of the eagle for airplanes to navigate the sculpture safely.

The creating of *The American* has been a challenge from the inception, pushing the design team toward the development of technological advancements that are the beginning of a change for the foundry industry. DDTM does have its drawbacks. Because it goes from maquette to computer to casting, there are no revisions as there might be in the latter stages (wax) of traditional casting. If an artist could think and carve using the negative shape, he or she could hand-carve into the foam. With the creation of robotic milling machines that mill on many axes, it would be possible to create more depth in smaller pieces. However, the artist would still have to do handwork and be able to think and carve on the foam as a negative space, instead of a positive sculpture image.

DDTM casting is an advancement in our technology and in the process of bronze casting that, until this time, has changed very little over thousands of years. Looking back from the future, we may one-day state, "It began with *The American*."

LIONEL T. DEAN

Tangle by Lionel T. Dean, FutureFactories. Selective laser sintering polyamide, followed by a "quick glass blast medium." Photograph by John Britton.

Puja by Lionel T. Dean, FutureFactories. Printed with Voxeljet in PMMA plastic, infiltrate of wax, or epoxy resin and electroform coating in copper, followed by plating in either silver or nickel. Photograph by Anwar Suliman.

THE FOUNDRY OF THE FUTURE?

HEATHER GORHAM

Heather Gorham creates her work using Geomagic Freeform software (http://geomagic.com). Combined with a haptic device, it allows her to make her digital work as she would her traditional art in the studio.

"Having come from more traditional mediums like bronze and wood, it took me a while to embrace digital sculpting for my own work. It wasn't until I held my first 3D printed piece and was able to recognize my own 'hand' in the work did I really begin to enjoy the process. I now use digital work as another tool, a really wonderful tool that gives me a new dimension of freedom and flexibility in my work."

Heather Gorham

One Grey Hare by Heather Gorham. Printed on a Connex500 in Vera White and painted with graphite paint, 15 × 17 × 9. Photograph by Barry Snidow.

Flowering Lamb of Odd by Heather Gorham. Printed on a Connex500 in Vera White and painted with automotive paint, 19 × 17 × 17. Photograph by Barry Snidow.

Beast Mountain by Heather Gorham. Printed by Voxeljet in a resin impregnated sand/silica and painted with acrylics, 27.5 × 12 × 13. Photograph by Barry Snidow.

JASON WEBB

Jason Webb also experimented with the "lost ABS" process of investment casting through the University of Nebraska at Kearney. He created his shapes using the math and code of superformula. Excited about computational art, Jason used bit.craft's Superdupershape Explorer to tweak the formula variables (www.k2dg2.org/blog:bit.craft, www.openprocessing.org/sketch2638). He used Super Shapes Script for Open SCAD to create a 3D model, before entering the "lost ABS" process of bronze casting.

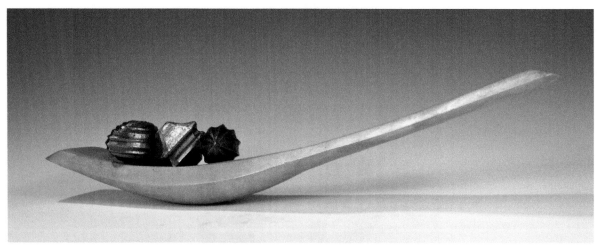

Lost ABS process with cast aluminum cradle, Jason Webb.

On the book's website at www.digitalsculpting.net you will find:

* Links to further descriptions on the process of creating the artwork featured in the galleries.
* Podcasts with the artists.
* Videos featuring the artists at work.

FACTUM ARTE

Factum Arte Isis Tripod
Piranesi Collection.
Edition of 6 numbered
copies. Made in silver
patinated bronze.
Dimensions: 90 cm high,
32 cm diameter. 3D model
created by voxel studios,
Madrid. Prototype worked
by hand after being
printed out by Materialise.
Proceeded through mold
making and the traditional
lost wax method of bronze
casting at Fademesa,
Madrid.

THE FOUNDRY OF THE FUTURE?

CHAPTER NINE

COPYRIGHTS, ETHICS, RESPONSIBILITIES, AND 3D TECHNOLOGY

———

With the emerging digital technology, we must take a look at ownership. Artwork is no longer just in the physical world, but it now also exists in the digital world. Intellectual property rights must evolve with the technology. The new technology brings great excitement, adventure, and possibilities. However, there are responsibilities that come with the technology. In this chapter, we will take a look at some basic information about copyrights, ethics, and responsibilities concerning artwork and 3D technology.

What is Copyright?

Intellectual property or IP refers to many different aspects of law that governments put into place to protect literature, artwork, music, discoveries, inventions, etc. Although many countries recognize IP rights, there are some differences between countries. The World Intellectual Property Organization (WIPO) tries "to promote innovation and creativity for the economic, social and cultural development of all countries, through a balanced and effective international intellectual property system."

There are several different kinds of intellectual property rights; copyright is one of them. Sparked by the invention of the printing press, copyrights were invented to protect those making creative works. A creative person, whether they are a musician, a writer, or an artist, owns the rights to the work that they have created for a designated amount of time.

In the United States copyright began in 1790, the total duration of protection was only for 14 years, and individuals needed to apply for a copyright. After a copyright expired, the creator could extend it for another 14 years before it went into the public domain. Works entering the public domain are those having expired copyrights or where an individual gives their works to the public domain. When works enter the public domain, no one else can claim ownership. They are available to the public. For example, Lewis Carroll wrote *Alice's Adventures in Wonderland*, and Sir John Tenniel created the illustrations for publication, in 1865. Many companies, including Disney, have recreated the story of Alice. They cannot claim copyright to the story because they recreated it.

According to the copyright law of 1976 (USA), the law protects everything that you create from the moment you create it, even if you have not registered it. This is the way copyright is handled throughout the world. It was defined by the Berne Convention, an international agreement concerning copyrights. The duration of copyright changed in 1988 from the creator's life plus 50 years, to the creator's life plus 70 years as it is today (USA). Having a piece of artwork protected by the very act of creating it is good for an artist because it means that they don't have to register every piece of work they make. Once something is in a tangible form, it is copyrighted. Many artists put their name on art along with the copyright symbol © and the year. It is surprising how many people do not realize that even if artwork does not have a copyright notice, the copyright law still protects it. Traditional sculptors have been fighting copyright infringement for years. Individuals think that they can copy a sculpture if a sculptor has not marked it with ©, the year, and the name of the artist. Sculpture is often recreated and sold as a reproduction without the permission of the artist.

Under the current copyright law, you do need to register your work with the copyright office if you want to collect for statutory damages for infringement. If you discover someone has stolen your work and you file suit, statutory damages are punitive and can be quite severe for those infringing on someone's rights. Financial penalties for infringement keep many people honest about "taking" other people's creations.

Many creative people make a living from their creativity. Authors make a living from the books they write, artists from the artwork they create, musicians from the songs they write and record. If there were no regulations to how others use these works of inspiration, it would be devastating for those who make a living creating.

Napster

Many have said that copyrights concerning 3D technology, especially as it pertains to 3D printing, rival what happened with MP3s and Napster. The story of Napster and copyright infringement is more than just a story for textbooks. It is a demonstration of how the way that we think and use our technology and what we expect out of our creative endeavors and our rights may have to change. Artists still deserve to be protected, but we may have to rethink how we work within that protection. Let's take a closer look, I'm sure it will become clearer.

In 1996 patents were filed for the audio compression file format we now know as MP3. MP3 stands for MPEG Audio Layer III. Just prior to 1996, music was shared on CDs or in uncompressed digital versions of files such as WAV, which were too large for digital transportation. This new MP3 format made files smaller with little loss of quality.

The first version of the online service known as Napster came out in 1999. A young college student named Shawn Fanning, who thought the Internet was a great place to search and share files with a primary focus on music, created it. The peer to peer (P2P) platform was shut down in 2001 due to the illegal sharing of copyrighted material. As everyone knows, songs are copyrighted. Musicians make money from the sale of their music. Radio stations pay a fee to play copyrighted music. Your store or gym pays a fee to play music while you shop or work out. However, the new MP3 format made trading music on the Internet easy. Some people who purchased and owned the music in other formats felt it was acceptable to download the same songs in the MP3 format; after all, they had already purchased it. Napster was successful (if its 80 million registered users were any indication). It was so successful that colleges were banning Napster as the downloading of music used up the bandwidth. Civil penalties for violation of copyrights were $750 per song and the 80 million people who were illegally downloading music could have all been held with civil and criminal liability. Instead, it was Napster which came under litigation.

Of course, while Napster allowed individuals to download songs, it did not pay royalties to the musician who created the music. Some artists such as Metallica and Madonna were influential in shutting down Napster. It is reported that Madonna's song "Music" came out on Napster before it was officially released by the artist herself. Napster lost in the lawsuit then tried to get the music industry on board for a paying website, but failed. Eventually Napster went bankrupt. There was an upside to the technology and process of sharing music. Some lesser-known bands felt that Napster helped them get their music heard. Some users felt that Napster offered them a selection of music of which they might not otherwise be aware.

It is important to note, and a bit hard to comprehend, that until this point in our history, the music industry created music in a hard format. Within the creation of music history albums led to tapes, which led to CDs, but a digital format of music to download made it very easy to obtain and transfer music. Many began to realize that convenient delivery of songs via the Internet was a viable need. It became a new way to work in the industry. Eventually iTunes was born. Some felt that the music industry did not get on board to the change in the technology but instead tried to halt it, suing makers of MP3 players and bringing down Napster. Also, remember that "digital" rights were not a part of the contracts between record companies and artists. Up until that point, "digital" didn't exist, so there was no need for digital rights.

Napster forced people to rethink how we distributed digital entertainment. It displayed the need of consumers to have easy access and a large selection of content. It paved the way for iTunes, Hulu, and others. Prior to MP3s, consumers never had the ability to sample a musical selection before buying it, unless you were in a record store. With MP3s, individuals could buy one song instead of buying an entire album.

The creation of the MP3 file format limited the need for packaging, distributing, manufacturing, marketing, and promotion of songs. Therefore, it cost less to produce the songs, savings the producers passed on to the market. MP3s offered an opportunity for listeners to try music for free and buy it if they liked it.

Napster had a profound impact on law and music, as well as highlighting the need to rethink digital distribution regulation. As digital technology evolves, the copyright laws need to evolve. We may also have to change the way we think about the distribution of creative work and what is acceptable. Musicians had a hard time grappling with the new MP3 technology and how they could use it to their advantage in the music industry. Some musicians saw positive aspects about giving away music as good marketing, offering free music to gain a mailing list or as incentives to purchase other music.

These same challenges will come up again, especially when it comes to 3D scanning and printing and the Internet. Those who feel violated will try to invent something to prevent others from infringement, as the Recording Industry Association of America (RIAA) did when they tried to secure a type of digital watermark (Secure Digital Music Initiative, SDMI). A digital watermark might help the industry to find the violators of copyrights. The Digital Millennium Copyright Act (DMCA) was added in 1998 in the hope of eradicating illegal file sharing. And many lawmakers are scrambling to keep up with the changes in technology, developing an entirely new field of the study of law called cyber law.

The Internet Crosses Borders

As the ease of transferring material increases, so does the risk. Although the ramifications of Napster were related to music, many realized that other forms of media—including video, publishing, and others—were soon to follow. It is easy to depict what our physical borders are. People from the United States go by one set of rules, and those from the UK have their set of rules, but what about the Internet? What borders and guidelines does it have, and how do we get all of the countries with physical borders and perhaps different intellectual property rights to play nice and follow the same rules?

The Orphan Works Act

An orphan work is one where the copyright owner is unknown, cannot be contacted, or perhaps has passed on. There are many scholars and archivists who would like to see these works enter the public domain and made available to the general public. Some propose that the commercial value on these works is limited. However, they believe that the copyright law withholds the release of these items to the public, sacrificing cultural and historical value. Many countries are working with orphan works in different ways. The United States is still in discussion over orphan works, and it is a heated debate.

With the fact that creative people do not have to register their work, it is difficult to know if a piece of work is copyrighted, in the public domain, or perhaps just abandoned—an orphan. Many think that the identification of an abandoned work should be clearer. That there should be a centrally located database that people can search. If they do not find the work, then that would mean it is not under copyright protection. However, that would mean that artists would have to register their work. Also, with the duration of copyrights lasting so long, many feel that the government should modify the copyright law as it stands, so that work can be accessible. The American Society of Illustrators Partnership (ASIP) consists of a variety of groups who are fighting for their rights as illustrators, and legislating against the Orphan Works Act.

According to the proposed Orphan Works Act, individuals wanting to use a work would be required to perform a "diligent search" to find who owns the copyrights. However, "diligent" is a subjective term. Initiating the Orphan Works Act also puts a hardship on the creator to register each and every thing they create.

Fair Use

It appears that many may infringe on copyright with the good of the public in mind. Many claim "fair use." The United States Copyright Office describes fair use as:

> Section 107 contains a list of the various purposes for which the reproduction of a particular work may be considered fair, such as criticism, comment, news reporting, teaching, scholarship, and research. Section 107 also sets out four factors to be considered in determining whether or not a particular use is fair.
>
> 1. The purpose and character of the use, including whether such use is of commercial nature or is for nonprofit educational purposes.
> 2. The nature of the copyrighted work.
> 3. The amount and substantiality of the portion used in relation to the copyrighted work as a whole.
> 4. The effect of the use upon the potential market for, or value of, the copyrighted work.

Google Books/Google Print

Just as Napster was making a collection of music, others began to see the Internet as a great place to collect material—a library of sorts. In 2002, Google began to digitize books. Their goal was to create a collection of books larger than anyone has done before. The mistake was that Google went to the libraries and contracted with them instead of contacting the book owners or publishers. In 2004, Google announced the Google Book Library. By scanning books, Google violated the rights of many authors, but called it "fair use."

Google has already scanned 20 million books without the authors' permission. On October 4, 2012, Paul Aiken, executive director of the Authors Guild, stated on the Authors Guild website, "Google continues to profit from its use of millions of copyright-protected books without regard to authors' rights, and our class-action lawsuit on behalf of U.S. authors continues" (www.authorsguild.org).

In 2004, the judge in the case against Google believed that to agree to allow Google to digitize every book would give them a digital monopoly. But time and technology seemed to be in Google's favor for the *New York Times* reported in November 2013 that Judge Denny Chin dismissed the lawsuit. The Authors Guild is planning an appeal.

Is Infringement of IP Becoming the Norm?

In 2012, Google had more than 55.2 million URLs reported per week that infringed on individuals' copyrights. In 2013, the amount doubled to 110.2 million.

3D Scanning

When 3D scanning, we take a physical object and translate it into points, or triangles, making it a digital file. Once you digitize a file you can send it anywhere via the Internet. Digitized files can be shared, modified, and even printed with a 3D printer or CNC milled. Digital scanning is becoming increasingly more affordable. We have seen several ways of scanning an object from probing, light, and laser scans to photogrammetry or the use of your cell phone.

As with other technologies, those incorporating 3D scanning into their workflow should take the time to familiarize themselves with IP laws. Remember it is impossible to look at an object and know if it has a copyright attached to it or if there is a patent on the object. The moment you take any object and put it in the scanner you could be infringing on someone else's copyrights or patents.

If you plan on using the 3D model that you have scanned as a base or armature to a design, you must be sure that you change the design. There is no formula for changing art to make it yours. A judge will not say, "you have changed the work 25 percent so it is now yours." There is no percentage that a judge will look at to say if you have infringed on another's design. They will not be comparing the differences; they will be comparing the similarities. They will be looking for "substantially similar" products.

There is probably no other 3D technology that will assist you in breaking the law by infringing on intellectual property rights quicker than 3D scanning. If you own a scanner or are preparing to scan something, even if you are going to use something like 123D Catch, before you do, be sure to familiarize yourself with the copyrights. If you own a scanner, you may be tempted to scan everything in your surroundings, but pay attention to intellectual property rights. Be sure to make yourself aware of how you could be breaking the law with your scanner. This is important. You can't just pick up anything in your household and scan it, even if there is no copyright symbol on it. Also, if you are using technology that incorporates outside sources, such as a 3D scanning bureau, you may want to be sure you have the necessary documentation to protect yourself. Finally, if you are using an online photogrammetry service such as 123D Catch, be aware of the website's policies. Read the fine print. Even if you don't make your scan public, if it has gone to their server, you may not own it anymore. Once you upload your data you may have given it away along with your rights to your artwork. If you are scanning your child for fun and upload the files, you may have just given away their image.

Ownership becomes hazy when it comes to scans. You might own an object, but do you own the scan? If you are hiring someone to scan something for you, be sure these details are clear. Anytime you can copy an object, you must ask yourself the question, "Am I allowed to copy this?" And when you send your files off or create work and then have it scanned, be sure you completely understand your rights and/or liability. Make the mailing of a simple nondisclosure agreement to your vendors a part of your production process. One of these is made available on this book's accompanying website. If you are an engineer creating data files of a new turbine prototype, a vendor would gladly sign a nondisclosure. Why should it be any less for fine art? Remember these files are easily transferred at the click of a button. Ask your vendors if they ever print additional copies of a client's file. Do they share the file? Do they use this image without the client knowing it? Do they use clients' images in their marketing? Is their network and the client's data protected? What happens to a client's data after they print my files?

Should we rethink how we are working with copyright infringement? Can we, instead of suing, figure out how to adapt the technology and infringement to our benefit? Think about Napster and giving the song away. How can we have another person's piracy work to our advantage as creators? How can we protect ourselves as we enter and create artwork with 3D technology?

The responsibility and the ramifications of 3D printing bring about a lot of discussion.

- Just because we can create something—should we?
- With 3D home printing, we are making "untested" products. What if someone is hurt using something that we have made on our 3D printer? Who is liable?
- We have talked a little about regenerative medicine and 3D printing. Science is making such wonderful strides in printing skins for burn victims, bone, and working towards replacement organs. These wonderful lifesaving processes bring up a world of questions.
  - In the future, who will guarantee my 3D printed organ?
  - Will organs become commodities making those of more wealth able to push themselves up on an organ donor list?
  - Will individuals place less importance on the care of their bodies if they know they can replace parts?

3D Printed Gun

Is open source always a good thing? In the United States, it is illegal to manufacture firearms without a license. In 2012, Cody Wilson announced his intention to create a working gun using 3D technology. He fired the gun that he printed on a Stratasys Dimension SST 3D printer in 2013 and made the blueprints of the gun available for download. Of course, the Department of Defense immediately took action.

———————

When technology threatens a livelihood or goes against the laws of the country, should it be controlled? There is great importance in having art in the public domain. Open source and the evolution of hardware and software through open collaboration can bring some wonderful advances.

Works, data, and information that are available to the public stimulate creativity in others. It gives an opportunity for others to build upon that work. We have seen it in several instances in this book such as Barry X. Ball's scans and Factum Arte's Piranesi project. Shared information can help us to remove our geographical boundaries. It plays a great part in education and historical and cultural exploration as we read about the scanning of cultural artifacts.

There is much more we could state on copyright ethics and responsibilities. 3D technology will change; we will change because of this technology in our lives. As we pursue this technology and advancement, we will continue to ask these questions, and you can bet that artists will create art to initiate such discussions. For more updated conversations on these subjects, visit this book's accompanying website at www.digitalsculpting.net.

Time Line

There is more that we can add to this timeline, but in the recognition of space, we will leave you with this.

1909   United States Congress enacted the Copyright Act.

1976   Congress rewrote copyright law to include the computer.

1976   "Fair use" is added to the copyrights "for purposes such as criticism, comment, news reporting, teaching (including multiple copies for classroom use), scholarship, or research."

1982   The Audio Home Recording Act (AHRA) allowed consumers the right to make digital copies of their analog music.

1983   *Sony vs. Universal*—when video tape recorders came out, people could tape one TV show while watching another. Universal felt this infringed on copyrights. Sony won, and that win set a precedent. It states that the maker of a machine, "capable of substantial non-infringing uses," cannot be held liable for those who use the machine to infringe on others' copyrights. (Here is another case where Universal felt that the recording of movies by these new machines would hurt the movie industry; however, this new technology had the exact opposite affect. It renewed interest and made movies more available.)

1996   Patents issued for MP3.

1997   The No Electronic Theft Act (NET Act)—with this act a person could be prosecuted for infringement even if they did not have a financial gain from the infringement.

1998   The Digital Millennium Copyright Act (DMCA)—this act has several different parts. In its basic form, it prevents piracy and copyright infringement as well as regulations concerning the process of reporting such infringement concerning websites and Internet service providers.

1999   Napster goes live.

2001   First iPod.

2002   Napster files for bankruptcy.

2003   iTunes music store established.

2005   Open source RepRap founded by Adrian Bowyer.

2008   Orphan Works Act failed to pass.

2008   Authors Guild and the Association of American Publishers sue Google.

2009   Fused deposition-modeling patents expired.

2009   MakerBot, developed from the RepRap open source project, incorporates and develops a DIY FDM open source printer.

2011   Several writers' groups sue five United States universities for digitizing copyrighted material and making it public.

2012   Google and publishers agree to disagree—Google gives publishers an option but the agreement does not make Google answerable to infringement.

2012   Instagram issues new policy.

2012   Class action lawsuit is filed by authors against Google.

2012   3D Kickstarter company Formlabs is sued by 3D Systems for patent infringement.

2013   MakerBot merges with Stratasys, closing the open source community.

2014   Patents preventing competition with selective laser sintering (SLS) expire.

APPENDIX

The book's accompanying website contains additional information. If you know of a company or service that would like to be listed on the website, please contact the author through www.digitalsculpting.net. The author has not personally used and does not personally recommend individuals, companies, or software mentioned in these lists, unless noted as "**author recommended**."

- Book's accompanying website, www.digitalsculpting.net
- Author's personal website, www.creativesculpture.com
- Podcasts, subscribe in iTunes or at www.digitalsculpting.net

Hackerspaces and Makerspaces

Hackerspaces and makerspaces are mentioned throughout the book. Fab Lab and TechShop are also terms associated with hackerspaces or makerspaces. A hackerspace is a physical community space or a creative workers' co-op. Tools, materials, and training are provided for a monthly fee. The learning at these spaces is self-directed. Even the White House is involved in the maker movement (www.whitehouse.gov/maker-faire).

A comprehensive worldwide user maintained list of all active hackerspaces can be found at http://hackerspaces.org/wiki/List_of_Hacker_Spaces. Makerspace meet-up groups are listed at http://makerspaces.meetup.com, while *Make* magazine can be found at http://makezine.com.

Be sure to look up libraries and makerspaces. Both public and private libraries are becoming a resource for makerspaces.

STEAM Education

The STEAM educational initiative is an interdisciplinary practice of the incorporation of science, technology, engineering, art, and math. The STEAM movement began with the Rhode Island School of Design (RISD). You can learn more about STEAM at http://stemtosteam.org.

Autodesk Software Company offers many free tools for teachers who want to incorporate STEAM education into their classrooms, see http://curriculum.autodesk.com/student/public.

Educators can use many of the resources in this book for their STEAM education.

- Learn about 3D scanning and 3D printing as well as history, culture, geography, and technology through the Smithsonian's X3D website at http://3d.si.edu.

- Explore the free educational material, again working with history, culture, geography, technology, and art at CyArk's website, www.cyark.org.
- Explore the free math programs listed below.
- Explore the free programs on making at 123D Catch.
- Visit the book's accompanying website for links to STEAM curriculum.

Math Resources

COMMERCIAL SOFTWARE
- Mathematica, www.wolfram.com/mathematica
- Maplesoft, www.maplesoft.com

FREE OR INEXPENSIVE GEMS THAT ENCOURAGE INDIVIDUALS TO PLAY WITH MATH
- Knot Plot, helps to visualize knots, www.knotplot.com/download
- Surface Evolver, visualizes minimal surfaces, www.susqu.edu/brakke/evolver/evolver.html
- TopMod, a topological mesh modeler, www.viz.tamu.edu/faculty/ergun/research/topology
- SeifertView, visualization of Seifert Surfaces, www.win.tue.nl/~vanwijk/seifertview
- Excellent tutorials on geometry and computation, www.christopherwhitelaw.us/?p=567

MATH CONFERENCES
- The International Society of the Arts, Mathematics, and Architecture (ISAMA), www.isama.org
- Bridges, www.bridgesmathart.org

3D Scanning Service Bureaus
- Synappsys Digital Services, www.synappsys.com, Norman, OK, (405) 366-6363, info@synappsys.com (**author recommended**)
- Direct Dimensions, www.dirdim.com, Owings Mills, MD, (410) 998-0880, info@dirdim.com
- Smart Geometrics, www.smartgeometrics.com, Houston, TX, Nashville, TN, Washington, DC, and Port of Spain, TT, info@smargeometrics.com (**author recommended**)

CNC Milling Companies—Foam
- Synappsys Digital Services, www.synappsys.com, Norman, OK, (405) 366-6363, info@synappsys.com (**author recommended—** excellent service, great communication, and very dependable)

- Across the Board Creations, www.acrosstheboardcreations.com, Porthill, ID, and Wynndel, British Columbia, (250) 866 5757, kevin@acrosstheboardcreations.com (**author recommended**)
- Blue Genie, http://bluegenieart.com, Austin, TX, (512) 444-6655, sales@bluegenieart.com

CNC Milling Companies—Stone
- Garfagnana Innovazione, www.garfagnanainnovazione.it/?lang=en

3D Printing Service Bureaus
- Shapeways, www.shapeways.com
- i.materialise, http://i.materialise.com
- Ponoko, www.ponoko.com
- Sculpteo, www.sculpteo.com
- Kraftwurx, www.kraftwurx.com

3D Scanners to Buy
- Next Engine 3D Scanner, www.nextengine.com (**author recommended**)
- MakerBot, www.makerbot.com
- 3D Systems Sense, www.3dsystems.com

Vendors Who Sell RAM
- Other World Computing, Mac, www.macsales.com (**author recommended**)
- Fry's Electronics, www.frys.com
- Micro Center, www.microcenter.com

Stains and Paint
- Sculpt Nouveau, www.sculptnouveau.com

Specialty Hardwood
- Houston Hardwoods Inc., www.houstonhardwoods.com

3D Printing Products
- Firecast, resin for investment casting, http://madesolid.com
- Formfutura, specialty filament, www.formfutura.com
- Fillamentum, specialty filament, www.fillamentum.com

Shipping Companies that Specialize in Shipping Art
- Acts Crating and Freighting, http://actsintl.com/crating, (713) 869-2269, crating@actsintl.com (**author recommended**, ask for Lace, friendly and very dependable)
- www.cratersandfreighters.com

Individuals Who Prepare Files for 3D printing

- Eric van Straaten, eric@ericvanstraaten.com, www.ericvanstraaten.com
- Vijay Dotsan, info@dotsan.com, www.dotsan.com
- Marco Valenzuela, marco3dart@gmail.com, www.marcovalenzuela.com

Software

- 3D Coat, $379 full version, $99 educational version, http://3d-coat.com, hard surface and organic
- Sculptris, free, http://pixologic.com/sculptris, hard surface and organic (**author recommended**)
- 3D-COAT, $419 full version, $99 educational version, http://3d-coat.com, hard surface and organic
- Mudbox, $495, www.autodesk.com, hard surface and organic (**author recommended**)
- ZBrush, $795, http://pixologic.com, hard surface and organic (**author recommended**)
- Blender, free—open source, www.blender.org, 3D modeling, animating, and much more
- Rhinoceros, $995, www.rhino3d.com, 3D modeling, NURBS modeling
- SketchUp, professional version $590, www.sketchup.com, 3D modeling
- SketchUp Make, free, www.sketchup.com/products/sketchup-make, 3D drawing
- 3ds Max, $3,675, www.autodesk.com, 3D molding and more
- Vectric Aspire, $1,995, www.vectric.com, modeling/signage and G-code
- Maya, $1,830, www.autodesk.com, 3D modeling and much more
- Carrara, $171, www.daz3d.com/carrara-software, modeling
- Cheetah 3D, $69, www.cheetah3d.com, 3D modeling and more

Posing Programs

- DAZ Studio 3D, free, www.daz3d.com (**author recommended**)
- Poser, $129 Poser 10, $449.99 Poser Pro, http://my.smithmicro.com (**author recommended**)

Where to Buy 3D Models

- Turbo Squid, www.turbosquid.com
- DAZ, www.daz3d.com
- Content Paradise, http://contentparadise.com
- Renderosity, www.renderosity.com

Software for Repairing Models

- Netfabb, $299 non-commercial, $1,799 commercial, some portions are free, www.netfabb.com,
- MeshMixer, free, www.meshmixer.com (**author recommended**)
- MeshLab, free, http://meshlab.sourceforge.net (**author recommended**)

Photogrammetry Software

- Autodesk 123D Catch, free, $9.99 a month for non-commercial use, www.123dapp.com
- Agisoft, $179 standard, $3,499 professional, www.agisoft.ru (**author recommended**)
- Acute 3D, $3,250 a year in the US, cross-platform, www.acute3d.com
- Photomodeler, $1,145, photo modeler scanner $2495, www.photomodeler.com/index.html, not cross-platform but will run on parallels 6

Other Free Fun Stuff

- JWEEL, browser-based jewelry design program, www.jweel.com/en
- Autodesk 123 Series, www.123dapp.com
  - 123D Catch, scan from your cell phone
  - 123D CNC, create files for CNC milling
  - 123D Creature, create creatures
  - 123D Design, create 3D models
  - 123D Make, helps you to make physical models out of designs
  - 123D Sculpt, sculpt using your iPad
  - 123D Meshmixer, helps to prepare your files for 3D printing
  - 123D Tinkercad, helps you to design 3D objects for printing

Learn Code for Art

- Processing 2, http://processing.org

Create 3D Models from Medical Imaging

- InVesalius, http://svn.softwarepublico.gov.br/trac/invesalius

Software to Transfer Files

- Cyberduck, $23.99, https://cyberduck.io
- Filezilla, free, https://filezilla-project.org
- Fetch, $29, http://fetchsoftworks.com

Search for Comparative Software

- http://alternativeto.net

Artists Featured in the Book

AERNI, MATHIEU, http://mataerni.com

AHMED, HASEEB, www.haseebahmed.com

ASHUACH, ASSA, http://assaashuach.com

BALL, BARRY X., www.barryxball.com

BEASLEY, BRUCE, http://brucebeasley.com

BOX, KEVIN, http://outsidetheboxstudio.com

BROWN, KEITH, www.art.mmu.ac.uk/profile/kbrown

BRUVEL, GIL, www.bruvel.com/

BURKE, PATRICK, www.facebook.com/patrick.burke.184

CARABALLO, LEONOR, http://objectbreastcancer.tumblr.com

CATTS, ORON, www.symbiotica.uwa.edu.au/residents/catts

CHAN, BRIAN, http://web.mit.edu/chosetec/www

CHOTOVINKSY, ONFRA, http://akemake.com

COOLEY, BRYAN, www.dinosaurresearch.com/brian_cooley.htm

DADELA, MAGDALENA, http://mdadela.4ormat.com/#0

DAVIS, BROOKE M., http://brookemdavisdesign.com/FS.html

DAWSON, IAN, www.iandawson.net

DEAN, LIONEL T., www.futurefactories.com

DEWEY, KATHERINE, www.elvenwork.com

DIRKER, MARTIN, www.dirker.co.uk www.slideshare.net/martindirker

DLVOYEB, WIM, www.wimdelvoye.be

DONDERS, PETER, www.peterdonders.com/index.php

EFFINGER, PAUL, http://effinger.us

EGGINTON, CLIVE, www.estudiosdurero.com/estudios_durero/opencms

ERVINCK, NICK, www.nickervinck.com

FARMAN, ABOU, http://objectbreastcancer.tumblr.com

GAUTIER, MATHIEU, http://mathieugautier.blogspot.com

GEVER, EYAL, www.eyalgever.com

GORHAM, HEATHER, www.heathergorham.com

GRAY, SHAN, www.theamerican.com

GROSSMAN, BATHSHEBA, www.bathsheba.com

HARKER, JOSHUA, www.joshharker.com

HAUER, ERWIN, www.erwinhauer.com

ISHERWOOD, JON, http://jonisherwood.com

JANKIJEVIC, VLADIMIR, http://unitvector.tumblr.com

KAHN, SOPHIE, www.sophiekahn.net

KEEP, JONATHAN, www.keep-art.co.uk

KEROPIAN, MICHAEL, www.keropiansculpture.com

KIRSH, JAN, http://jankirshstudio.com

KLEMENT, CINDEE TRAVIS, www.cindeeklement.com

KRIKAWA, LISA, www.krikawa.com/unique-wedding-bands

KUDLESS, ANDREW, http://matsysdesign.com

LAARMAN, JORIS, www.elvenwork.com

LANG, ROBERT J., www.langorigami.com

LAVIGNE, CHRISTIAN, http://christianlavigne.free.fr

LAZZARINI, ROBERT, www.robertlazzarini.com

LIA, www.liaworks.com

MACK, KEVIN, www.kevinmackart.com

MADOZ, CHEMA, www.chemamadoz.com/a.html

MIEBACH, NATHALIE, http://nathaliemiebach.com

MILLER, JORDAN, http://bioengineering.rice.edu/faculty/Jordan_Miller.aspx

MINKIN, LOUISA, www.louisaminkin.com

MIRHABIBI, NINI, www.anarmo.com

MONGEON, BRIDGETTE, www.creativesculpture.com

MONGEON, JOEL, www.joelmongeon.com

NEUBAUER, MARY, www.sculpture-digital.net

O'MICHAEL, MICHELLE, www.omichael.com/Welcome.html

PERRET, RAPHAEL, http://raphaelperret.ch

PETCHKOVSKI, GREG, www.users.on.net/~gjpetch/temp

RAMIREZ, STEVE, www.smashthedesign.com

ROARTY, DAN, www.danroarty.com

ROSENKRANTZ, JESSICA, http://n-e-r-v-o-u-s.com

SCHAIE, CHRIS, www.schaie.com

SILKE, ANDREW, www.andrewsilke.com

SMITH, ROBERT MICHAEL, http://iris.nyit.edu/~rsmith/index2.html

SNELSON, KENNETH, http://kennethsnelson.net

STAAB, GARY, www.staabstudios.com

STANDLEY, ERIC, http://ericstandley.30art.com

VALENZUELA, MARCO, www.marcovalenzuela.com

VAN HERPT, OLIVIER, http://oliviervanherpt.com

VAN STRAATEN, ERIC, http://ericvanstraaten.com

VIJAY, PAUL, www.Dotsan.com

VISSER, MARY HALE, www.mavissersculpture.com

WATSON, GREGG, www.gwatsondesigns.com

WEBB, JASON, http://jason-webb.info/category/3d-printing

WEBER, HARRY, www.harryweber.com

ZURR, IONAT, www.symbiotica.uwa.edu.au/residents/zurr

INDEX

Printed and bound by CPI Group (UK) Ltd, Croydon, CR0 4YY

24/10/2024

01778551-0001